English Society
1580–1680

Jennifer Hicks
February 1996

English Society 1580–1680

Keith Wrightson

London

First published in 1982 by Hutchinson
Sixth impression 1990

Reprinted in 1993 by
Routledge
11 New Fetter Lane, London EC4P 4EE

Printed and bound in Great Britain by
Mackays of Chatham PLC, Chatham, Kent

British Library Cataloguing in Publication Data

Wrightson, Keith
English society, 1580–1680
1. England – Social conditions
941.506 HN385

ISBN 0–415–09915–3

To my mother
and in memory of
my father

Contents

Preface

No historian writes a book alone and this book is no exception to that rule. It would never have been conceived had it not been for the wave of new thinking about English social history which swept through the universities of the English-speaking world in the 1960s and 1970s. It could not have been written but for the painstaking research and constructive imagination of dozens of scholars in recent years and the pioneering efforts of the more isolated scholars of earlier generations upon whose shoulders they stand. In attempting a general study of English society in the later sixteenth and seventeenth centuries, my intention has been that of rendering some of the findings of recent research more accessible, while at the same time suggesting ways in which the discoveries and insights of the last two decades can be worked into a coherent whole. I have not, however, attempted a comprehensive account of English society in this period. To do so would be premature. My aim has been to provide a selective, interpretative approach to the period viewed from a particular personal perspective. Selectivity, of course, implies the existence of lacunae. Personal interpretation inevitably involves the likelihood of disagreement. Nevertheless, I have chosen to argue a case as I presently see it.

In preparing and writing this book I have incurred many debts. The greatest and most long-standing is to the many research students and scholars of diverse nationality who contributed, however briefly, to the discussion of English social history in and around the Cambridge research seminars of the early 1970s. No-one who participated in that activity, much of it informal, is ever likely to forget it or to escape its influence. It was historical inquiry at its best: generous and constructive; spirited indeed, but free of the dogmatic posturing which sometimes disfigures academic debate. A second debt is to the members of the Modern History Department of the University of St Andrews, who from 1976 encouraged me to teach the social history of this period as a special subject. That experience forced me to explore more deeply the printed sources for the subject, to consolidate and articulate my ideas and to expose them to the critical evaluation of successive groups of students of signal ability. Their enthusiasm persuaded me to undertake a general study of this kind and their perceptive comments in discussion did much to shape the final form of many of the arguments presented here, as they will recognize. In the actual writing of the book, I owe a special debt of gratitude to all those who allowed me to refer to or quote from their unpublished theses (several of which will shortly be available in published form). A number of good friends gave particular help. John Walter was generous both with material and with comment upon my manuscript. Rab Houston and Lorna Weatherill also read over the manuscript and helped me with advice and discussion of specific points. Above all, David Levine subjected each chapter as it was written to detailed and forthright criticism. If I sometimes winced as I read his letters and groaned as I set about the rewriting, I am grateful for his judgement and his frankness now. My wife Eva knows what she contributed to this book over several years and what it meant.

My manuscript was completed in the early autumn of 1980, but in an important sense work of this kind is never finished. In a rapidly developing subject any attempt at interpretative synthesis must of necessity remain provisional in its conclusions. Challenging new work continues to appear. Scraps of thought float up time after time to disturb the smooth surface of what I mistook for my final formulation of an idea. I recognize only too well the ultimate insufficiency of any effort to capture the rich complexity of the past. It will be enough, however, if I have succeeded even partially in my two most important objectives. One is that of conveying something of the texture of the social experience of this period to those as yet unfamiliar with its history. The other is that of putting forward arguments about the nature and development of English society in the past which will stimulate as much as persuade.

Introduction

On 28 October 1647 the General Council of the New Model Army met in Putney church to discuss the settlement of the kingdom in the aftermath of the first civil war. At an early point in the proceedings the debate was suddenly enlivened by a short interjection from one of the cavalry troopers present. He was a bold man, for he intervened to express disagreement with Oliver Cromwell himself. He was articulate, propounding a clear and coherent argument. Moreover, he was a man of spirit, an avowed supporter of the Levellers' *Agreement of the People*, determined to forestall any fudging over the securing of 'the people's rights'. Beyond this, however, we know nothing of him, not even his name. The secretary of the council, unaware of the identity of this obscure soldier, but perhaps recognizing his accent, took down his words under the heading 'Bedfordshire Man'.[1*]

For all too long historians of sixteenth- and seventeenth-century England were in a position comparable to that of the secretary of the army council. Most of the English people were either excluded from the account of national development or else admitted only when they forced themselves upon the attention of the arbiters of history. They stood in the background, in the penumbra of historical consciousness, while matters of significance were left to the consideration of a narrow circle of their betters. When they appeared they did so either as exceptional individuals or else in the form of anonymous statistics, demographic units, aggregated producers and consumers, members of the mob. They were both faceless and passive: deprived of identity, divorced from any meaningful cultural context, denied any recognition of their active contribution to the making of their own history.

In the last two decades, however, both our knowledge and our understanding of the English people in the sixteenth and seventeenth centuries

*Superior figures refer to the Notes and references on pages 229–57.

have been immeasurably expanded. For a significant minority of English-speaking historians have devoted an unprecedented amount of time and energy to the rediscovery of English society within that period. New questions have been asked. Neglected sources have been investigated. Novel methods have been devised and adopted. A 'new social history' has appeared, a history in which a deliberate effort has been made to recover the experience of the mass of the English people, to rediscover them as members of a distinct and vigorous culture and to understand their part in the making of their history. It is an effort which continues. Much remains obscure. The subjects of this study still stand too often in half-light, modelled in shadow rather than clearly realized. Yet enough is known to permit a description of their ways of life, an assessment of their characteristic patterns of behaviour and an interpretation of their changing experience over time.

This book represents a personal attempt to bring together, to come to terms with and to make sense of what has been revealed both of the nature of English society and of the course of social change within the century 1580–1680. As an historical period this century is in some respects arbitrary. Social history cannot easily be contained within the walls of neat chronological compartments. There were many features of English society in this period which were essentially enduring and to this extent the century might be seen simply as a convenient unit of time within which to explore some of the long-term structural characteristics of 'pre-industrial' society in England. Nevertheless, the years between 1580 and 1680 also have a special significance of their own for they witnessed significant developments in English society. For this reason they were deliberately chosen as a period appropriate to the writing of a history which is intended to be not simply an essay in historical sociology, an account of the enduring elements of social structure, but also a social history, an interpretation of social change.

Society is a process. It is never static. Even its most apparently stable structures are the expression of an equilibrium between dynamic forces. For the social historian the most challenging of tasks is that of recapturing that process, while at the same time discerning long-term shifts in social organization, in social relations and in the meanings and evaluations with which social relationships are infused. As a means of expressing the interrelationship of continuity and change in English society within our period, I have adopted the simple device of dividing the discussion into two broad sections. In the first of these, I have described what I believe to have been some of the persisting characteristics of English society in the later sixteenth and seventeenth centuries. In the second, I have tried to chart the course of social change.

Neither of these sections is exclusively concerned with either continuity or change. Nevertheless, this broad division seems to me the clearest method of presenting both an account of English society in these years and an interpretation of its development. My argument is that within the context of continuity in some of the principal structural characteristics of English society, the forces of social change interacted in such a way as to produce two crucial developments. On the one hand local communities were penetrated more deeply than had been the case previously by forces of economic, administrative and cultural integration which bound them more closely together into a national society and economy. On the other hand, however, there was a simultaneous enhancement of the extent and the complexity of social differentiation within local communities. The process of social change acted not only to unify, but also to divide. Interrelated demographic and economic developments brought an enhanced prosperity to the upper and middling ranks of society, a prosperity based upon exploitation of the opportunities provided by an expanding national market. They also brought about a marked polarization of living standards and a massive growth in poverty and deprivation. Administrative and cultural changes provided new opportunities for people of middling status and above to participate directly in the political and cultural life of the nation. However, they also served to promote a differentiation of attitudes and values which added a cultural dimension to the age-old inequalities and conflicts within local communities.

These developments were cumulative rather than catastrophic. They were selective rather than all-embracing. They were not revolutionary, if by that term we mean an abrupt transition in social structure and social relations. They were singularly uneven in their impact, giving rise to different outcomes in communities of different type. They occurred partly in response to the pressures of impersonal forces of socio-economic development, and partly as a consequence of deliberate programmes of innovation. Above all, they were the outcome of the moulding and channelling of the forces of change by the continued strength and intractability of some of the persisting elements of the social structure.

English society in the later seventeenth century was still in many respects what it had been in the reign of Elizabeth. It remained an amalgam of small-scale communities, based upon nuclear family households, and held together by bonds of co-operation between neighbours and kin and ties of patronage and deference between superiors and inferiors. But it was also a society which had been irreversibly altered. Local communities had been deeply penetrated by forces which both weakened their localism and gave a sharper edge to their patterns of social stratification. Inequalities of wealth were more marked. Sharper distinctions of education, religion, attitudes, beliefs and manners had emerged to reinforce the polarizing effects of demographic and economic development. Inter-group conflicts of interest had arisen which produced fiercer antagonisms and demanded readjustments of social relations if they were to be defused and contained. The social alignment of individuals and groups of differing rank had been modified in such a manner as to facilitate the dissociation of polite and plebeian cultures which has been identified as a fundamental feature of English society in the eighteenth century.[2]

These changes gave the later sixteenth and seventeenth centuries their significance in the development of English society. Their interaction with the enduring characteristics of social existence gave the period its distinctive texture as human experience. In the pages that follow I have drawn upon the pioneering work of a generation of scholars in the attempt to recapture that experience and to express something of the satisfactions, sufferings, elevated aspirations and common humanity of four earlier generations which did more than a little to shape the subsequent development of modern English society.

Part One

Enduring structures

1 *Degrees of people*

When sixteenth- and seventeenth-century Englishmen set out to describe their society, they began by making distinctions, by classifying and ranking. 'We in England,' commenced William Harrison in 1577, 'divide our people commonlie into foure sorts.' A century later the curate of the Kent parish of Goodnestone-next-Wingham, in listing the local population, automatically divided the householders into five social categories.[1] This mental habit, of which many more examples could be cited, is of the first significance. It bears witness to the fact that the most fundamental structural characteristic of English society was its high degree of stratification, its distinctive and all-pervasive system of social inequality.

The reality of inequality was displayed everywhere. Massive and very visible distinctions of wealth and living standards impressed themselves on the casual observer who travelled the countryside or walked the streets of the towns. Hierarchical distinctions of status were reflected in styles of address. Rank and power were recognized in dress, in the conventions of comportment which governed face-to-face contacts between superiors and inferiors, in the order in which seats were taken in church, in the arrangement of places at table and in the ordering of public processions. Order, degree, rank and hierarchy seemed self-evident, even natural.

That English society was highly stratified and that such stratification reflected major differentials in the social distribution of wealth, status and power, all historians of the period would agree. Their disagreements derive from their different conceptions of the relative importance of the actual criteria upon which social stratification was based and their varying interpretations of the nature of the relationships between individuals and social groups of different rank. Was English society, as some would assert, essentially a hierarchy of status, based upon the estimation accorded to different social functions, or was it, as others would argue, a hierarchy founded upon the possession of wealth? How far did relative position in this hierarchy affect the experience and opportunities of individuals? Were relationships between people of different social position characterized by vertical ties of patronage and clientage, or by the animosities generated by horizontal class solidarities?

These questions are fundamental to our understanding of the nature of English society in this period and they are not easily answerable. It is easier for the historian to be aware of the system of social inequality than to generalize about it in more than the shallowest manner. Once familiar with the records of the period we can more readily feel its force, almost intuitively, than analyse its characteristics with real precision. Yet such an analysis must be made. In attempting it, we must take care to steer between on the one hand, an uncritical acceptance of contemporary perceptions of the social order and on the other hand, the forcing of the complex historical realities of the time into conformity with our own, perhaps anachronistic, conceptions of the nature of social inequality. We can best approach the problem by asking first a number of simple questions. What were contemporary ideas about social inequality? What do they reveal about the criteria of evaluation upon which social distinctions were grounded? How far do these ideas conform to what we can discover of the actual distributions of wealth, status and power in society? By answering these questions we may arrive at a description of the social order which encompasses both contemporary perceptions of its nature and discoverable historical reality. Such a descriptive analysis can provide a firm foundation. The further and ultimately more fascinating and significant questions of the influence of social position upon the life experience of individuals, and the relationships between social groups can then be pursued as we go on to explore social behaviour and the dynamics of social change in later chapters. For the moment it is enough to begin by establishing the structure of inequality itself, the distinctions which existed between what Harrison called 'degrees of people'.

Perceptions of the social order

It is a commonplace to assert that sixteenth- and seventeenth-century Englishmen were deeply preoccupied with the problems of order and degree. In their most elevated discussions of the nature of the universe they envisaged a 'great chain of being' stretching down from the deity to the very elements, in which each creature, each created thing, had its appointed place. In their accounts of the 'tree of the commonwealth' or the 'body politic', they presented society as an organism of functionally interdependent, though unequal, parts. Such accounts of society were at once an explanation of social inequality and a scheme of values. They portrayed society as it *ought* to be, providing a prescription for an ideal harmony in social relations. The scheme of social order thus propounded was the conventional bombast of sermons and homilies, of proclamations and of preambles to statutes. That it was platitudinous is not to say that it was not employed with sincerity often enough, but even its most enthusiastic protagonists knew very well that it was an ideal, an aspiration.

In trying to describe society as it *was*, or rather as it seemed to them to be (for systematic social investigation was to await a later age) contemporary writers came down to earth more firmly. They invariably put forward a scheme of ranks or degrees, of hierarchically arranged social categories which were intended to simplify the complexity of reality and clearly distinguish the principal social groups. The nature of the actual ranking frequently varied, usually in accordance with the principal concerns of the writer (in general sixteenth-century writers were primarily interested in the polity; those of the seventeenth century gradually turned their attention to questions of national resources and manpower). Despite these variations, however, contemporary analyses of the social order usually have at least two features in common. By and large they present accounts of what is recognizably the same society, though with different degrees of detail and clarity. Again, they tend to show an overlap, even a confusion between different criteria of social rank. The broad structure of society emerges clearly enough, yet the social order was also far too complex to be anatomized in terms of any single criterion. It had burst through the constraints of traditional classifications into functional 'orders' and only with difficulty could its component parts be adequately defined.

William Harrison's scheme of society can provide an example.[2] Of the four 'degrees of people' distinguished by Harrison, the first degree consisted of gentlemen. Though internally differentiated into the titular nobility, knights, esquires and 'last of all they that are simplie called gentlemen', this group was defined in general as 'those whome their race and blood or at least their vertues doo make noble and knowne'. Next in Harrison's scheme came the citizens and burgesses of England's cities, a group defined by their occupations and by their possession of the freedom of their cities. Third came the yeomen of the countryside, defined either as freeholders of land to the value of 40s. a year, or as farmers to gentlemen, and further as possessing 'a certaine preheminence and more estimation' among the common people. Finally came a category embracing day labourers, poor husbandmen, artificers and servants, people who had 'neither voice nor authoritie in the common wealthe, but are to be ruled and not to rule other'.

Harrison's classification is significant, and not untypical in several ways. Its author was confident about the broad structure of society, yet the sharpness of his focus varied considerably. Distinctions of rank within the category of gentlemen were carefully defined, yet below the level of the yeomanry the internal differentiation of the common people was minimized. Indeed, even when dealing with the middling ranks of society, Harrison was curiously silent about, or made only glancing references to, certain groups which did not fit neatly into his classification: notably the professions. Another striking feature of his account is the multiplicity of criteria employed in the allocation of rank. Gentility, as we have seen, was broadly defined in terms of birth and blood. Yet in his account of different degrees of gentlemen Harrison showed himself very aware indeed of the importance of wealth to the establishment and maintenance of station. Knights, for example, were described as being not born, but made; for their valour in war, their service to the monarch in peace, but 'most commonlie according to their yearelie revenues or abundance of riches, wherewith to mainteine their estates' at a level appropriate to 'a knight's living' – though he quickly added that not all gentlemen of sufficient wealth were knighted. Again, gentle status itself could be achieved as well as inherited; by obtaining a university degree, by appointment to governmental or military office, or by any man who 'can live without manuell labour, and thereto is able and will beare the port, charge and countenance of a gentleman'. With these qualifications Harrison passed from the ideal of gentility as an independent condition conferred by blood to its reality as a status dependent upon a compound of occupation, wealth and life-style in addition to and sometimes independent of birth. He also gave frank recognition to the reality of social mobility, to the fact that the social order's apparent stability was a condition not of stasis, but of dynamic equilibrium.

These features are equally apparent in the account given of lower degrees in the social scale. Citizens and burgesses were distinguished partly by their distinctive occupations, partly by their legal status as possessors of the freedom of their cities, but even more by the fact that they were of sufficient 'substance to beare office in the same', while the wealth upon which their civic position depended might enable some of them, in time, to found gentle families. Yeomen bore a status rather than an occupational designation, yet in the final analysis the 'preheminence' and 'estimation' which they were accorded among countrymen was a product of their wealth and life-style as substantial farmers who were able to 'live wealthilie, keep good houses and travell to get riches' and of their essential, though subordinate role in local administration. They too might see their sons set up as gentlemen. Membership of Harrison's fourth degree depended upon occupation, lack of wealth and virtual exclusion from positions of authority; of their chances of social mobility he said nothing.

Finally, it can be observed that Harrison was concerned only with adult male rank. The status of women and children was assumed to follow that of their husbands and fathers, while the problem of the relative position of such transitional adolescents and young adults as servants and apprentices was not considered.

Both the broad structure of society described by Harrison and the difficulties he experienced in constructing a consistent scheme of classification in the face of numerous competing criteria of rank are equally evident in other social analyses of the period. Sir Thomas Wilson, writing around the year 1600, divided the English people into nobles, citizens, yeomen, artisans and rural labourers. Of these groups, he was primarily concerned with the first, carefully distinguishing the parliamentary peerage from 'the meaner nobility' of knights, esquires and gentlemen, and explicitly placing a variety of professional men – lawyers, officers, graduates and middle rank clergymen – among the gentry.[3] Only slightly different was the hierarchy of 'Ranks, Degrees, Titles and Qualifications' drawn up by Gregory King in 1695 as part of his famous attempt to estimate the state of national resources as they had stood in the year 1688.[4] King followed the gradations of gentility from the peerage down to the level of plain gentlemen much as Harrison and Wilson had done (with the addition of baronets, an order created only in 1611). Thereafter, however, he dropped both the usual division between townsmen and countrymen and such status terms as citizen or yeoman, providing instead a simple ladder of occupations. First after the gentry came a mercantile and professional cluster of 'Persons in offices', merchants, lawyers and clergymen. Next came freeholders, farmers, 'Persons in sciences and liberal arts', shopkeepers and tradesmen, artisans and officers in the forces, and finally, common seamen, 'labouring people and outservants', cottagers and paupers, common soldiers and vagrants.

Like Harrison, Wilson and King viewed wealth as an important determinant of social status. Wilson related gradations of status within the gentry to complementary scales of wealth, and further distinguished the 'great yeomanry', who aspired to gentility, from 'yeomen of meaner ability', on the basis of wealth. King's ladder of status conformed, to a large extent, to his estimates of the average family income of different social groups, while his fundamental distinction was that between those 'increasing the wealth of the kingdom' (that is, those whose incomes exceeded their annual living expenses) and those decreasing national wealth. Nevertheless both also recognized that the social hierarchy could not be reduced simply to a succession of economic categories. Relative wealth, though a necessary, was not a sufficient condition of social standing. While very much aware of the great wealth of some leading citizens, Wilson would not accord them the gentility which he granted professional men. Again, the lesser yeomanry were distinguished from copyholders, who held land from manorial lords, on the basis of their superior mode of land tenure, though Wilson was aware that some copyholders were men of substantial means. Similarly with King, there are more than enough exceptions in detail to the general convergence of status and wealth in his table to make it clear that even at the end of the seventeenth century other criteria of social estimation retained much force. Merchants whose income was equal to or greater than that of many landed gentlemen were nonetheless placed firmly below the gentry. Freeholders ranked higher than farmers. Lesser clergymen came above farmers and tradesmen of equal or superior wealth. Even among those groups 'decreasing the wealth of the kingdom', common soldiers and vagrants, whose incomes King reckoned to be superior to those of cottagers and paupers, were placed below them.

Finally, it can be observed that Wilson, like Harrison, frankly recognized the existence of social mobility in English society, though King's table, by its very nature, provides no information on this issue.

This brief review of three of the best known and most available contemporary descriptions of the social order, which could be expanded by the inclusion of many other similar accounts,[5] helps to reinforce a number of points. The broad pattern of society emerges clearly and consistently from Harrison to King, despite variations in detail, disagreements over the exact positions of certain middling groups in society and a general tendency to minimize distinctions at the lower end of the social scale. Again, rank and status emerge as having been far from autonomous conditions. Rather, they were perceived as compounds made up of several elements of social estimation in varying proportions, including (in no particular order of significance) birth, conferred title, wealth and the nature of that wealth, life-style, occupation, form of land tenure, tenure of positions of authority and legal status. Finally, social mobility was recognized as a structural feature of society, an element of dynamism which, in the context of a society acutely conscious of social stratification, served to confirm and highlight rather than to abrogate social distinctions.

The characteristic features of contemporary perceptions of the social order are clear enough. How far did they conform to the discoverable reality?

Wealth, status and power

There was no doubt among contemporary commentators that gentlemen occupied a place of special estimation in the social order. The very term 'gentlemen' was employed by them as a group expression, implying a certain homogeneity of social position and identity of interests, perhaps even a collective consciousness, which was attributed to no other single social group – though they might on occasion speak broadly of 'the common people', or 'the poor'. Gentlemen stood apart, and the possession of gentility constituted one of the most fundamental dividing lines in society. At the same time, however, it was recognized that the line dividing gentlemen from the rest in the body of society was a permeable membrane and that the collective identity of gentlemen concealed a considerable degree of internal differentiation. Both features are well confirmed by independent evidence.

In the first place gentlemen as a whole were not a legally defined group in English society. Different degrees of gentility were defined with more or less precision. Thus the peerage of dukes, earls, marquises, viscounts and barons was distinguished by its heritable titles, its favoured position before the law, and its privileged parliamentary status. Lords were born or created by the crown. The order of baronets, on the other hand, enjoyed a heritable title, but had no legal privileges or seats in the House of Lords. Originally created in 1611, baronets technically had to be drawn from families which had been entitled to display arms for at least three generations and to be possessed of lands to the annual value of at least £1000 – a double qualification which in itself is significant. In fact baronetcies were virtually auctioned off under the early Stuart kings. Knights were created by the monarch for service and, more generally, from among those of armigerous family who could afford the accoutrements of a knight: a medieval property qualification which had become meaningless by the seventeenth century. They were in fact sparingly created among crown servants and leading county families under Elizabeth I, more lavishly under her successors. Below the knights in the scale of precedence came esquires, officially including the heirs male and descendants of heirs male of the younger sons of peers; the heirs male of knights; certain office holders (such as Justices of the Peace) who held the title by courtesy; and finally those whose direct male ancestors had held the title by long prescription. Gentlemen were in strict definition the younger sons and brothers of esquires and their heirs male.[6] So much for definitions. As to the proportions of gentlemen of different rank, the peerage was always a tiny minority – Sir Thomas Wilson listed sixty-one temporal lords, while in 1688 (after the flood of Stuart creations) Gregory King reckoned that there were 161. The baronetage was originally to be limited to 200 creations, though Stuart financial needs led to something over 400 grants by 1641 and Gregory King estimated that there were 800 baronets in 1688. King also thought that there were 3000 esquires and 12,000 mere gentlemen in the England of his day, though for more precise information on the relative proportions of gentlemen of different degree we do better to rely on detailed county studies. Lancashire on the eve of the civil wars, for example, had seven baronets, six knights, 140 esquires and 641 mere gentlemen. Yorkshire had thirty baronets, seventy knights, 256 esquires and 323 mere gentlemen (though a rather more restricted definition of mere gentility applies in the case of these Yorkshire figures).[7]

The definitions given above seem clear enough. In practice, however, the qualifications for rank below the level of knight were never rigorously maintained. The College of Heralds, it is true, kept an official register of gentility, and on the occasion of heraldic visitations of the counties, claims to gentility were rejected as well as confirmed by the Heralds. But visitations were rare and could never keep pace with the waxing and waning of family fortunes in the counties. Although the Heralds could snub the more obvious and most recent interlopers in county society, on the whole they tended to grant a formal legitimacy to those whose claims rested on grounds less precise, but much firmer than those of genealogy. Moreover their visitation books never included all those whose claim to gentle status was informally recognized in their localities. Far more significant for the attainment of gentility, for the distinctions between gentlemen and for the place of the gentry in society as a whole than formal qualification, was the recognition accorded to wealth, life-style and the exercise of authority.

Gentlemen, taken together with their immediate families, constituted a tiny minority of the English population – around 2 per cent of the populations of Kent and Lancashire in the early seventeenth century and something similar over the nation as a whole.[8] Yet they controlled an immense proportion of the nation's wealth; most notably, of course, by virtue of their positions as landowners. Estimates of the distribution of English landownership in the mid seventeenth century suggest that perhaps 50 per cent of English land was owned by the gentry while a further 15 per cent or more was the property of the peerage.[9] Such global estimates, of course, involve a good deal of reasoned guesswork, but there can be little doubt that they reflect broadly the realities of the situation. Gentility was based on landed wealth, a wealth conspicuously displayed in the superior houses, diet and clothing of gentlemen, in the leisure which they enjoyed, in the numbers of servants they employed and in the memorials which they erected to perpetuate their memory after death.

There were, of course, variations in the wealth of individual gentlemen, ranging from the immense incomes commanded by peers such as the Earl of Derby, who had vast estates in no fewer than thirteen counties, to the modest holdings of mere gentlemen supported by a single estate. In general, despite individual variations and some fluctuation over time in its fortunes as a group, the peerage stood apart, both in the scale of its wealth and in the extent and geographical dispersal of its estates. As for the gentry proper (using the term in the customary sense to mean gentlemen of baronet status and below), a variety of close county studies agree that they can be subdivided on the basis of wealth into 'greater' or 'upper', 'middling' and 'lesser' or 'parish' gentry – divisions which, much as Harrison, Wilson and King suggested, correspond roughly, though by no means necessarily, to the status distinctions of baronets and knights, esquires and gentlemen. The actual landed incomes necessary to place a man in any one of these categories varied from region to region (it was not infrequently remarked that many a southern yeoman was worth more than many a gentleman in the relatively poorer north), yet within counties the broad distinctions were clear enough. In early seventeenth-century Yorkshire, for example, the lesser gentry generally had estates of between fifty and 1000 acres, the middling gentry, estates of 1000–5000 acres and the upper gentry, estates of 5000–20,000 acres. In terms of actual income the 679 heads of Yorkshire gentry families in 1642 broke down into 362 with annual incomes of under £250 (53.3 per cent), 244 with incomes of £250–999 (35.9 per cent) and seventy-three with incomes in excess of £1000 (10.8 per cent). In Kent in the same period, the range was from around £200 a year for 'parish' gentry to as much as £10,000 for the greatest gentlemen. Lancashire gentlemen ranged from very substantial landowners like John Calvert of Cockerham, who had a landed income of approximately £913 (of which some £850 was received in the form of rents), to men who were essentially large farmers, though rarely themselves engaged in manual labour, like John Hoghton of Park Hall of whose total landed income of £77, some £60 came from the profits of his own home farm.[10]

Gentility thus derived from a degree of landed wealth sufficient to afford a certain life-style, which in turn gave rise to local recognition. Part of that process of recognition was selection for office and the exercise of authority. As the lords of manors and leading figures in their parishes, lesser gentlemen exercised considerable influence and authority in their communities. But the true test of status was selection for county offices. Thus in Lancashire, Essex and elsewhere, 'parish' gentlemen might be chosen as High Constables of their hundreds or serve on the grand jury at quarter sessions. Middling and upper gentry, by virtue of their greater prominence and established positions served in the more prestigious offices of local administration. Similarly in Somerset the greatest baronets, knights and esquires provided the county's Members of Parliament, deputy-lieutenants and leading justices, while lesser esquires filled the judicial bench and mere gentlemen, the subordinate posts.[11]

The gentry of provincial England thus formed an élite of wealth, status and power, internally differentiated and yet united by their shared interests as substantial landowners and agents of government and by their common claim to bear the name of gentlemen. They were not, however, a closed caste. Whatever the definitions of gentility itself and of different degrees of gentility, the very complexity of the criteria which, in practice, established a man's rank meant that there was always room for movement both into and within the ranks of the gentry. Over time some families became extinct. Others failed to maintain the wealth necessary to uphold their position. Where such opportunities arose there were aspirants ready to press forward, backed by the wealth upon which subsequent recognition and the establishment of a lineage depended.

Of the 963 known gentry families of Yorkshire in the period 1558–1642, nine were elevated into the peerage, sixty-four removed from the county, 181 are known to have died out in the male line and a further thirty simply disappeared from the records. They were replaced in county society partly by cadet branches, partly by newcomers from other counties, partly by successful lawyers and merchants who crowned their careers with the purchase of estates, but above all by men of yeoman origin patiently building up their lands until they were recognized as gentlemen. In the case of Lancashire the painstaking research of B. G. Blackwood reveals the full extent and complexity of the process of social mobility. Over the seventeenth century as a whole the numbers of gentle families in the county varied: there were 763 gentle families in 1600, 774 in 1642 and 662 in 1695. These broad trends were the product of a constant flux, involving shifts of relative position within the gentry and even more a steady turnover of families on the lower edges of gentility. In each of the three periods 1600–42, 1643–64 and 1665–95, for example, as many as one third to a half of the families claiming gentility changed.

Taking the first of these periods, Blackwood found that the overall numbers of gentry slightly expanded. Of those families recognized as gentry in 1600, 485 retained their gentility (forty-eight of them rising relatively within the gentry, thirty-four declining relatively and a further thirty-five holding their position, though only in the face of economic difficulties). Less fortunate were the 278 gentle families of 1600 which had lost their places among the Lancashire gentry by 1642 (twenty by failure of the male line, twelve by removal from Lancashire, thirty-five by disastrous economic decline enforcing the sale of their lands and the rest by less dramatic failures to maintain their social position). Finally, 210 families were able to achieve recognition of gentle status for the first time over the period, while a further seventy-nine probably did so. Of these rising families some were wealthy townsmen establishing themselves on estates, but the majority were prosperous yeomen who crossed the indefinable but crucial threshold of recognition as gentlemen.[12]

Such independent evidence confirms that, as contemporaries were aware, social mobility was a constant phenomenon in English society, though one which might vary in its significance from district to district and over time. The question of variations in the intensity of social mobility is one to which we will return. For the moment, however, the structural point suffices. Its implications are clear enough: that in the final analysis the establishment and maintenance of gentility depended upon the acquisition and retention of landed wealth. Birth, a genteel life-style and activity in places of authority were secondary criteria, buttressing the fact of substantial landownership. Those ranked next in the social hierarchy were those best placed to achieve the necessary qualification for gentility: the wealthier merchants and professional men of the towns and the prosperous yeomanry of the countryside.

The position of these two aspirant groups must, however, be distinguished. Yeomen clearly occupied a lower position in the same hierarchy of rural society which was headed by country gentlemen. They were measured on the same scale. The place of wealthy townsmen, however, was different. In the first instance they could not be placed on the same land-related scale as the gentry. They belonged rather to another and, to some extent, an independent ladder of status. That their urban status was inferior to that of established landowning families, there was no doubt. Nevertheless, contemporaries generally agreed in placing them higher in social estimation than the rural yeomanry and in assimilating them more closely to the gentry. Was there a real basis for this commonly repeated judgement?

Although the careful study of both urban elites and the professions is undeveloped in comparison with the now extensive literature on the gentry, the evidence shows clearly that there was such a basis, and for several reasons. One of the most compelling reasons was that many leading merchants and professional men enjoyed close familial ties to the landed gentry: they were, to a significant extent, recruited from the younger sons of the gentry. Again, the most successful among them were able to accumulate substantial wealth, certainly far greater than that of country yeomen and not uncommonly greater than that of many gentlemen. Finally, such men were able to hold positions of authority in urban government, or in administration, comparable to the positions monopolized by the gentry in the countryside. A few might aspire to places of great influence in national affairs – in Parliament and royal administration. Let us examine these matters in more detail.

There can be no doubt that the attitudes of the English gentry towards mercantile occupations were somewhat ambivalent. Trade lacked the prestige historically associated with the tenure of manors and its traditional military and administrative obligations. The constant attention to business required of the successful merchant denied him the leisured pursuits of the country squire. Nevertheless, no formal inhibition prevented the gentry from participating in commercial activities, while careers in trade were generally regarded as suitable opportunities for those younger sons of the gentry who could not be set up independently on estates. As a result a considerable number of adolescent sons of the gentry received their inheritances in the form of the often substantial fees necessary for their apprenticeship in England's cities. Of more than 8000 apprentices bound to the members of fifteen London companies in the years 1570–1646, for example, some 12.6 per cent were the sons of knights, esquires and gentlemen, the remainder of the entrants being drawn largely from the middling ranks of rural and urban society. Gentry recruitment to these companies was clearly far in excess of the proportion of gentlemen in the population at large. Moreover, in the most prestigious and wealthy companies (broadly speaking those trades which involved wholesale and retail dealing rather than manual labour) the proportion of apprentices of gentle birth was far higher – amounting to one quarter to one third of all entrants.[13] Once apprenticed, of course, not all these sons of the gentry necessarily thrived. Some were overtaken by fellow apprentices of less elevated social origins. Nevertheless, the fact remained that the upper ranks of urban society maintained strong familial ties with the upper and middling ranks of rural society. Less than 10 per cent of the great merchants of Elizabethan and early Stuart London and only a quarter of its Elizabethan mayors had been born in London, and the experience of the other cities of the kingdom was much the same.[14] It was a fact of real significance for the relationships between rural and urban society and between the possessors of landed and commercial capital in England.

What was true of the great merchants of the cities was even more true of the professions. Military officers and officials of the royal civil service were generally of gentle origin – though neither profession offered very numerous opportunities before the late seventeenth century. The law, the church, and to a less extent medicine, however, did so, and while apprenticeship to trades was one means of providing well for sons, outlay on education in the universities or Inns of Court was another. Formal education at university or the Inns of Court was by no means essential for entry to any of these professions in this period, but it was necessary to those who aspired to reach the higher echelons of their profession. Since education cost money it is scarcely surprising that studies have revealed some three-quarters of common lawyers and half to two-thirds of civil lawyers to have been of gentry origin, most of the remainder being the sons of prosperous tradesmen and professional men. Only the clergy provided something of an exception, many of them being of yeoman stock, though the proportion of gentry sons entering the clergy rose steadily over the course of the seventeenth century.[15]

Once established in their trades or professions, the merchant, the lawyer and the rest could attain at least a decent living standard and sometimes indeed a degree of wealth which put them on a par with the landed gentry. A notable few (such as the plutocrats of London and the provincial cities, or the leading lawyers of the age) became immensely rich. Such money might lack the prestige of broad acres, but it could be turned into land readily enough when the time came. With distinction in a man's trade or profession came not only wealth, but also status and power. The successful merchant could climb the ladder of urban office to the aldermanic bench or mayoral office, taking his place among the self-perpetuating oligarchies which ruled England's cities, wielding authority comparable to, and sometimes far in excess of, that of a country justice. Similarly, the clergy occupied a position of considerable status in their communities, and high clerical rank brought with it wealth, power and authority, while successful lawyers could progress to the judicial bench and ultimately to the great offices of state.

Entry into trade and the professions thus placed able youths upon semi-independent ladders of rank which could carry them, with luck and ability, to positions far superior to that of the rural squire. As Sir Thomas Wilson, himself a successful lawyer and crown servant, remarked of younger sons, 'many times we become my master elder brother's masters, or at least their betters in honour and reputation, while he lives at home like a mome'.[16] Even for those who attained only modest success, however, the comparability of their positions to those of at least the lesser gentry, to say nothing of family ties which remained strong, ensured their effective assimilation to gentle status, their pseudo-gentility, to borrow Professor Everitt's apt phrase.[17] When possible that assimilation was made complete by the purchase of an estate and removal back to the countryside. This eventual exodus to the country should not be exaggerated. The extraordinary rates of turnover among leading urban families (which incidentally ensured that there were always opportunities for newcomers in the towns) owed at least as much and probably more to the extremely high mortality rates in the towns and to the instabilities and insecurities of trade as to the passage of the successful to country estates. But it was a very real phenomenon nonetheless, one much commented on by contemporaries and very well evidenced in individual case histories.[18] In part it reflects the fact that land remained the best and most secure form of investment for wealth gained in trade or the professions, but it also demonstrates that whatever a man's urban riches, the ideal of rural gentility retained its superior prestige and cultural force. Moreover, the constant process of interchange, of which it was part, worked against the development of any self-conscious urban interest group ranged in opposition to the landed gentry.

Careers in trade or the professions thus constituted a kind of social oscillation for many younger sons of the landed gentry, a way of retaining, or of recapturing after an interval, the place and 'port' of a gentleman by means other than the undisturbed possession of land. Other recruits to the civic élite, to the professions (at least the clergy and the lower ranks of the law) and indeed to the gentry, enjoyed upward social mobility of a less ambiguous kind, starting from humbler origins among the yeomanry of the countryside and the 'middling sort' of townsmen. Recognition of their opportunities for upward social mobility helps to place these middling groups in context as regards the upper ranks of society. If we are to understand their position correctly, however, they must also be placed in the context of the remainder of rural and urban society. Their distinction from the gentry and from the tiny urban élites is clear enough. But equally important was their distinction from the mass of the common people. On this question contemporary commentators were persistently vague, beyond their usual recognition of the yeomen as a distinct status group. Looking down the social scale from their own superior positions they tended to ignore, or dealt only cursorily with social distinctions of singular importance, while the quality and precision of their comments on groups below the yeomanry was generally poor. Such condescension is perhaps to be expected of men of their time, position, purposes and prejudices. There is no reason why historians should share it.

Yeomen, Harrison tells us, were regarded with superior 'estimation' among countrymen. On that all of his contemporaries would have agreed. Where they diverged was on the question of defining yeoman status. The word 'yeoman' itself is a status term of obscure origin, rather than an occupational designation of the kind usually applied to the common people. Occupationally, yeomen were tillers of the soil, 'husbandmen' in the contemporary usage. Yet as Peter Laslett has observed, while all yeomen might be husbandmen, not all husbandmen were yeomen: the term husbandman generally being reserved for a lower rank in rural society.[19] In what lay the superior standing of the yeoman?

In general, contemporary descriptions of the social order defined yeomen as men possessing land in freehold to the value of 40s. a year or more. Such a definition was resonant in two separate ways. On the one hand, freehold was considered a superior form of land tenure. It gave relative independence. While the freeholder might owe a nominal rent to the lord of the manor on which his land lay, he possessed a fully secure title to his land and was free to sell, exchange or devise it by will as he saw fit. The freeholder was thus distinguished from the majority of copyhold tenants who rented land for a period of lives or years, paying an annual rent and a substantial 'fine' whenever the copyhold came up for renewal; from the leasehold tenant renting his land for a specified period according to the terms of his lease; and from the mere tenant-at-will, who possessed no right save that of gathering his growing crop should his landlord decide to terminate his tenancy. On the other hand, a 40s. freehold entitled a man to vote in the parliamentary elections of his county; it conferred political rights.

Freehold land tenure might therefore appear an admirable means of distinguishing the yeomanry from other villagers. As such it was emphasized by contemporaries and by more than a few historians. Unfortunately it is a broken reed. Research has shown that many yeomen were indeed freeholders, but that many were leaseholders, many were copyholders, while some held land by a variety of tenures. Conversely, seventeenth-century England had many 40s. freeholders who did not aspire to call themselves yeomen. In fact, as local research has clearly revealed, social status among countrymen depended far less upon the form of a man's land tenure than upon the amount of land he held. Yeoman status was accorded to men who farmed a substantial acreage, usually in excess of fifty acres, though there was no precise norm and the holdings of yeomen varied considerably. Farmers of smaller acreages, say between five and fifty acres, were generally accorded the name 'husbandman' in conventional usage, while below them in the rural social scale came cottagers and labourers who might hold a few acres but who were distinguished by the fact that they needed to undertake wage labour for others to a greater or lesser extent if they were to eke out a living. The exact proportion of these different groups in the populations of particular villages, of course, varied. At Laxton in Nottinghamshire a survey of 1635 reveals that the manor of Laxton had 106 tenants of whom 24 (22.6 per cent) held farms of from 40 to over 200 acres, 49 (46.2 per cent) held between 5 and 40 acres and 33 (31.2 per cent) held less than 5 acres. In addition, 8 villagers held no land at all. At Willingham in the Cambridgeshire fens, the field book of 1603 reveals a situation in which a single tenant held 59 acres, 48 held between 5 and 38 acres each and 9 held less than 5 acres, while 67 householders were entirely landless.[20]

With different farm sizes went different levels of wealth and different living standards, differentials which are most graphically illustrated in surviving wills and probate inventories. Take, for example, three near-contemporary County Durham cases. Ralph Singleton of Gainford, yeoman, died in 1587. He had held several parcels of land, some by leasehold, some by customary tenure. He left bequests of £60 in cash and in addition goods to a total value of £74 8s. 6d., including animals worth £36. His inventory indicates that his house was relatively well furnished, containing two beds, a table, cupboards and a good deal of brass, pewter and other furnishings. In the same year Peter Madison, husbandman, of the same village died. He held one tenement by leasehold, lived in a simple two-room house and left his bequests in the form of grain and animals, rather than in cash. His total goods were valued at £38 12s., of which his animals accounted for £22 and growing corn for £13 more. He possessed some pewter and brass utensils, but little furniture, his household goods being valued at only £1 13s. 4d. and his clothes at 6s. 8d. Four years earlier John Smith of Pittington had died. He was accorded no occupational designation, but was clearly a landless labourer or cottager. The total value of his goods was £2 10s. 8d. He possessed some linen and pots and pans, but no bed and no table, only a board and some stools. His table vessels were of wood, his clothes were described as old and his only livestock were two hens and some 'lytle chikkens'.[21]

The economic realities underlying such differentials at the village level can be quite simply stated. Dr Bowden has calculated that an early seventeenth-century husbandman with an arable holding of thirty acres might expect to make a net farming profit of perhaps £14–15 in a normal year. Of this sum perhaps £11 would be needed to feed a man, wife and four children, leaving a surplus of £3–4: 'a tolerable, though by no means easy existence'. Given that many husbandmen held smaller farms, we can see why William Harrison described husbandmen as merry at their occasional celebratory feasts, 'divers of them living at home with hard and pinching diet and some of them having scarce inough of that'. Bread, cheese, bacon and beer were their usual fare and if they ever obtained wine, strong ale or venison 'they thinke their cheere so great and themselves to have fared so well as the lord Maior of London, with whom when their bellies be full they will not often sticke to make comparison'.[22]

That was in good times. In a year of poor harvest the modest surplus of the husbandman was wiped out. Only the man with more than fifty acres under the plough could expect to be insulated from such fluctuations and perhaps even to make a bigger profit as a result of soaring scarcity prices.

In contrast to the position of the husbandman, Campbell estimates that even lesser yeomen had incomes of £40–50 a year, while £100–200 was not uncommon among more substantial men. The farming accounts of the Berkshire yeoman Robert Loder for 1613 indicate that his profits after the costs of maintaining his household amounted to £185 15s. 7¼d. He spent £12 per head on his family and servants, who enjoyed a diet of wheaten bread, beer, meat, cheese, fish, milk, butter and fruit. He could make generous allowances for fuel and clothing, for soap, starch and candles and could also afford other small luxuries and gifts to friends and relatives.[23]

This is to state the contrasts sharply. Of course there was much middle ground in the scale of rural wealth, in which the smaller yeoman and the wealthier husbandman overlapped, just as the greater yeomen and smaller gentry overlapped higher in the scale. In an analysis of inventories from the Lancashire Forest of Pendle in the seventeenth century, some 45 per cent of husbandman inventories had total values of over £50, while some 14 per cent of yeoman inventories had values of under £50. Yet the basic realities of the yeoman/husbandman distinction remained clear. While almost half the yeoman inventories were valued at over £100, the highest total for a husbandman was £87. Similar results have been obtained in a comparable study of Oxfordshire inventories.[24]

Such blurring at the edges of conventional social categories was equally evident in the case of small husbandmen and village labourers. Some husbandmen occasionally undertook wage labour, sometimes working for their landlords at harvest time, for example. Labourers and cottagers, however, were much more dependent on day labour. The more fortunate among them might hold an acre or two, or enjoy the benefits of customary common rights. At Nassington, Northamptonshire, for instance, the fifty-two cottagers were each allowed to keep three cows and ten sheep on the common, while at Alberbury in Shropshire they were allowed unstinted pasture in the woods for their cattle and hogs. Such a situation was most common in the woodland, moorland and fen areas of England where extensive commons existed to supplement the produce of numerous smallholdings. Over the country as a whole, however, Professor Everitt estimates that perhaps two-thirds of labourers held only their cottages and garden plots.[25]

For most labourers, then, wages were crucial to their subsistence: generally at rates of around 1s. for a day's work in the seventeenth century, with higher rates for some specialized tasks and sometimes additional perks such as free housing in tied cottages, the right to gather fuel or to keep an animal on their employers' land and perhaps the opportunity to buy food cheaply from farmers. Both the annual income of a labouring family and their enjoyment of such small additional advantages depended largely on the regularity of their employment, something which could vary greatly. The accounts of the Petre family for 1580–1, for example, reveal that six labourers were employed regularly on the home farm, while a further two were given fairly regular work in the summer months. Peak periods of the agricultural year saw many more taken on: twenty-two to help with weeding in June, nineteen in harvest time and twelve for hay-making. The accounts of another Essex farm, that of Thomas Cawton of Great Bentley, for 1631–2 presents a similar picture. Three men worked regularly throughout the year for Cawton, while several more obtained an occasional day's work. At the times of weeding, hay-making and harvest others were employed in addition to the wives of the regular labourers and a number of village women. In Kent in 1693–4, Sir John Knatchbull employed five labourers for 226–84 days each, three for 121–67 days each, ten more for between nine and fifty-one days, and twenty-two more at peak times.[26]

Given such variations in the regularity of work, the approximate incomes of labourers are extremely difficult to assess. Dr Bowden has calculated that a regularly employed man in the south of England in the early seventeenth century might earn a maximum of around £10 8s. a year, while Miss Clark's estimate suggests a figure of around £9 on average. In the Essex village of Terling in the late seventeenth century an annual income of about £15 was probably the maximum for a labouring family, a figure which matches Gregory King's estimate of the income of cottaging and labouring families in 1688. As for the costs of subsistence for an average family, various estimates suggest that around £11–14 would be necessary for food, clothing, fuel and rent in normal years: substantially more in times of scarcity and high food prices.[27]

On whatever estimate we employ, the glaring fact is that the life of the labourer was a constant battle for survival. Labouring families lived in poor one-room cottages for the most part, with little furniture, and on a diet of bread, cheese, lard, soup, small beer and garden greens, occasionally supplemented by better fare at harvest feasts provided by employers. (At one early seventeenth-century harvest home, for instance, the farmer provided boiled beef, bacon, puddings, apple pie, hot cakes and ale.)[28] But such occasions were rare. As contemporaries often remarked, labourers (and indeed small husbandmen) and their wives lived best during the transitional years of adolescence and early adulthood when they worked as resident farm servants and were at least tolerably well housed and fed, in addition to receiving small wages which could be put by for the future.

The broad distinctions in village society between yeomen, husbandmen and labourers are clear enough. Rural craftsmen and tradesmen are somewhat more problematic in that they might have belonged to any of these levels in terms of wealth. Indeed, as an occupational group they can be said to have lacked a distinct identity, primarily because many of them had dual or even multiple occupations. In the Leicestershire village of Wigston Magna, for example, the miller, baker, butcher, carpenter, smith and wheelwright were all small farmers in addition to pursuing their crafts and trades; a situation which also obtained in many other villages, and was even more prevalent in areas of domestic industrial production. There were yeomen–craftsmen, husbandmen–craftsmen and labourers who possessed also some specialist skill. A craftsman whose skills were in regular demand, such as a smith or carpenter, might spend his time largely at his craft, while others might occupy themselves primarily in agriculture. At the same time, however, there were areas of domestic industrial production where a landless or near landless industrial proletariat had emerged, wholly or very largely dependent on its wages. To generalize broadly, it can be said that the most prosperous craftsmen, engaged largely in the more highly skilled trades, tended to enjoy incomes and living standards comparable to those of lesser yeomen and husbandmen, as is evident from taxation assessments and the evidence of wills and inventories. Others more sporadically engaged, or plying less well-paid trades, or employed at piece rates in domestic industry, were often more akin to labourers.[29]

Social stratification in the villages thus tended to be dictated by levels of wealth rather than by the mere fact of landholding in itself or by the mode of land tenure, though in an overwhelmingly rural society the former obviously depended largely on the latter. Social status and participation in positions of authority followed the same pattern. In the Essex village of Terling, the yeomen, the most substantial husbandmen and the wealthier craftsmen were most sought after as sureties for recognizances and as witnesses to wills. In addition the distribution of office-holding in village life followed the distribution of wealth: churchwardens, vestrymen, overseers of the poor and quarter sessions jurymen tended to be drawn from among the petty gentry and the yeomanry of the village. Husbandmen and craftsmen served much more rarely in such prestigious positions, but most commonly held the humbler posts of sidesman and constable. Labourers and poor craftsmen scarcely ever participated in village administration at all. Similarly at Kelvedon Easterford in the same county the village yeomen formed 'a sort of informal oligarchy', at Hawkshead in Lancashire the yeomen ran the parish, and at Solihull in the Forest of Arden the wealthier villagers occupied the key offices as churchwardens, parish bailiffs and feoffees of charities, while lesser villagers played a part only in the subordinate offices of the parish. Such findings support Harrison's assertion that England's yeomen were to be included among those who governed the nation, while husbandmen, artificers and labourers (though occasionally holding village office) could be generally dismissed as having 'neither voice nor authoritie in the common wealthe'. It was an overstatement, but substantially true.[30]

Social stratification in rural society can thus be anatomized with some degree of precision. Of the towns much less is as yet known in satisfactory detail. Nonetheless, a few clear points stand out, which may be further elaborated by the findings of future research. The occupational structure of towns of any size was, of course, of much greater complexity than that of the countryside – Worcester records of the period 1600–49 mention 100 different occupations – and this complexity was enhanced by the existence of dual and multiple employments. Among the urban crafts and trades a certain hierarchy existed, based largely, it would seem, upon the relative wealth of their practitioners. Beyond distinctions of this kind, the basic status division of the towns was between freemen who could engage independently in trade and who possessed political rights (perhaps one third to a half of the male population) and the rest. Independent urban craftsmen could live comfortably enough, though even freemen had comparatively little voice in urban government except at the level of parish administration. Below them were various categories of wage earners, ranging from journeymen–craftsmen employed by a master, to the mass of casual labourers of whose existence very little is known beyond the fact that many of them lived in grievous poverty.[31]

Although our knowledge of the complex urban situation remains inadequate, the evidence of social stratification among the common people of England is at least sufficient to make it clear that contemporary writers were mistaken in regarding those below yeoman and citizen level as a homogeneous mass. The reality of social distinctions in the lower reaches of the social hierarchy was just as complex as among the gentlemen, who may have appeared as indistinguishable to a labourer as the common people appeared to some of their superiors; and, as among the gentry, the enduring overall structure of inequality was a framework within which constant movement took place. Some farm servants would eventually become husbandmen or yeomen, some urban apprentices or journeymen would become independent masters. As among their superiors, such social mobility both gave flexibility to and confirmed the established distinctions between men. Inadequate as contemporary social descriptions may have been in detailing the complexities of the distinctions that existed among the common people, they were generally right, however, in insisting upon the special place of yeomen and full citizens in the social order. Indeed the evidence which we have reviewed suggests that the gap which separated them from their social inferiors was in some respects greater than that which removed them from their immediate superiors. This point deserves some emphasis, for it serves to remind us that however finely graded the hierarchy of English society may have been, certain strata were more closely placed than others – there existed what might be thought of as clusters of social groupings presaging a simpler profile of stratification. Contemporaries recognized this to some extent when, in less formal moments, they simplified their terminology and spoke of 'gentlemen', 'the middling sort of people' and 'the poor'. These expressions reflected a slow shift in both the structure of inequality and in its perception, to which we shall return.

One final point remains to be made – one which contemporaries, in their emphasis on the broad national picture, tended to overlook. This is simply that considerable local variation can be discerned in the profile of social stratification. The gentry were unevenly distributed across the English countryside. In Lincolnshire, for example, they were notably thin on the ground, while in Lancashire, which had many gentlemen, they were to be found more in the lowland than in the upland areas of the county and more in arable than in pastoral parishes.[32] Again, variations in both the distribution of wealth and in occupational structure existed in areas with different agricultural and industrial structures. In Wiltshire the cheese and butter producing areas had many small family farms, the sheep–corn region had bigger farms and large numbers of landless labourers, while the area of cloth production had numerous poor industrial workers. Broadly speaking, lowland fielden regions exhibited a greater degree of inequality in the distribution of wealth than did poorer, but more egalitarian pastoral regions of the woodlands and the highland zone.[33] In short, great variety existed and such variation could be singularly important in its influence on the social dynamics of particular communities. The fact of such plurality of circumstances is of vital importance. Yet equally important is the fact that it existed within a known range, within the broad parameters of a structure of social inequality which had general validity across the nation and which was recognized as such.

Having described that social order and having established its principal characteristics, we are the better prepared to approach the larger questions which force themselves upon the social historian. For if we are to understand how the English people in the later sixteenth and seventeenth centuries lived and thought, how they contributed to and experienced the processes of social change, it must be constantly remembered that their experience was neither equal nor uniform. Where it exhibited regularities, these were most commonly related to the underlying structure of relative social position. It is for this reason that the social hierarchy has been examined here in such detail. For the differences which existed among the English are vital to any understanding of their collective history. To ignore or obscure them, to fail to appreciate their significance, is to smudge our picture of the past.

2 *Social relations in the local community*

In the year 1700, at the age of 66, the Shropshire yeoman, Richard Gough of Myddle, set out to write the history of his parish. A year later, having completed a creditable, though largely conventional, antiquarian and institutional study of the parish, he added to it an altogether more original piece of writing: his 'Observations concerning the Seates in Myddle and the familyes to which they belong'. Beginning with a seating plan of the parish church, he proceeded to provide individual histories of the families who occupied its pews. In this compilation of anecdotes, spiced with his own sometimes censorious, sometimes wryly humorous comments, the seventeenth-century village community, which Gough knew so well and viewed with both affection and candour, is resurrected 'warts and all'.[1]

Gough's starting point in his approach to the local society which he brought vividly to life was not dissimilar to our own. For in his plan of the parish church pews and their occupants he provided a swift sketch of the profile of social stratification in Myddle. In the front pews sat the gentry, in the south-west corner of the church, the cottagers, each rank in its appointed place. With Gough, as with us, however, this could be no more than a starting point. The individual characters of the people of Myddle and the nature and quality of the social relationships, which bound together their society in a living whole, emerge not from the static description, but from the tangled skein of incident which Gough spun into the threads of his narrative. In his ability to construct this dynamic picture, Gough, of course, had an advantage over us. The norms which informed behaviour, the characteristic social relations of that society, were matters which he could take for granted. They were familiar, unproblematic, and therefore portrayed but never analysed. To the historian, however, for whom that society is in some respects comfortably familiar and yet, in so many others, puzzlingly alien, these matters present themselves as problems demanding analytic reconstruction. What were the social bonds of primary significance in local society and how did its members relate to one another, as kinsmen, as neighbours, as people of differing rank? It is to these matters which we must now turn; for it was these things, just as much as and perhaps more than its patterns of stratification, which gave English society its special character in terms of social organization and its distinctive texture in terms of human experience.

Localism and mobility

Richard Gough was very much a man of his parish. He knew its topography intimately. He was aware of its history. His knowledge of the customs of the manor and of the working of parochial institutions – in which he had served as an officer – was extensive. He knew exactly where his neighbours sat in church and was well acquainted with their business and characters. His sense of place and local loyalty was sufficiently developed to make his parish the object of the literary endeavours of his old age. In all this Gough was not untypical. English society was composed of thousands of relatively small rural communities, interspersed with a smaller number of towns and a handful of great cities. Its various subdivisions, the village, the parish, the county, the town, all had their own integrity as social units. Although we must take care to avoid the pitfall of assuming too much when we employ the term 'community', it is nonetheless clear that each of these was to a greater or lesser degree not only a geographical or administrative unit, but also a local social system. Both the fact of geographical propinquity and their constellations of local institutions focused the interactions of their inhabitants. Shared relationships, concerns, speech, manners, rights and obligations contributed to a powerful sense of place which had a role in personal identity and could excite fierce local loyalties.

Such sentiments should never be underestimated, but neither should they be exaggerated. Localism was an important element in both the social experience and the mentality of sixteenth- and seventeenth-century people, but it was only one element, however strong its influence. Moreover, its significance varied for different purposes and for different social groups. The diversity of English provincial society was contained, as we shall see, within a strong framework of national integration. Similarly, at the most intimately local level, the real strength of social ties must not be held to imply that local communities were either bounded or static.

The myth of the relatively isolated, self-contained and static rural community is a powerful element in our conception of the past. For this very reason it is the more important to stress that it is at best a half-truth. In the upper reaches of society, the gentry belonged to a much larger social world than that of the country parish. Their community was that of the county, their neighbours the members of their own class with whom they hunted, exchanged visits, and served in county administration. If they possessed the wealth and time to participate in the developing seasons of London or the great provincial capitals, then their social world took on national or regional dimensions. By virtue of their role in government, their preoccupations embraced those of the kingdom. This much is readily recognized. Yet we do an injustice to their social inferiors if we exaggerate the degree of their necessarily more circumscribed existence.

However much they belonged to their villages and parishes, the country people of the period also moved in a larger world. The village was their place of residence and the parish their closest unit of administration, but they lived in broader social areas for each of a variety of other purposes; in their economic activities, for example, in their family relationships, or in their general sociability. Richard Gough was primarily concerned with the seven townships and 600 inhabitants of his parish of Myddle, but he also had broader social horizons, was aware of national events and issues and had numerous extra-parochial contacts. The diary of the Lancashire apprentice Roger Lowe, written in the 1660s, provides a lively account of Lowe's relationships with his fellow inhabitants of Ashton-in-Makerfield, but it also reveals that both he and they had regular contacts over a larger area, serviced in Lowe's case by a good deal of gadding about the neighbouring towns and villages of south Lancashire. The recorded social relationships of the villagers of Terling in Essex with outsiders – economic, marital, familial and other kinds – reveal that they enjoyed contacts with outsiders resident in London, Kent, Hertfordshire, Cambridgeshire, Norfolk and Suffolk and no fewer than 108 towns and villages in Essex. Though the core of their social area was the district within ten miles of Terling, it could also, and frequently did, extend much further.[2]

Village communities, it is clear, were not social isolates, something which common sense would lead us to expect, though not a few historians have chosen to deny common sense in this matter. Much more significant in terms of its effects upon local social structure was the fact that the population of England was surprisingly mobile; a startling finding of recent social history which is supported by several kinds of evidence. The surnames recorded in parish registers, for example, indicate a considerable degree of turnover of population. At Honiger in Suffolk, of the sixty-three family names recorded in the period 1600–34 only two can still be found in the register for 1700–24. Such evidence alerts us to the long-term movement of population, but the evidence of rare consecutive census-type listings of village populations provides an even more unexpected indication of the degree of short-term mobility. Just over half the population of Cogenhoe in Northamptonshire disappeared and was replaced between 1618 and 1628, while at Clayworth in Nottinghamshire the turnover of population between 1676 and 1688 approached two-thirds, only a third of those disappearing being accountable for by death. Skeletal individual biographies, provided particularly in the depositions made before church courts, add to the picture by making it clear that most country people had lived in more than one settlement in the course of their lives. To take the more explicit example of Richard Wood, a dyer of Eccleshall in Staffordshire, recorded in a late seventeenth-century survey of population, we find that he had been born twelve miles away at Stoke-on-Trent, and had lived as a servant for six months in Newport, Shropshire, for a year in Eccleshall, for two years in Aston, Shropshire, and for a year in Bucknall hamlet in Stoke before returning to Eccleshall for a further year's service, following which he married and settled there as a tradesman.[3]

As this example suggests, a good deal of the population mobility of the period can be accounted for by the movements of adolescent servants, who left their home villages in their early teens, moved here and there as servants on annual contracts and then ultimately found permanent employment, married and settled down, only to send out their own children in due course. Such mobility has been revealingly analysed by Ann Kussmaul, who finds that farm servants moved often, but rarely far – describing a kind of orbit around their villages of origin in the case of one well-documented district of Lincolnshire – and that such mobility was a temporary phase of the life cycle, curtailed in adulthood. Similar in kind was the mobility of some youths as apprentices and of some single women as servants moving to the cities, part and parcel of a constant flow of migrants to those 'devourers of mankind' – some of them encouraged by contacts with kin, friends or former neighbours now established in town.[4]

There were other kinds of mobility too. Seasonal labour was one – as in the case of the annual movement of workers from Cleveland to the farms of southern Yorkshire at harvest time. In addition there was movement not only of the young and of temporary workers, but also of whole families. Peter Laslett found that, although the largest component in the turnover of population in Clayworth and Cogenhoe was the mobility of servants, there were also established families which chose to move on. This phenomenon is further revealed in the settlement papers produced by the administration of the Law of Settlement, which sought to regulate mobility in the later seventeenth century, and can be quantified by careful use of parish registers to 'reconstitute' the histories of individual families. The message is plain: most of those children born to the families of English parishes did not marry and settle in their parishes of birth, many of those marrying and starting families came from outside, and a considerable number of families chose, for whatever reason, to move on.[5]

Mobility varied in its nature. It also varied in terms of the social composition of the mobile part of the population. At Powick in Worcestershire and at Kelvedon Easterford in Essex, the farmers, yeomen and husbandman families were comparatively stable, while the labouring families experienced a much more marked turnover. At Myddle in Shropshire and also at Terling in Essex, the labouring poor were similarly mobile, but their mobility was matched by that of the largest tenant farmers of these parishes, while the most stable element in local society was composed of middle-rank yeomen and husbandmen. Perhaps further research will reveal regional patterns in these matters (a possibility raised by the work of Peter Clark), which might in turn be related to the nature of local economies, to such matters as inheritance customs, or to regional variations in the density of urban settlements.[6] These questions remain tantalizingly open, but certainly it would appear that the degree and social structure of mobility were influenced on the one hand by the attraction of economic opportunities and on the other hand by the pressure of economic deprivation. The more substantial members of a village might be attracted by better opportunities elsewhere, land to buy, a good farm to lease, trade opportunities. The poor were drawn by the prospect of employment, pushed by the lack of it and often enough shuffled on by the unwillingness of settled neighbours to recognize them as permanent inhabitants. In analysing patterns of migration to Kentish towns, Peter Clark proposed a distinction between 'betterment' and 'subsistence' migrants, the former moving short distances, the latter long distances, the former originating usually in the countryside, the latter including a proportion of inter-urban migrants.[7] This useful distinction helps clarify the problem, though it too may need much eventual qualification. But whatever the motivation of population mobility, and it was undoubtedly complex, the facts remain that it was part of the life cycle for a very substantial part of the English population and that it was a not infrequent phenomenon among their elders and betters. Indeed, for a substantial minority of the casualties of social change – the vagrant poor – restless movement became, as we shall see, a way of life. The problem of vagrancy and that of variations over time in the degree of general population mobility are two matters to which we will return. For the moment it suffices to emphasize that a steady turnover of population was a vitally important structural characteristic of local society in England.

Kinship

The implications of such a situation should not be exaggerated, but they must be recognized and taken into account. In terms of local social organization, the most striking of these is that we must learn to think of the local communities of the period, in the countryside no less than in the towns, as being to some extent fluid. Given that fact, we may well ask what was the nature of the social bonds which held them together?

One not uncommon suggestion has been that the principal social bonds within local communities were the ties of kinship; that each was in a sense an aggregate of kinship groups, sometimes co-operating to serve mutual interests, sometimes thrown into conflict with one another.[8] This suggestion might derive some support from comparisons between England and those peasant societies studied by social anthropologists in which ties of extended kinship are of the first importance. Yet, slowly accumulating evidence now provides reason to believe that this view must be seriously modified, for in this important respect English society, far from being analogous to modern peasant societies, may have been significantly different.

In the first place, analysis of the structure of households in English settlements, based upon surviving census-type listings, reveals that since the sixteenth century at least, the overwhelmingly predominant household form has been the simple 'nuclear family': households consisting of husband, wife and children, with or without servants. The large and complex households containing resident kin, or even several cohabiting conjugal families, which are known to have existed in some continental societies, are notable by their comparative rarity. It must be said at once that this pattern was by no means rigid. More complex households were formed on occasion for a variety of reasons. Again, there was a degree of variation between different social groups. In a sample of communities covering the period from the sixteenth to the early nineteenth centuries, Peter Laslett found that 27.6 per cent of gentry households contained resident kin, as compared with only 17 per cent of yeoman households and 7.9 per cent of the households of the poor. Such exceptions and variations were doubtless occasioned by a number of factors, ranging from the peculiar circumstances of individual families to differences in the provision made for the elderly and for siblings, not to mention the question of the degree of wealth necessary to house and maintain a more complex family group. The fact remains that the great majority of English households consisted of simple, nuclear families, and this was true of town and country alike.[9]

Be this as it may, the possibility remains that each of these families may have had kin living nearby, occupying separate houses, yet perhaps frequently co-operating; that the neighbours, in short, were also kin. Early research on this problem, however, suggests a further negative conclusion – that links of kinship between households in English villages were fewer than might have been expected and that, in terms of kinship, the families of English villages were relatively isolated. In the Essex village of Terling in 1671, less than half the 122 householders had relatives among the other householders, while such networks of kinship as can be discerned were far from dense: most of those related to another householder having only one such connection in the village. Whether local variations existed in this matter, which might be explained in terms of differences of economic organization, of inheritance customs or of settlement patterns, remains a fascinating but as yet unanswered question. In the northern upland parish of Kirkby Lonsdale, very different in its economy and settlement pattern from lowland, fielden Terling, Alan Macfarlane nevertheless finds no evidence of dense kinship networks. In woodland-pastoral Myddle, however, a good deal of interrelationship may have existed among the longest established small-farming families. Doubtless the reason lay in the relative immobility of this particular group, a matter to which attention has already been drawn. Where mobility was higher, in particular the mobility of adolescents leaving their home village and moving off as servants to settle eventually elsewhere, dense clusters of interrelated households can scarcely be expected. Kin, it would appear, were generally spread over a quite considerable area, some of them no doubt near enough to maintain occasional contact, others effectively lost. Whichever was the case our current working hypothesis must be that kinship ties beyond those of the nuclear family were of limited significance in the social structure of village communities.[10]

If this hypothesis should be confirmed by further research it would be a matter of considerable significance. Even so, we must recognize that it would still tell us very little about the actual quality of relationships between kinsmen living within a single village, or scattered by the accidents of seeking out a living and a home over a rather broader social area. The social significance of kinship, after all, depends not simply upon the question of the immediate availability of kinfolk locally, but to a much greater degree upon the extent to which kinship provides the basis of individual social relationships. Despite all the circumstances discussed above, kinship might still have been a very significant social bond and a vital element in social organization.

There are a number of ways of testing this proposition. In the first place we may consider the problem of the 'recognition' of kin; that is, the conventions according to which sixteenth- and seventeenth-century people recognized others as kinfolk and the genealogical depth and breadth of that recognition. This established, we may attempt to explore the effective importance of the kinship ties recognized in the everyday lives of individuals.

A number of structural features of the English kinship system of the period suggest that those recognized as kin were relatively few in number, and that recognized kinship groupings were to a large degree personal and impermanent. The tracing of ancestry and descent, for example, conformed to neither the patrilineal nor the matrilineal forms most familiar to social anthropologists; rather it was traced bilaterally, through both father and mother. Surnames, to be sure, were passed patrilineally, but the system itself was not patrilineal. It was ego-centred, pivoting on the individual who traced kin outwards from himself, rather than placing himself in a line of descent reckoned from a particular ancestor. As a result, every individual in each new generation possessed a unique range of kin, and the lack of exclusive criteria of kinship meant that kinship groupings lacked structural persistence over time. Corporate kinship groups with firm structures, unambiguous rules of membership and a continuing identity generation after generation, were absent, with the arguable exception of parts of the Scottish borders where the notorious 'surnames' enjoyed a unique significance. Again, the kinship terminology employed in England was relatively simple when judged by the standards of many human societies. Since the time of the Anglo-Saxons no distinction had been made between the terms used for relatives on the father's as against the mother's side of the family.[11] The terms actually in use were strikingly vague beyond the confines of the nuclear family and the nuclear families of origin of a person's parents. Father, mother, grandfather, grandmother, brother, sister, uncle and aunt were clear enough. For the rest, the terminology for the more extended kin was singularly unspecific: 'kinsman', 'cousin', even 'friend', being commonly employed without further specification of the exact nature of the relationship. Finally, it may be observed that few binding formal obligations were recognized to kin other than to members of the individual's own nuclear family and to grandparents and grandchildren; a point illustrated by the fact that the

Tudor Poor Laws, when laying down those relatives for whose welfare individuals might be held responsible at law, went no further than parents and children, grandparents and grandchildren.

The implication of these structural characteristics is that the recognition of kin was flexible, that it must have varied a good deal from person to person. Some individuals recognized a wide-ranging cousinage. Others concentrated their attention upon their closest kin. Moreover, such differences could be influenced by the needs and circumstances of particular social groups and the peculiarities of particular local conditions. It is undoubtedly true, for example, that both the titular aristocracy and the upper gentry were deeply preoccupied with ancestry and lineage and that they tended to recognize a wide range of kinsmen. Birth and descent were, after all, matters of much significance, indeed vital where hereditary titles were at issue. Hence the lively interest in genealogy of many gentlemen like Sir Thomas Pelham, one of the leaders of Sussex society, who spent £30 on the drawing up of an elaborate pedigree, or of another Sussex gentleman, Anthony May of Tinhurst, who desired memorial brasses representing four generations of his line to grace his tombstone.[12] Lower in the social scale, however, the evidence suggests that people were considerably less preoccupied with ancestry and indeed less conscious of blood relationships with their living kin. Alan Macfarlane's painstaking analysis of references to kin in the diary of the Essex clergyman Ralph Josselin makes it clear that Josselin's recognition of kin was genealogically shallow (extending only to his grandparents) and narrow (extending to first cousins). Other diaries and autobiographies of people of middling rank give a similar impression, while the range of kin mentioned in wills of villagers again indicates a lack of concern with kin beyond the nuclear family and nuclear family of origin of testators and their spouses.[13] None of these forms of evidence is, of course, wholly satisfactory, and the only truly adequate method of exploring this problem – direct questioning – is impossible for the historian of any period of history beyond those covered by today's 'oral historians'. Nonetheless, what we have points to a somewhat circumscribed degree of kinship recognition, subject to a number of qualifications. The gentry and aristocracy were certainly different in this respect and had their own good reasons for being so. In some thinly peopled upland regions kin may have been of greater significance, a matter still awaiting further exploration. Finally, we must remember such northern border areas as the 'debatable land' of Cumberland, where in 1603 the Graham 'surname' included some 200 members, headed by fifteen to twenty 'surname leaders' who were all direct descendants of Long Will Graham. This was a remarkable situation and one which may seem romantic to the sentimental, but it was an utterly untypical product of very special conditions and was increasingly regarded at the time as an anachronism.[14]

Consideration of the question of kinship recognition thus suggests that the extended kin were of relatively small significance for most late sixteenth- and seventeenth-century people, who were for the most part unaware of broad kinship networks. But what of the practical significance, the effective importance of kinship ties? It is only when we approach this question that the social variations in the strength of kinship sentiments, already pointed to, are clarified and confirmed, and that the reasons for these variations become plain.

Among the gentry, kinship was undoubtedly a matter of great practical significance. For persons of this rank, their community was the county society made up of their approximate social equals. Their habit of marrying for the most part within that county society (a matter to be examined in more detail in Chapter 3) meant that extensive kinship links existed within the gentry community. Not only did they exist; they were used. Anthony Fletcher has argued that in Sussex county society 'kinship was the dominant principle'. Networks of extended kinship were the basis of the round of social life, of county administration and of political activity. Where ties of actual kinship did not exist, friendships and alliances could be reinforced by fictional kinship through the choice of godparents – a highly significant fact. Other writers on the 'county community' are in broad agreement with Fletcher and though the uses of kinship among the gentry still awaits systematic analysis, the broad reality of the situation is clear enough. To take the example of a single gentleman, the diary of Nicholas Assheton of Downham in Lancashire for the years 1617–18 reveals that of the people whom Assheton recorded meeting in the period, as many as 30 per cent were kinsfolk, while of those he mentions without meeting, as many as 40 per cent were kin. The more frequently individuals were met or mentioned, the more likely were they to be kin. Assheton's social life revolved around family gatherings, the greatest of these being at Christmas 1617. He supported kin in times of trouble, while his kinswomen aided one another in time of childbirth. In short, Assheton's life was heavily oriented by ties of kinship.[15]

Assheton was a scion of a leading county family. Whether such a situation was common among the minor gentry is more doubtful. John Morrill has suggested that the bond of kinship was much less significant for the lower gentry of Cheshire as compared with leading gentry families, a point which receives some support from Lawrence Stone, who has argued that the influence of kinship was slowly declining among the propertied classes in general. There were other particular groups besides the gentry for whom kinship was of much practical significance, however. The lawyers of Elizabethan and early Stuart Kent were members of a profession closely knit by ties of kinship which reinforced professional solidarity, while the clerical profession saw the emergence in this period of a considerable number of clerical dynasties whose members offered one another aid and support in their careers. Again, the extent to which kinship was used by the merchants and businessmen of the period as one way of establishing trustworthy contacts in the chronically insecure world of commerce is well known, the Hostmen of Newcastle-upon-Tyne providing only one outstanding example of the way in which particular trades and industries, in this instance the coal industry, could be dominated by networks of kinsmen.[16]

Lower in the social scale and outside the special conditions of gentle, professional and mercantile life, however, kin were of less practical significance. Ralph Josselin, a clergyman, though not a member of a clerical dynasty, had very strong emotional ties within his own nuclear family, and was helped in his youth by his paternal uncle, but most of his practical and emotional support in life came from his neighbours rather than his extended kin. Josselin, it might be objected, had been carried by his career far from his kinsmen and therefore may have been untypical, but this does not seem likely. Adam Eyre, a Yorkshire yeoman, lived quite close to his kin. Both he and his wife visited their most immediate relatives, and at various times in 1647–9 he was involved in exchanges of aid and support with kinsmen, notably his father-in-law and cousin Joseph. But his social life was dominated by unrelated neighbours and most of the practical aid which he gave and received was exchanged with friends in the neighbourhood. Close analysis of the relationships of villagers in Terling, Essex, throughout our period reveals that, although testators exhibited a considerable preference for their kin (usually their closest kin) when naming executors and overseers of their wills, thereby showing a greater confidence in kinsmen to handle family property or look to the interests of their children, they showed no such preference in most matters. When seeking aid and support of other kinds they turned above all to their neighbours, even when kin were available. In short, the many forms of assistance given by individuals to one another were not regarded, as they might be in some societies, as essentially the sphere of kinship activity. On the contrary this was an area of non-kinship activity, which sometimes happened to involve kinsmen.[17]

For the mass of the English population, then, it would appear that ties within the nuclear family were strong and that these were, when possible, maintained once children had left home and formed their own nuclear families. Contacts were relatively close with surviving parents and siblings on both sides of the new conjugal family, with what Talcott Parsons has called the 'families of orientation' of both spouses.[18] Otherwise, for most social groups kinship would appear to have been something which, if not unimportant, was nevertheless rarely of *overriding* significance. In a sense it may have been something of a reserve, a resource which was selectively drawn upon. The impression is that kinsfolk were selected for certain purposes if they were locally available and all other things were equal. Kinship shaded into friendship in its practical importance. It was one of many social bonds, rather than a dominant principle in the social structure, one of many foundations on which the individual might build up a network of social contacts. Kinship was a good basis for co-operation, certainly, but there were few ascriptive elements in the relationships of most English people with their broader kin. They reveal instead a marked optional quality, permitting considerable individual variation within this broad situation.

In all these respects English kinship may appear to have been essentially flexible and permissive, a dependent rather than an independent variable in social organization. Indeed, in its essential characteristics it was closer to the kinship system of modern England than to that of the peasant societies with which sixteenth- and seventeenth-century England has been too readily assumed to have shared features of its social structure. But we must ask, in conclusion, what influenced its varying significance socially and perhaps geographically?

A number of factors may have influenced the simple availability of kin locally, such as different rates and patterns of population mobility; variations in settlement patterns in particular areas; the question of settlement size, which might affect whether or not children found land, work, or marriage partners near to one another; the nature of inheritance customs, which might influence the dispersal or holding together of heirs to family property; the prevailing demographic rates, age of marriage and life expectation, which would influence the size of kinship groups. As to the effective significance of kinship, this might be related to the state of development of social institutions (for example, the Poor Law) which might compete with kinship obligations, and to economic factors such as whether labour was available for hire, whether credit facilities were available, or whether kinsmen needed one another for help. These issues demand further research, but all in all the crucial factor must have been the relative balance of advantage or disadvantage which would be derived from maintaining a particular pattern of social relationships. For some, the merchant, the politically active gentleman, the insecure inhabitants of a turbulent and badly policed border area, the maintenance of strong kinship bonds and obligations had manifest advantages (though this is not to say that they coldly calculated them by some kind of social accountancy). But to generalize from the special experience of these historically prominent or notorious social groups is as mistaken as the uncritical importation and application of inappropriate social anthropological models. For most of the English, more vital social bonds were those which they individually established and maintained not with an extended kinship group but within another social grouping: the neighbourhood.

Neighbourliness

'Neighbourliness', unlike kinship, is a somewhat vague concept, lacking in precise definition. Yet it was a notion much employed by sixteenth- and seventeenth-century people. Indeed 'good neighbourliness', as Mildred Campbell has argued, was a virtue which stood 'perhaps first in the criteria by which the social and ethical standing of an individual in a community was measured'.[19] Quite what was meant by neighbourliness is something which can be inferred from contemporary usage of the term. At its simplest it can be defined as a type of relationship between people established on the basis of their residential propinquity; but this too is inadequate. Two further characteristics of neighbourliness were that it involved a mutual recognition of reciprocal obligations of a practical kind and a degree of normative consensus as to the nature of proper behaviour between neighbours. Finally, and crucially, it was essentially a horizontal relationship, one which implied a degree of equality and mutuality between partners to the relationship, irrespective of distinctions of wealth or social standing. The reciprocity of neighbourliness was a reciprocity in equal obligations, the exchange of comparable services between *effective*, if not actual, equals. It is this aspect above all which distinguished neighbourliness from those other types of relationship between local inhabitants in which the element of social identification was overlaid and qualified by the realities of inequality.

Neighbourliness is most visible to the historian in the many practical forms of aid and support rendered to one another by neighbours, services which might often enough be vitally important to people who shared an environment which could be chronically insecure. Of these perhaps the most significant were the many occasions for simple economic aid. The small farmers of the period were in many respects individualistic economic agents, a point which has recently been stressed by Alan Macfarlane. But it is equally important to recognize the strong limitations which existed on their economic individualism. Quite apart from the continuing significance of communal regulation of open field agriculture or common pasture, there was abundant need for informal co-operation in economic matters. In the village of Wigston Magna, Leicestershire, for example, many of the poorer tenants did not possess their own ploughs; presumably they arranged to borrow implements from their neighbours.[20] Of this kind of daily co-operation, comparatively little trace is left to the historian as compared with the abundant evidence of individualistic property rights. Yet it must have been of major significance in the ability of many families to make their living. One aspect of such relationships, however, is fortunately extremely well documented in the abundant references to debt and credit relationships between villagers which were recorded in wills and probate inventories. These may serve to illustrate the numerous instances of aid and support which certainly existed, but of which we have only occasional evidence.

It is a striking feature of English village society in this period that debt and credit were not matters which were either controlled by specialist moneylenders, or reduced to simple financial contracts on the basis of the payment of interest by the debtors. Specialist moneylenders, of course, existed, but what is more significant is the extremely widespread participation of villagers in the provision of credit. In a study of some 4650 probate inventories taken in Lincolnshire, Leicestershire and Norfolk in the period 1650–1720, B. A. Holderness discovered that some 40 per cent listed debts owed to the testator, a finding which receives general support from Margaret Spufford's research on debt and credit in Cambridgeshire villages throughout the later sixteenth and seventeenth centuries. Of those involved in the lending of money, a number of particular categories of people stand out – widows, single people, professional men and gentlemen, for example. However, the broad point remains that involvement in this kind of activity was extremely widespread. Not only did many local people lend money, but it is also clear that the same people were often involved as borrowers. In the absence of developed banking facilities, it would appear that people with spare money were ready to lend it to neighbours, doubtless knowing that they would borrow in their turn when need arose. Thus the diary of Ralph Josselin reveals that on 19 November 1651 he lent £3 to one Young of Halstead, 'who was in great straites to make his rent up to his landlord'. Ten days later he received back £3 10s. he had lent to one Caplin and promptly lent him £1 10s. more. Josselin was clearly in funds at this point, for he paid off £4 of an £8 debt of his own to William Brand. On 12 and 13 December Josselin received the £3 he had lent Young and the £1 10s. from Caplin, paid off another £4 debt of his own to Nicholas Hurrell and lent £4 to John Smith an 'oatmeale man' until 26 December; and so it went on. On 23 January, however, Josselin recorded: 'I was quite out of moneys and went where some was owing me.' Failing to get this cash, he trusted that 'god would provide for mee against my needs' and was rewarded with the unexpected payment of money owed to him by a tenant and some others, part of which he promptly used to pay off more of his own debts.

It is clear from Josselin's diary and from other evidence that the network of debt and credit might extend beyond the bounds of a single village, but that it was densest within the immediate neighbourhood, especially where relatively small sums were concerned (and many lists of debts include sums of a few pence as well as sums of several pounds). Of equal significance is the fact that interest does not usually seem to have been charged on small sums, though both interest and the drawing up of formal bonds becomes apparent in the case of substantial sums of money. Doubtless the interest on small sums was in the form of the 'social interest' of goodwill and the tacit assumption of reciprocal aid in time of need, something on which no cash value could be placed.[21]

The examination of debt and credit in the local community thus helps us to discern both the concrete benefits of neighbourliness and the limits within which neighbourly sentiment operated. The willingness to lend was there, together with the willingness to forgo interest, but within limits. Where large sums were concerned which could not easily be forgone in the case of default, formal financial transactions came in to replace casual neighbourliness. Similarly with regard to the moral dimension of neighbourliness, the evidence suggests that neighbourly relations were surrounded by both positive and negative boundaries, vaguely defined, but doubtless well-recognized within a particular local context. What were these frontiers of the 'moral community'?

On the one hand, there were negative limits, minimum standards below which a neighbour fell only at risk of losing the benefits of local goodwill. A neighbour should at the least live peaceably and harmoniously, recognizing his obligations and placing no unreasonable burden upon the tolerance of the community. Such limits are vividly displayed in local petitions and presentments to the courts of church and state. The inhabitants of Bromsgrove for example, petitioned the JPs of Worcestershire in 1623 on behalf of their neighbour William Flavell, explaining that he was 'of good and honest parentage, not litigiously given, no drunkard, quarreller, contentious, or profane person, but such a one as in our judgement feareth God and followeth a godly and painful course to live, paying Scot and Lot according to his abilities'.[22] Flavell was an exemplary neighbour. In contrast, the same JPs, like many of their fellows throughout the kingdom, received numerous complaints against bad neighbours who failed to maintain such standards. Such were those who were quarrelsome and litigious, who abused their neighbours, spread malicious gossip, caused general nuisance, were drunken and idle, mistreated their wives and children, took in and harboured suspicious strangers, or caused unnecessary expense to the parish. Individuals of this kind had placed themselves outside the boundaries of the moral community. In less extreme circumstances, the negative limit of neighbourliness is nicely encapsulated in the ecclesiastical concept that one should at the least not 'be out of charity' with one's neighbours. Such a passive definition of harmony was enforced by the symbolic exclusion from holy communion of people notoriously out of charity with neighbours. Thus in 1625 the churchwardens of one Sussex parish went so far as to complain to the church courts of the action of their minister who had defied local opinion by admitting to communion an 'open contender' who, they explained, 'will not reconcile himself, though it hath been sought by some of the parish'. As this example indicates, formal action came only after informal mediation and appeal to the canons of neighbourliness, as when William Baker and Thomas Hall quarrelled outside Durham Cathedral one day over the impounding of Hall's cattle by Baker. Hall called Baker a knave and his wife a whore, and matters might have escalated but for the prompt intervention of Nicholas Turpin who appealed: 'Fye, thes ar no meet wordes or communication emongest neighbours.'[23]

The positive dimension of neighbourliness involved recognition of the obligation to render aid and support in all the ways already discussed and a willingness to accept the neighbours as a reference group in matters of behaviour and to promote harmonious relations among them. Conformity to these standards made a 'good neighbour'. Adam Eyre was one such. He participated in a good deal of borrowing and lending, helped a neighbour at shearing time, played a role in parish administration, organized 'ales' to help needy neighbours and paid his share towards them, mediated quarrels and accepted mediation in a quarrel of his own and finally maintained good general social relations with his neighbours in his leisure hours whether at sport, over a drink, or in visits 'only to be merry'.[24] The limits of such positive neighbourliness are less clear, but basically involved recognition of the points beyond which too much could not reasonably be demanded of one's neighbours. This, as we have seen, was clearest in money matters, where the risk involved in giving aid might be too great to be sanctioned by neighbourliness alone.

Beyond the boundaries of mere neighbourly duty, any heightened positive content in either practical or emotional support carried a relationship to a higher plane; that of friendship. Here an altogether unusual degree of emotional compatibility and trust distinguished relationships based upon personal selection and going far beyond the obligations owed to either neighbours or the broader kin. 'Friends' was, of course, a term which could be used to denote kinsfolk, but it was at least as often employed to indicate friendship in the modern sense and many examples of such close personal bonds exist to bring into question the interpretations of historians who place an undue stress upon conflict in the village community, or who infer from contemporary child-rearing practices the predominance of a combative, hostile and neurotic personality type. Ralph Josselin's deep friendship with Mary Church has been well described by Alan Macfarlane, while many wills of less spiritually preoccupied and articulate people reveal testators who left the oversight of their wills or the care of their wives and children to a 'good neighbour and friend', 'speciall trustie friends' or 'gossips', who were turned to by many dying men and women, or were left tokens of esteem to carry their memory beyond the grave.[25]

Neighbourliness and friendship thus operated both to promote harmonious and co-operative relationships among groups of largely unrelated householders and to overcome personal or familial isolation in a relatively fluid society in which individuals and independent nuclear families were little cushioned by kinship ties and obligations. The importance of these bonds implies a form of social organization which was highly flexible and even individualistic, but which was far from unstructured. As a general summation of the nature of the social bonds of primary significance in this society and of their relative importance, we might do worse than to accept as a working model, those prayed for by Ralph Josselin on his fortieth birthday, 26 January 1656, when he desired God to 'blesse the soule of those I call mine; wife, children, sisters, friends, kindred, people'.[26]

If this was probably the general pattern, however, we must also take into account a number of possible qualifications and variations. That local differences may have existed in the proximity and relative importance of kin and neighbours is a possibility to which attention has already been drawn, with reference to England's heterogeneous agrarian structure. A further possibility is that of variation between countryside and town. This matter is one which awaits systematic examination, but it is one which deserved brief discussion in the light of the common assumption of the existence of a marked dichotomy between rural 'community' and urban 'anonymity'. Whether urban society was indeed markedly less structured and more impersonal than rural society remains an open question. Certainly the urban population was fluid, even sometimes transient, but this, as we have seen, was equally true of rural parishes, though the *degree* of fluidity, if it can be measured, may well have been higher in the towns. On the other hand, there may have existed stronger elements of stability and neighbourhood within the towns than is commonly imagined. For craftsmen, the urban guilds performed many services akin to those of the rural neighbourhood, though obviously only among the members of these bodies. Beyond such exclusive institutions, however, we should not discount the possible existence of parish sub-communities within the towns and cities. Dr Dyer has argued that the parishes of sixteenth-century Worcester had a community ethos. This may have been equally true of other cities, perhaps even of London where, in the sprawling suburban parish of Stepney it seems of possible significance that in 1606–10 some 63 per cent of people marrying chose partners from within the same hamlet of the parish, while a further 16 per cent married people from within Stepney, though from different hamlets. Street communities may also have existed in the cities, perhaps reinforced by occupational solidarities where it was often the case that craftsmen in particular trades congregated in particular streets or districts; the leatherworkers of Kendal in 1695, for example, resided for the most part in the lower stretch of Highgate. If 'urban villages' existed, then these may have had special characteristics worthy of study. Some may have been one-class communities, given the already considerably developed nature of residential zoning in the larger towns, though this seems never to have been so absolute a segregation as it was to become in the industrial cities of a later age.[27]

These questions remain tantalizing, but as yet unanswered. Nor are they the only issues relating to the social structure of local communities which demand investigation and resolution. The special place of women within the neighbourhood and the possible existence of youth groups as a distinctive element in local communities are matters only now beginning to attract careful exploration, and it is perhaps in these areas that significant additions to our knowledge are most likely to be made in the immediate future. Another form of distinctive experience, however, is much more clear-cut. For the gentry, the bonds of community and neighbourliness extended far beyond any village or parish to embrace large areas of their counties of residence. The network of friendship and neighbourliness of Francis, Lord Dacre, as reconstructed by Anthony Fletcher, extended throughout east Sussex, while that of Sir Thomas Pelham embraced the entire county. Neighbourly interaction among the gentry overlapped to a considerable extent, as we have seen, with kinship activity. But in other respects it was much like that of the village. The Sussex gentry were heavily interconnected as overseers, executors, trustees and beneficiaries of one another's wills. They had relationships of debt and credit with one another and shared in business enterprises, administrative activities and general sociability.[28] All this is familiar enough. The difference lay in the geographical area over which these relationships were maintained and in their social exclusiveness. The latter characteristic may serve as a reminder that neighbourliness was a relationship based upon reciprocity of comparable services between effective equals. The relations of the gentry both with their own social superiors and with their social inferiors in the villages where they resided were of a distinctly different quality.

This brings us to a final qualification of the picture of neighbourly interaction that has been drawn; the necessity of recognizing that neighbourliness, however vital its role, should not be uncritically extended to encompass the entire range of social relationships in the local community. Its sphere of operation was largely confined to the more settled inhabitants (and to those newcomers accepted into the neighbourhood), while even among these, it embraced only one dimension of local social relations. In a society so permeated by gross inequalities it was, of course, impossible for all social ties to be established on the basis of reciprocity among effective equals. Just as the canons of neighbourliness governed relations between effective equals, so also there were norms to govern relationships between superior and inferior, between patron and client. These were the conventions of paternalism and deference.[29]

Paternalism and deference

Relationships of patronage and clientage, paternalism and deference, involved, like neighbourliness, a degree of reciprocity and a sense of social obligation. What distinguished them above all was the fact that this was a reciprocity in *unequal* obligations. Such relationships stemmed from the existence of *permanent* inequalities and were based upon the recognition of the power of one party and the dependence of the other. Moreover they were conducted on terms largely, though not wholly, defined and determined by the relative superior.

These relationships were of many kinds. A landlord might extend preferential terms to certain of his tenants, as in the case of the Catholic William Blundell of Crosby who allowed his established tenants (many of them his co-religionists) long leases with security of renewal and asked of them renewal fines only half the size of those demanded of newcomers. He might aid them in times of emergency, as when Sir Ralph Assheton of Whalley ordered his steward to abate the rents of tenants hard hit by the harvest failure of 1648. A gentleman or substantial farmer might give certain favoured clients regular employment, help find places in service for their children or supply character references. He might provide support with the authorities, stand surety for a recognizance, help get a licence to erect a cottage or open an alehouse, or intervene in a court case. Thus in 1621 Sir Henry Oxinden wrote to his brother-in-law, Robert Bargrave JP, on behalf of one Goodwife Gilnot who had been accused of witchcraft, explaining that she was 'troubled and perplexed in mind' and might be 'utterly undone' by an accusation made 'either maliciously or ignorantly', and explaining the circumstances which had led to this unjust allegation. Such aid could be invaluable, as could the more commonplace gifts of money, Christmas treats, old clothes or fuel to needy dependants.[30] In all these ways a social superior could, if he chose to, protect a client from the manifold insecurities of existence.

Such relationships were based upon a recognition of their social obligations by the rich, by the landlord, the yeoman farmer and parish notable, by the clergyman – by those for whom such obligations were part and parcel of their social position, and who often thought no more deeply on the matter. Yet they also served a latent function; for paternalistic behaviour of this kind gave stability to a society which, as we have seen, embraced gross inequalities and which was, in the final analysis, based upon the individualistic pursuit of self-interest. The paternalistic gentleman, the generous patron, legitimized and justified his position by his actions, in his own eyes, in those of the world and in those of God (and not a few of them were deeply self-congratulatory about it). Such beneficence cost little, and in return a price was tacitly demanded – in terms of deference, obedience and implicit recognition of the legitimacy of the prevailing social order. The assistance rendered might vary in its content and its regularity, and so no doubt did the degree of genuine deference elicited in return. It was, nonetheless, an exchange of essentially unequal obligations: crumbs from the table, relatively speaking, in return for at least an outward subscription to a world-view and a tacit rejection of alternative definitions of the situation. Moreover, the social 'rate of exchange' in such relationships was to a large extent determined by those who possessed the wealth and power to meet the needs of their inferiors.

The remarkable memorandum book of the Lancashire landlord James Bankes of Winstanley, written in the first decade of the seventeenth century, vividly illustrates paternalism in action; its benefits, its terms and its limitations. Bankes was a godly man and subscribed to paternalistic conceptions of the landlord's duties. 'Be vere kynd and loving unto youre tenantes', he advised his children, 'and so they wyll love you in good and godly sort.' Moreover, he went far to practise what he preached. Drawing up a list of his tenants, he observed that Margaret Ranford's eight-acre tenement would be better consolidated into his demesne lands, but advised his son to do no harm to her family for 'the father and the sones have done good sarvis to this houes'. The lease should be bought in if possible, but 'plaise them in some other tenement, in Godes name – of the lyke or better'. Again, John Winstanley's three-acre tenement was worth 40s. a year more than the present rent and a twenty-one-year lease might fetch a fine of £16. But he was poor, therefore 'if his son wyll geve you tene pondes for the sam, lett him or his have it. He is a power man. Lett him remaine and his sid'. Bankes could be generous. He could also use his power to punish those who had slighted him or offended his standards. A number of undeserving tenants were named whose lands he advised his son to take into his own hand, like Roger Adlington who had taken a lease of land occupied by a poor widow and evicted her. Adlington's land could be taken when opportunity arose, 'for the said Roger is a most baid man sondre waies and so apparanly knowe of all his nebores and it is thowght well not mend'. Bankes was also realistic enough to recognize from experience that the deference of his tenants diminished in proportion to the length of their leases, and advised his children 'if God shall send you to be lordes of any tenantes, se that you never make ane les above won and twente yeres, for so shall you kipe yor tenantes in good and dowtefull obedeinces tow you'. Where no sense of special obligation impelled him to generosity, he had a sharp eye for profit – his lists of tenants were drawn up for the specific purpose of estimating how far the rents of their holdings might reasonably be raised above existing levels.[31]

Paternalism had its limits when it came too sharply into conflict with the interests of the landlord. How far Bankes's heirs followed his advice we do not know. There were many landlords, however, for whom traditional values had no compulsive power when ranged against the need to expand income from rent in a period of inflation. Walter Hawksworth of Hawksworth in Yorkshire advised his son in his will of 1619 to be a good lord and not to raise rents. The son ignored this advice and went ahead with a programme of increases. How much credit then should we accord his own pious advice to his son in his will of 1652 to treat his tenants fairly and maintain their rents at present levels? Landlords were ready enough to abrogate traditional obligations when need arose, as in north Lancashire, Cumbria and Northumberland after 1603, when the demise of border tenure heralded sharp rent rises, the refusal to recognize rights of inheritance and even attempts to reimpose moribund labour services on tenants.[32]

In these instances we see revealed the fundamental contradiction between the realities of an individualistic agrarian capitalism and the ethics of traditional social obligations which so often surfaced in the course of the sixteenth and seventeenth centuries. Given this constant tension, the maintenance of the ideological underpinning of the relations between superior and inferior assumed particular importance. Moralistic preachers and pamphleteers constantly reminded the rich of their duties, while an even greater stress was laid upon the duty of inferiors to obey those placed in authority over them by God. The 1562 Book of Homilies of the Church of England provided, as Dr Marchant has wryly observed, three officially sanctioned discourses on 'Repentance and true Reconciliation unto God', but six 'Against Disobedience and wilful Rebellion'. Young people catechized by their parish ministers were taught their duties not only to honour their parents and to do as they would be done by with their neighbours, but also 'to submit myself to all my governors, teachers, spiritual pastors and masters; to order myself lowly and reverently to all my betters . . . and to do my duty in that state of life unto which it shall please God to call me'.[33] These were quite deliberate and barefaced efforts to shape the social consciousness of inferiors in a form consistent with the definition of the situation espoused by their superiors. The submissive attitudes which they were intended to inculcate can be illustrated from occasional descriptions of admirable inferiors set down by some of the 'betters' referred to in the catechism. William Blundell of Crosby described the 'virtuous, patient soul' Bridget Stock, who though lame, impoverished and unrelieved by her parish, nevertheless refused to beg and cheerfully did what she could to earn a penny a day. Henry Newcome praised Ann Haslom of Bury, an abused but uncomplaining wife and a diligent worker, who placed her whole trust in God: 'a contented poor woman that hath learned how to want'.[34]

These women were admirable indeed, though more for the maintenance of their dignity in conditions of appalling deprivation than for the submissiveness which struck the observers who patronized them even as they praised them. How often the teachings of church and state on the relations of superior and inferior were so thoroughly internalized it is impossible to say. Their effective hegemony, however, was perpetuated by the lack of any practical alternative conception of the nature of the social order. In practice, of course, many must have recognized the iron hand behind the velvet glove of paternalism and performed their expected role largely out of a canny self-interest, manipulating thereby the prejudices of their social superiors to their own advantage. Others undoubtedly kept their place only within limits, for as we shall see, deference and obedience could dissolve when the relationship became too obviously exploitative and superiors abdicated their traditional responsibilities or betrayed the expectations established in the minds of their inferiors. Nevertheless, given the existing nature of society and the lack of alternative definitions of the situation, most had to play the game according to the given rules.

As a result, there existed networks of patronage and clientage stretching up, in what Mervyn James has called, 'a graduated ladder of dominance and subordination' from the humblest villagers, through the leaders of parish society to the gentry, and from the gentry to their own social superiors.[35] The actual quality and durability of these relationships were governed above all by the relative dependence of the subordinate partner. If a gentleman or independent yeoman, then he might be relatively free to give allegiance to, or withdraw it from, a patron, and the price of continued deference might be higher. If he was a village labourer then freedom of action was altogether more circumscribed. Whatever its ideological legitimation, deference was ultimately a social bond based upon the dual foundations of interest and dependence, and deriving its strength therefrom. At best it might seem a fair exchange on the part of the client in return for tangible benefits. At worst it was a necessary acceptance of the realities of social power.

Conflict and community

We have, then, a picture of local communities which were subject to a considerable degree of population mobility and which were held together less by dense ties of kinship than by relationships of neighbourliness between effective equals, and ties of patronage and clientage between persons of differing status, wealth and power. These characteristics of the grid of social relations in local communities seem clear enough. It should never be forgotten, however, that the reality of local society exhibited a complexity far greater than can adequately be described in a general account of the kind presented here. The relative significance of the different social bonds which we have examined could vary considerably from place to place, from social group to social group and from person to person. Again, it would be a mistake to allow ourselves to assume that the predominant patterns of relationships described were in any way static or that they functioned to produce a local society that was a comfortable idyll of order and harmony. On the contrary, such equilibrium as local society possessed was the product of a constant dynamism in its social relations and the impetus of this dynamic came, as often as not, from conflict.

Conflict between individual neighbours was an essential feature of the constant process of readjustment of social relationships at the local level, as we will see in more detail when we come to examine the problem of order. At times it might ramify into feuds between rival groups or be carried by the interconnections of patronage across the social scale. Such was the case in the Sussex village of Cuckfield in the 1570s when a quarrel between the vicar and the squire began by splitting the community from top to bottom, was carried first to county and then national level by the patronage connections of the two main protagonists, and ended only when Sir Francis Walsingham intervened in 1582 by securing the vicar's deprivation.[36] Nor was conflict invariably between either individual neighbours and families or vertically aligned groups. It could also exist, albeit temporarily and locally, between lord and tenants, rich and poor; for the finely graded hierarchy of social description could give way under pressure to the much simpler group alignments of social conflict. Given these possibilities, the maintenance of order, harmony and subordination in particular local societies required a constant, if usually undramatic, attention to balancing the forces of tension and co-operation, of differentiation and identification, thereby preserving the emotional force of the values of neighbourliness, paternalism and deference in the face of the undermining inconsistencies of reality. How was this achieved?

A significant contribution was made by the numerous popular recreations of the period, activities which did much to excite feelings of mutuality and communal identity both among particular peer groups, such as the village youths, and between people of different rank in local society, often enough including resident gentry. 'Community' after all, is not a thing; it is a quality in social relations which is, in some respects, occasional and temporary, and which needs periodic stimulation and reaffirmation if it is to survive the centrifugal forces of the inevitable tensions which arise in local society. Village sports and games, dancings, wakes and 'ales', 'rush-bearings' and parish feasts were of singular importance in this respect, as contemporaries well knew. They punctuated the calendar of the working year and reaffirmed in merriment the neighbourly ties and collective identity which, as we have seen, could be of vital importance to the physical and emotional security of individuals and families. They were occasions to 'increase a love among neighbours' in the contemporary phrase, providing recognized opportunities for the resolution of conflict and the formal burying of quarrels. They were organized and conducted according to established custom and lent a sense of communal identity over time to communities which were relatively fluid in their membership. They served also to redistribute wealth in some degree, by the manner in which parishioners contributed to a common fund of money or provisions according to their means, or more directly when the proceeds of an 'ale' were intended for the relief of a particular individual. Moreover, they helped defuse tensions not only between individuals but between social groups, not simply through common participation, but also by virtue of the fact that some festivities included elements of ritual reversal of the structure of rank and authority. The world could be turned upside down for a day, a safety valve which made it the stabler when once again it stood the right way up. Such activities did not go unchallenged in this period, as we shall see. Nevertheless an appreciation of their complex functions is necessary if we are to understand the significance of their ultimate impoverishment in some areas, their continued vitality in others, for the gradual process of social change.[37]

These aspects of the major formal festivities of the period are well known to historians and have been much discussed. Less familiar, though certainly of at least equal significance were the weddings, christenings, 'churchings' and funerals which might involve a substantial proportion of the neighbourhood, or sections of it. There was also the daily round of informal recreation – as when the neighbours met in the numerous ale-houses to drink, talk, sing, play at bowls or 'shove-groat' – and indeed the whole world of regular personal contact, at work, after church services, in the streets, the field and the market place. What was vital in this daily social intercourse was the regularity of direct face-to-face contact both between comparative equals and between superiors and inferiors. Indeed in the latter case, individual demeanour in direct personal interaction was of singular importance, for it could simultaneously reinforce consciousness of the bond of personal identification and the reality of social differentiation upon which the whole structure of paternalism and deference rested. The Kentish squires Nicholas Toke and John Clopton personally mediated in quarrels between their workers, while their wives attended at the sickbeds and childbeds of their dependants. William Blundell chatted with his people in the street – 'I asked a poor woman how many children she had. She answered "Six." "Here," said I, "here is sixpence for them." "No, sir," said she, most simply, "I will not sell my children." ' Was she really so simple? Perhaps yes, or perhaps she adopted a role. Nevertheless she showed due deference, called him 'sir', and doubtless curtsied, while he was well pleased with the exchange and his generosity was stimulated. It was the manner which was important, for it defined the relationship. This was equally so where social distance was less pronounced. The apprentice Roger Lowe bought drinks for his equals, but never for his superiors. They bought drinks for him and he in turn, as a promising lad, listened deferentially to their opinions and advice. Through the institution of service, young men and women of humble birth interacted daily with their masters and mistresses and showed them due obedience for the most part, even if they could also sing in the alehouse of their ability to 'doe my master too/when my master turnes his back'. Doubtless for the most part these conventions of demeanour and address were simply taken for granted, though some exceptional people might become conscious of their function. The minister Henry Newcome was prompted to reflect upon the matter when he found himself 'much troubled that some durst swear before me and . . . humbled that I had not more authority and presence with me'. 'One help to a profitable converse with the people', he decided, 'is that a man should not admit of any other talk but divine. It should not be an ordinary thing to keep him company.' He resolved 'to let some savoury thing fall where I had spoken merrily; or to count myself truly in debt for as much serious discourse for every jest I had told'. Newcome was learning an important lesson which many others in positions of authority knew instinctively: that in the maintenance of the relationships upon which the local social order rested face-to-face contact was vital, but effective only when conducted according to convention. These relationships were not, in the final analysis, personal. They were *personalized*: they served an impersonal function.[38]

In the successful functioning of both formal festivity and informal social interaction, localism was crucial. Despite the fluidity of its composition over time, the locality was sufficiently stable to constitute a relatively complete social situation in which the prescribed norms of neighbourliness, paternalism and deference appeared to work for the most part, and from which alternative definitions of the social order could be effectively excluded. The most vital of social relationships were established and maintained within a specific local context and it was in this context that the hegemonic activity of the national ruling class, their domination of the social consciousness of their inferiors, was most successful.

Where localism was so important, of course, a degree of variation in the quality of local social relations is only to be expected and undoubtedly existed. The presence or absence of a resident landlord, variations in settlement pattern, in the nature of the local economy, in population size, in the degree of social differentiation locally and in the institutional structures of particular localities, were all matters which could exercise their influence, as contemporaries well knew. Yet this was variation within a known and recognized range of experience. The broad structural characteristics of local society were common. It was not a society dominated by class affiliation; for however strong the awareness of status within a specific local context, broader class consciousness was inhibited for those below the level of the gentry by their lack of alternative conceptions of the social order, their envelopment in relationships of communality and deference, by the localism which gave those ties force and meaning and by a lack of institutions which might organize and express a horizontal group consciousness of a broader kind. It was perhaps a society which possessed an *incipient* class dimension in its distribution of wealth, productive relations and market situation, and in which antagonisms between social strata undoubtedly existed. But these were too limited to a specific social situation and too temporary an element in cognitive experience to allow us to speak of class as a dominant principle in social relations. That was to come, above all when and where the relationships which we have been examining lost their effective force and gave way to new forms of social organization and new dimensions of meaning in social relations.

In the local communities of the sixteenth and seventeenth centuries a constant process of accommodation served usually to maintain the balance between co-operation and conflict, between identification and differentiation. It was a complex and delicate matter, and from time to time it could be upset, as we shall see. Yet for the most part it served.

3 *Family formation*

Vital as the local community was in the lives of sixteenth- and seventeenth-century people, it was not the basic unit of society. That distinction, as Richard Gough well knew, belonged to the family. The family was the basic unit of residence, of the pooling and distribution of resources for consumption. For many a small farmer and craftsman it was also the basic unit of production. Through the family, society reproduced itself; children were born and reared and property was transmitted from generation to generation. Within the family, individuals found security and identity and the satisfaction of both physical and emotional needs not catered for by other social institutions. The family was fundamental.

Of the many functions of the family, contemporaries were well aware. In January 1588 when the puritan diarist Richard Rogers steeled himself to consider the consequences for his family of the threatened death of his wife Barbara, he listed not only the emotional deprivation of 'forgoing so fitt a companion' but also the dislocation of 'care and looking after children', 'care of household matters' and 'loss and decay in substance'.[1] Yet what most preoccupied contemporaries was less the manifold practical significance of the family, than the family as a set of relationships. To William Perkins, author of one of the many moralistic guides to family life published during our period, the family could be defined as 'sundry combinations or couples of persons', a 'couple' being 'that whereby two persons standing in mutual relation to each other are combined together, as it were, into one'.[2] In writing of the family, Perkins, in common with other authors of 'domestic conduct books', sought to advise his readers on the best ordering of these relationships. Like modern sociologists, the moralists of the time explored the principal 'dyadic relationships' of the family; between husband and wife, parents and children. Again, like modern students of the family, they pursued these relationships through the developmental cycle of the family from the selection of marriage partners to the rearing and 'setting forth' of children. It is an example that we may do well to imitate, beginning where they began with marriage, the choosing of a spouse and the process of family formation.

Marriage and marital opportunity

Marriage, according to William Perkins, was 'the lawful conjunction of two married persons; that is one man and one woman into one flesh'. It was an honourable condition, 'ordained of God in paradise' for four principal ends: the procreation of children, the perpetuation of the church, the containment of sexual desire and finally for the mutual assistance and comfort afforded one another by the married couple. For all these reasons, marriage might be considered 'the foundation and seminary of all other sorts and kinds of life in the commonwealth and in the church'.[3]

In ecclesiastical law three forms of 'lawful conjunction' were recognized. The first and only fully satisfactory form of marriage was an ecclesiastically solemnized union, performed in the face of the church after the calling of the banns, or after the procurement of a licence exempting the parties concerned from this formality. Unlike the continental churches, however, the church of England continued to recognize as legally binding two other forms of valid, though irregular marriage. A promise to marry expressed in words of the present tense in the presence of witnesses constituted a binding marriage, as also did a promise made in words of the future tense, provided that it was followed by sexual union. Consent to a marriage could be given by any person over the age of 7, while marriage could be sexually consummated by boys at 14 and girls at 12 years of age. Persons already married, or parties to binding contracts, could not, of course, contract a valid marriage, while marriages between people falling within specified degrees of consanguinity and affinity were prohibited. For the rest, as Perkins put it, marriage was 'free to all orders and sorts of men without exception'.[4]

All this seems clear enough. Yet marriage in England was in reality far more complex and far less homogeneous than was allowed for by the conventional definitions of the moralists or the neat prescriptions of the law. Marriage was indeed a fundamental institution, but marital behaviour was far from uniform. In the relative ability of English people to marry, in the age at which they did so, in the manner in which spouses were chosen and in the criteria upon which choice was based, English marital practice reflected less a uniform code of behaviour than the varying needs and opportunities of people of different social position.

Marriage, as we have seen, was 'free to all', yet not everyone married.

Perhaps 10 per cent or more of women who achieved adulthood passed their lives unwed.[5] Marriage could be contracted and consummated by any boy or girl who had attained the age of consent. Yet the English married late. The average age of first marriage for men in the period 1600–49 was 29.1 at Aldenham in Hertfordshire, 29.2 at Bottesford in Leicestershire, 27.4 at Colyton in Devon, 27.8 at Hawkshead in Lancashire and 26.7 at Willingham in Cambridgeshire, while the average ages for women in the same parishes over the same period were respectively 25.3, 25.9, 27.3, 24.8 and 24.8. Within this pattern of comparatively late marriage, variations were observable between the age at first marriage of people of different occupation and social status. Though this issue demands much more thorough investigation than it has received hitherto, it seems clear that in general members of the aristocracy and upper gentry married younger than their social inferiors, while among the common people, wage-earning artisans and labourers married somewhat earlier than landholding yeomen and husbandmen.[6]

In the broad characteristics of their marital behaviour, the English were firmly within what has been dubbed the 'European marriage pattern', the combination of relatively high age at first marriage for women together with the celibacy of a substantial proportion of women which has been historically confined to those parts of Europe west of a line extending from the eastern Baltic to the Adriatic.[7] The origins of this pattern remain obscure. Its demographic implications, however, are plain enough, for such behaviour clearly placed a considerable degree of restraint upon the reproductive capacity of the population. Given an age of menarche in the mid to late teens, women spent much of their potentially fertile lives unwed, while a sizeable minority never enjoyed the opportunity to bear legitimate children. It is doubtful, however, that contemporaries considered the matter in quite this way. As E. A. Wrigley has argued, the demographic rationality of the system was largely unconscious. It was maintained less by a calculating awareness of its demographic effects than by adherence to 'unconsciously rational' social conventions surrounding the question of the qualifications deemed necessary for marriage.[8] These factors underpinned the marital and familial system of the period and shaped the everyday reality of marital opportunity. By far the most significant of them was the fact that young people, and in particular young men, were considered ready for marriage only at the point when they were capable of establishing and maintaining an independent nuclear family.

As we have seen, the vast majority of the households which constituted the basic units of England's local communities consisted of a simple nuclear family, with or without resident servants. A minority of extended family households, including co-resident kin, existed, usually as the product of special circumstances, but only rarely did newly married couples share the same roof as the parents of one of the partners. Such a situation existed in some aristocratic families in which children had married very young. It might also be found lower in the social scale as a temporary expedient or as the outcome of parental retirement and inheritance. But unlike some European peasant societies, arrangements of this kind were not the norm in England. Indeed a strong cultural prejudice existed to discourage such living arrangements. 'When thou art married,' William Whately advised prospective bridegrooms, 'if it may be, live of thyself with thy wife, in a family of thine own.' Two masters and two dames under one roof led in his opinion to 'unquietness of all parties', especially among the common people, and was a situation to be avoided whenever possible.[9] Young couples should start married life under their own roof and standing on their own feet; and usually they did.

Given these circumstances, marriage needed to be deferred well past the legal or physiological minimum age until the point at which a sufficient degree of independence could be secured. This might sometimes involve waiting for parental death and inheritance, though this would not usually appear to have been the case. More often the prospective couple seem to have reached the necessary stage by a mixture of personal saving, perhaps putting aside their wages as servants, and parental assistance. Among property-owning families, ranging from prosperous husbandmen and craftsmen to the aristocracy, parents assisted the couple by providing their marriage portions of goods or money, though among the common people these were rarely large enough to do more than contribute to the setting up of the new family. Where no such assistance could be expected, couples had to provide for themselves and among the labouring poor the chance of regular employment and a cottage for rent may have been the prime consideration, rather than the wherewithal to obtain land or stock a shop, though even so they would need some savings to provide their basic household goods. Such preparations took time and they also involved both partners, except in those cases where a substantial dowry was available for a girl at an early age. The extent to which these realities pervaded popular expectations is revealed in many instances, ranging from paternal advice, such as that given by James Bankes to his son not to marry until he was 'sofecant of abelete to manetane yor estaitt', to the answers given by humbler people questioned by the church courts about their marital intentions. Thus in 1584 Edward Thornton of St Nicholas's parish, Oxford, told the Archdeacon that he had promised to marry Bridget Fayreberne 'uppon condicon that she wold stay untill he cold provide him of an howse', while John King of Dunstow declared his intention of marrying Ursula Saule 'at Michaelmas next, when he hath provided a living for her'.[10] Providing that house and that living might come sooner or later for differently placed individuals, and it is for this reason that variations in average marriage age can be observed between different social groups and areas with different economic structures and differentials in economic, and therefore marital, opportunities. Whatever the particular case, the general situation was that marriage and family formation in this society was a privilege rather than a right. It was something to which all might aspire, yet which some would never achieve, while those who succeeded would do so at a relatively high age – indeed a very high age when we consider the comparatively short life expectation of the period. Economic independence, then, was the principal prerequisite for marriage, and differentials in attaining that independence deeply affected the marital opportunities of both individuals and social groups. Once it was within reach, the crucial issue became not so much that of ability to marry as that of the choice of a spouse and it is to this question that we must now turn.

The selection of marriage partners

The selection of marriage partners is an issue of central importance, in part because it might affect the age of marriage and marital opportunity, but much more because the manner in which spouses were chosen might establish the whole character of marriage in this period and deeply influence the quality of relationships within each newly formed nuclear family. Indeed, for Lawrence Stone it is in this matter that the shifts in familial behaviour which he discerns in the later sixteenth and seventeenth centuries can be most clearly perceived. In the 'low-keyed, unemotional, authoritarian' 'Open Lineage Family' of the sixteenth century, Stone argues, 'marriages were arranged by parents and kin for economic and social reasons, with minimal consultation of the children'. In the last decades of the sixteenth century and the early seventeenth century, however, a new form of family emerged which was both more closed to the influence of the extended kin and emotionally warmer in its internal relations. In this 'Restricted, Patriarchal, Nuclear Family', parental power over the choice of marriage partners remained absolute, but a right of veto was conceded to the young parties to a match. This situation persisted until the later seventeenth and eighteenth centuries, when a double shift took place. Parental choice moderated by the child's veto gave place to choice by the child subject to parental consent. Economic and social interest gave way to personal affection and companionship as the principal criteria of choice. These changes heralded the emergence of a third form of family, the 'Closed Domesticated Nuclear Family', in which greater autonomy was allowed to wives and children and in which strong affective ties developed. These successive developments in affective relations within the English family amounted in Stone's view to 'the most important change in *mentalité* to have occurred in the Early Modern period, indeed possibly in the last thousand years of western history' for they laid the foundations of the family as we now know it. In that momentous process the pace was set by the upper and middling ranks of English society, from which change spread downwards by a process of 'stratified diffusion' and the seventeenth century saw the most critical breakthrough from distance, deference and patriarchy in family relations to the rise of 'affective individualism'.[11]

Stone's powerful arguments and adventurous hypotheses constitute the most ambitious attempt yet undertaken to interpret the development of the English family over time. Nevertheless they are seriously open to question in both their characterization of family life in later sixteenth- and seventeenth-century England and in their account of change within this period. Although he is undoubtedly aware of the major distinctions which may have existed between social groups in England, Stone has devoted insufficient care to the exploration of the experience of the mass of the population. As a result his interpretation has been elaborated on the basis of the historical experience of the aristocracy, upper gentry and urban plutocracy with which he is primarily concerned and retains at its heart the tacit assumption that analytical categories derived from their experience can somehow be extended to encapsulate phases in the history of the English family. This is a mistaken assumption. For whatever their historical prominence, the familial behaviour of the English élite was very far from representative of that of their countrymen. Nor can shifts in their behaviour be asserted to have been significant advances in familial development when set in the full context of the already established and persisting characteristics of the family life of their social inferiors. Both points can be well illustrated by considering in turn the issues so central to Stone's argument: control of the choice of marriage partner and the criteria upon which selection was based.

Matchmaking

There can be no doubt that in the opinion of the moralistic authors of the 'conduct books' it was one of the chief duties of parents to 'bestow' their children in marriage. This is not necessarily to say, however, that they advocated parentally arranged marriages. Indeed, the frequent employment of the term 'arranged' by historians, with its implication of unilateral parental choice, may be said to have blunted our perception of this problem. Perkins, for example, was much more subtle. He maintained that the parental duty might be discharged *either* by providing matches for children *or* by advising children on the suitability of prospective spouses. Elsewhere, he made it clear that even where parents took the initiative in proposing a match, they should never force the marriage of a child. Bishop Barnes of Durham was prepared to go so far in his injunctions of 1577 as to lay down that 'yonge folkes by the lawes of God may not marry without consent of their parents', but he did not say that parents should initiate or dominate matchmaking. There was a degree of flexibility, even of ambivalence in the prescriptions of these churchmen which has sometimes been overlooked by historians. To neglect it is to do them less than justice, for as J. L. Flandrin has shown, it was their allowance of a greater degree of freedom in this matter to the young which most distinguished English moralists of the period from their French counterparts.[12]

When we turn to the evidence of actual behaviour, it rapidly becomes clear that the initiative in the making of a match might come from either parent or child, much as Perkins suggested. What mattered was less the identity of the initiating party than the securing of the consent or 'goodwill' of all those concerned. Within this broad framework, however, the degree of parental restraint placed upon children could vary, and where such variation is observable it sprang most commonly from the differences which existed in the needs and interests of families of different rank.

Among the aristocracy, the urban élite and leading gentry families, as Stone has demonstrated, marriage was a matter of too great a significance, both in the property transactions which it involved and in the system of familial alliances which it cemented, to be left to the discretion of the young people concerned. By the later sixteenth and early seventeenth centuries both child marriages and crudely arranged matches which took no account of the opinions of the prospective spouses were largely things of the past. Nonetheless, parents commonly initiated matches and parental influence on the choice of a spouse frequently remained decisive, even though the formal consent of the parties to the match was sought.[13] In some cases such consent was willingly given, as when John Bruen of Bruen Stapleford in Cheshire returned home from Oxford in 1579 to find that his father proposed matching him with the daughter of the Mayor of Chester. John 'did entertain the motion with such respect and reverence as became an obedient son' and gave his assent once he was assured of the affection and willingness of the young woman herself. At other times the consent of the child might be a mere formality, exacted under pressure. Margaret Russell assented to a marriage with the Earl of Cumberland more 'on the ground of common good than any particular liking' and commenced a married life which brought her little happiness. The Yorkshire heiress Margaret Dakins, who was far more fortunate in her husbands, was nonetheless essentially a passive participant in the matchmaking of her elders. Between 1589, when she was 18 years old, and 1596 she was married three times. On each occasion the match to which she assented was proposed and forwarded by others, notably her former guardian the Earl of Huntingdon, though Lord Burghley and Lady Russell took a hand in her third and final marriage to Sir Thomas Hoby.[14]

Such circumstances may well have been the norm in the highest ranks of English society. It is, nonetheless, important to appreciate that even for the children of the social élite, marital initiative did not lie solely in the hands of parents. Among the aristocracy, parental domination of matchmaking may have been stronger in the marriages of daughters than was the case in the matching of sons, while younger children were generally accorded greater freedom of choice than was the case in the marriages of heirs and heiresses.[15] Again there is evidence that in the lower ranks of the gentry where less depended upon a particular match, courtship could become a more personal affair. Anthony Fletcher finds that among the leading families of the Sussex gentry the marriages of heirs and heiresses were usually 'arranged', subject to the assent of the young couple to the match. Courtship among the lesser gentry, however, was a more personal, intimate and romantic process, with the initiative in proposing a match often lying with the couple concerned. G. E. Mingay takes the view that 'among the propertied classes generally the individual's interest in marriage was subordinated to the interest of the family'. Yet he too allows that the child might well initiate matters and subsequently seek formal parental consent and backing in the furtherance of a match. Thus in 1649 Bridget Oglander sought to marry a young gentleman of whom her father Sir John initially disapproved. Yet upon 'her importunity' and her declared resolve 'to have him whatsoever became of her', he gave way and consented to the match.[16]

The question of the frequency with which children took the initiative at this level of society may have depended very much upon the relative freedom accorded to the young in their contacts with other young eligibles and the consequent opportunities afforded them to initiate their own courtships. In this regard it is perhaps of some significance that foreign visitors to England were often struck by what they saw as the surprising degree of freedom allowed to English women.[17] Even among the social élite, women were not cloistered and a fair degree of unsupervised contact was permitted between young people of both sexes. The round of gentry social life in the countryside afforded opportunities enough for the formation of marital preferences among the young which might later form the basis of formal parental overtures. Again, among gentry families participating in the developing London 'season', young people did a good deal of visiting without adult supervision, though girls were commonly accompanied by a chaperone of their own age. As a result, courtships were often initiated well before parental involvement was sought and the making of 'secret vows' was not uncommon.[18] Of course the situation must have varied a good deal from family to family and young men certainly had greater scope for independent action in courtship than was the case with their sisters. Nevertheless, it is clear that even in the higher social ranks where families had most to lose by an imprudent match, the situation was far from monolithic when it came to the selection of future spouses. The 'arranged' match, initiated by parents, which left the child with nothing more than a right of veto was undoubtedly a reality throughout our period. But even among the social élite it presents a picture which is too stark unless accompanied by considerable qualification. The key to the situation may well have been less parental 'arrangement', with or without subsequent consultation of the child, than the seizing of the initiative by one of the parties concerned and the subsequent securing of the consent of the other.

If the choice of marriage partners among the aristocracy, gentry and urban élite was a considerably more complex matter than has been alleged, there is no doubt whatever that lower in the social scale the initiative in selecting a spouse already lay with the young people concerned. However ambivalent the behaviour of their betters, the vast majority of the English people awaited no fundamental transition of their marital norms. Adolescents of both sexes enjoyed considerably more freedom from parental tutelage than was usual even in the most generous of gentry families by virtue of the simple fact that they usually left home to enter service in their early teens. Moreover, if, as was common enough, they had already lost one or both parents, they were very rarely subject to the constraints of wardship. Among fellow servants, at hiring fairs, in the alehouses, at village dancings and at church, they were free to make their own moves in courtship. Such inhibitions as they experienced in the matter were the outcome not of their parents' marital strategies but of their common recognition of the desirability of gaining consent to, or at least approval of, their matches from a variety of interested parties. Even so, the significance of such endorsement varied a good deal between social groups, and between the sexes.

Among the propertied 'middling sort' parental consent could be a matter of considerable practical importance to the future well-being of a couple, if only by virtue of its bearing on parental willingness to transfer property to children at their marriages in the form of dowries and marriage portions. That such arrangements were the norm among small property holders is clear from the evidence of their wills, some of them specifying that married children had already received their 'portion' from the testator, while most allocated goods and cash to be given to unmarried children at the time of their weddings. Indeed, consent to their children's marriages was sufficiently important to some testators for them to attach strings to bequests made to unmarried children. William Ingleby, a yeoman of Great Haswell in County Durham, for example, made a will in 1632 leaving each of his daughters a substantial portion of both land and money if they married with the consent of their mother and two uncles. If they did not marry with such consent, however, they were still to receive the money, and in some cases even more money, but they were not to receive land.[19]

As this example indicates, the right of parents to approve their children's matches was valued, but not insisted upon. Sons in particular were relatively free to go their own way as is made clear by the testimony of three well-known clerical diarists or autobiographers of the period. Adam Martindale, son of a yeoman, described how in the 1630s two of his three brothers not only chose for themselves but braved and faced down parental disapproval of their choices, while a generation later Martindale's son made his own match in London. Ralph Josselin's courtship began when his 'eye fixed with love' upon Jane Constable in church in October 1639. By January 1640 he had proposed to her and they had given one another a 'mutual promise'. They then sought consent to the match before proceeding to a formal contract in September 1640. Such niceties, however, were ignored by their son John, who in due course married without his parents' knowledge. Henry Newcome, whose parents were dead, chose his own bride in the 1640s, though he later admitted that he had 'sinned in that I took not that advice I should have took of my friends in it'. His sons Daniel and Harry both married without either their father's consent or even his knowledge and though this grieved him, he accepted it.[20]

The relative freedom with which young men pursued prospective brides is amply illustrated by the diary of Roger Lowe, an apprentice mercer. Lowe's remarkable diary provides us with the viewpoint of a young man on the lookout for a bride for some five years from the time in 1663 when he recorded 'this was the first night that ever I stayd up a wooing ere in my life' until his eventual marriage to Emm Potter in 1668. Lowe's courtships generally revolved around such activities as walking in the fields, visiting nearby towns, drinking in the alehouses, or attending weddings and funerals with other young people of Ashton, while he formally courted one of his sweethearts by 'sitting up' with her in her father's parlour. He first approached his future wife Emm Potter in an alehouse during Ashton wakes, though he had spotted her before. They courted on and off for four years, falling out on numerous occasions and once needing a mediator to effect a reconciliation, until in 1668 they 'consummated [their] grande designe of marriage'. In all of this there is no reference to formal seeking of parental consent, though Roger often drank with men of the Potter family and may well have had their tacit approval.[21]

There is little in Roger Lowe's account of his courtships which would be unfamiliar to a modern youth. It does, however, represent a male viewpoint and that of a young man whose parents appear to have been dead. Other examples suggest that while young men were free enough to make their approaches to a girl, young women were rather more constrained by the need to secure the advice and consent of parents and 'friends' (who might or might not include kin). To this extent their independence of action might be considerably more circumscribed. Henry Newcome, for example, recorded the case of a Manchester girl thrown into deep depression when initially crossed in her desire to marry a suitor turned away by her family. Adam Martindale went so far as to remove his daughter Elizabeth from service when she fell for a fellow servant who was 'an unsuitable match for her'. He feared that the girl was being used and tried to compensate by providing 'a farre more lovely match', though understandably the girl refused this parental initiative and Martindale, to his credit, did not press the matter. The marital hopes of daughters could thus be effectively thwarted by failure to gain parental approval for their matches. Nevertheless some young women could show considerable independence in their matchmaking. Katherine Marshall, a Newcastle girl, forced the issue of her marriage to Christopher Robson, a tanner's son, by herself approaching his father, stating her intention, and proceeding to settle the terms of the match. Or again Mary Cooling, daughter of a London linen draper, went so far as to get contracted to a young man of her father's trade and then won her father over, though he was 'much discontented that they had proceeded so far without his consent and blamed his daughter muche'.[22]

It is perhaps significant that Francis Cooling's discontent was not with his daughter's taking of the initiative in finding a suitor but rather with the fact that she had gone so far before informing him and winning his approval. This provides a clue to the probable norm for young women. Ralph Josselin was a father who was prepared to defend the theoretical right of the patriarchal father to choose his children's spouses, but in fact it is clear that in the courtships of his daughters, the initiative usually belonged to the young couple. Suitors presented themselves and sought his approval to woo formally, while once matters were under way the girls themselves were allowed the final and absolute say over the completion of the match. The implication is that the girl concerned had already given the young man sufficient encouragement to make his formal approach but that matters would not proceed further without parental approval. This situation is clearly exemplified by one Somerset case, which may well represent the normal circumstances of a match at this social level. The girl in question informed her father that one Walter Woodrow wished to marry her and requested permission for him to call at the house. Her father replied 'that if she liked the man and was disposed to bestow herself in marriage he should be welcome to his house'. The next Sunday Walter appeared, together with his sister and in the course of a meal asked the father for his goodwill, receiving the reply 'that they should have his goodwill if he and the maid were so agreed'. That accomplished, they settled down to some hard bargaining over the dowry, with the father cannily using Walter's declared affection for his daughter as a lever to reduce his demands in the matter of the marriage portion![23]

Parental consent, then, was desirable if the match was to be amicably concluded and a satisfactory dowry negotiated. The role of 'friends' is more obscure. It might often have been the case that close relatives such as uncles, or else family friends, acted in the place of a dead parent, perhaps in accordance with the guardianship provisions sometimes to be found in paternal wills. Certainly church court records provide many instances of the influence of friends at work, as when John Stacie of Sandon in Oxfordshire reported to an inquisitive Archdeacon in 1584 'that theare hath beene good will and motion of marriage betweene this respondent and Jane Banister but noe perfett contract because the frendes of this respondent and the same Jane have not yet concluded'. In matches between individuals for whom lack of property rendered the question of settling dowries and portions irrelevant, the advice of personal friends among their peers may also have been of some importance, the more so if they were servants living at some distance from their parishes of origin. At this social level, however, it would appear that in the final analysis agreement to marry was very much a matter for the couple themselves, for the match had little direct bearing on anyone else. Parents, who as likely as not were geographically distant, seem to have been informed largely as a courtesy, and indeed were often presented with a *fait accompli*. Thus, husbandmen's daughters living as servants in London and marrying by licence rarely expected a portion from their parents and many stated explicitly that they had none and that they were therefore at their own disposition. One Hertfordshire girl might speak for many. She asserted 'that her said father doth not as yet knowe of this intended marriage but when he shall understand thereof he will be verie glad of it because yt is for her preferment (her father being but a poore man and having more children is not able to give mutch at marriage with her)'.[24]

It seems reasonable to conclude that among the greater part of the common people marriage partners were freely chosen, subject to the advice of friends and a sense of obligation to consult or subsequently inform parents if they were alive and within reach. Among the very poor, however, a further form of consent might be required in the form of the willingness or otherwise of the parish authorities to countenance a marriage which might threaten a future charge on the poor rates. They had no legal right to do this, but they could make their opposition effective by informal means such as withholding rights of settlement, housing or employment. In 1618 Anthony Addames of Stockton in Worcestershire 'fortuned to marry with an honest young woman', but the parishioners were 'not willing he should bring her into the parish saying they would breed up a charge among them'. He had to find a cottage elsewhere while continuing to earn his living in Stockton. Or again the case of the Rector of North Ockendon in Essex could be cited, who, when asked to read the banns for the marriage of a poor cripple, departed from the set form and 'signified to the parishe that they would marry and goe a begging together and asked if any knewe lawfull cause why they might not doe so'. Such instances are far from rare and merely illustrate a practice described by Carew Reynel in 1674 as 'an ill custom in many country parishes'.[25] They serve as a sombre reminder that if the marriages of the labouring poor in some respects appeared free, that freedom could be severely qualified. It was at best a freedom accompanied by a marked insecurity in the actual completion of proposed marriages, as will be further illustrated when we come to consider the problem of illegitimacy.

Having reviewed the evidence relating to the selection of marriage partners at different social levels, it would appear that interpretations based upon the conventional dichotomies of arranged as against free matches, and parental choice as against self-determination by the child, do less than justice to the complexities of reality. There is little evidence of cold-bloodedly 'arranged' matches outside the very highest ranks of society. The likelihood of parents initiating or proposing a match was not uniform even at the highest social levels, while even when they did so, children usually seem to have enjoyed a right of refusal. Below the level of the aristocracy, upper gentry and urban plutocracy, the actual initiative usually seems to have lain with the young people, subject to the advice and consent of parents, friends and even principal neighbours. The significance of that advice and consent would appear to have varied according to both sex and wealth, but on the whole it seems rare for it to have been withheld when a couple were determined to marry.

Finally, it can be observed that the period does not appear to have witnessed significant changes in these matters, except possibly among the aristocracy, upper gentry and leaders of urban society. Professor Stone's interpretation of change may well be sound for the highest social groups, with which he is primarily concerned and of which his knowledge is unrivalled. But neither his characterization of conventional practice, nor his account of change seem adequate as descriptions of the experience of the greater part of the English people. There was no single 'English' norm in this matter, but rather a persisting variety of coexisting practices, a range of experience broad enough to call into question the validity of any single evolutionary schema. The position as regards the selection of marriage partners, then, seems established. It remains to explore the question of the criteria upon which that selection was based.

The criteria of a match

Marriage in the sixteenth and seventeenth centuries was usually for life. Given that fact, great care needed to be exercised in the choosing of a partner and this was a matter to which the writers of the conduct books devoted considerable attention. William Perkins distinguished the criteria of selection into two basic categories. First, there were what he called 'essential' qualities: that the couple be of different sex; that there be no impediment of consanguinity according to the forbidden degrees recognized by the Anglican church and displayed in most parish churches; that neither partner be already married; that both be free from contagious diseases and of 'ability and fitness for procreation'. Matches which contravened these requirements were in Perkins's view prohibited. All other matches were, by the same token, permitted, but this was not to say that they were to be preferred. On the contrary, Perkins also offered a second guide to the criteria for the optimum match, with a list of what he called 'accidental' qualities. Like most other writers on this subject he recommended the seeking of a degree of 'parity or equality' between partners in age, condition (by which he clearly meant social status and wealth), 'public honesty and credit' and, of course, 'Christian religion'. Some, though not many, moralists also added that personal compatibility was desirable.[26]

Parity of age, status, wealth, reputation and religion, together with personal attraction, made the perfect match. All this seems straightforward enough. Yet in reality the relative significance given to these various considerations might vary considerably. Among the aristocracy, for example, Stone argues that although other factors were given some consideration, 'marriage was not a personal union for the satisfaction of psychological and physiological needs; it was an institutional device to ensure the perpetuation of the family and its property'. Consequently 'the greatest attention was . . . paid to the financial benefits of marriage' and 'wealth was the most important single consideration' even in the early seventeenth century when children were being accorded greater consideration in matchmaking – indeed it may have actually grown in importance at a time of financial stringency for many aristocratic families.[27]

The aristocracy may not have been alone in this, for historians of the gentry seem largely agreed that throughout the landed class as a whole considerations of property and the status which it conferred weighed very heavily as compared with other criteria of a good match. In Sussex in the later sixteenth and seventeenth centuries 'continuity in the estate and advancement of the family were the gentry's prime considerations in marrying their children'. In Yorkshire the gentry sought above all partners of comparable wealth and status. For the upper gentry Verney family, marriage was 'a relationship characterised by social and economic rather than romantic considerations' and 'the emotional and physical needs of the couple were peripheral considerations'. All in all, as Mingay has argued, the safeguarding of property, the assertion and advancement of status and the forging of alliances between families figured most prominently in the preferred matches of England's landlords.[28]

This situation must not, however, be exaggerated into assertions that the gentry and aristocracy showed a monomaniacal concern with questions of property, for this is demonstrably untrue. The ideal match was rarely conceived of solely in terms of economic gain, but comprehended a range of desirable traits and was not uninfluenced by romantic expectations fuelled by the romantic literature of the day.[29] Nevertheless financial considerations were inevitably of major significance to those whose maintenance of their élite position depended above all upon the consolidation of their landed wealth, and this fact gave to their matchmaking a strongly commercial flavour. Moreover, among families in which the initial proposal of a match often came from the parents, their recognized duty to make the best bargain they could for their children weighed heavily, and even children free to choose for themselves had commonly been brought up to share their parents' attitudes. To judge by his letters, Thomas Hoby was genuinely delighted with his bride's personal qualities, but he had commenced his suit before he had even met her at the instigation of a mother anxious to secure him the hand of a well-connected heiress. When James Bankes advised his children on the choice of wives, he hoped that they would choose girls 'that feareth God and are obedeant to the prince's lawes and of good parentage borne', but his most specific recommendation was that they seek out heiresses, for this was 'the sonist way to increas yor howsus, as mane wyes men have done'.[30] His preferences were clear enough.

Lower in the social scale, among the propertied 'middling sort' of town and country, with whom the initiative in proposing a match more often lay with the couple themselves, property remained an important consideration. Naturally enough a realistic attitude had to be taken to the question of how the new couple would live and both they and their families could bargain with a will to secure an equitable or advantageous property settlement. Sometimes this could weigh very heavily indeed, as is suggested by the fact that, in a sample of first marriages by London craftsmen and tradesmen, Dr Elliott found that no fewer than 25 per cent married widows, thereby ensuring a good start for themselves. Or again, such cases as that of a Cumbrian husbandman who broke off an otherwise acceptable match when he 'did demaund in mariadg hir fathers farmehold, which he refusyd to graunt' are not unusual.[31] Among small property holders, however, it would appear that a rough parity of wealth was more a necessary than a sufficient condition of a good match and that other considerations were at least equally important, if not more so.

Personal or family reputation could be significant, as when the mother of Ralph Wilson of Durham expressed her dislike of his courtship of Isobel Thompson on the grounds that Isobel's father had been accused of theft and that Thompson's 'evill gotten good' should not be conjoined to the Wilsons' 'well gotten good'. Roger Lowe discovered that Emm Potter's unwonted coldness towards him at one stage of their courtship was the result of her having heard a false rumour that his mother had borne him out of wedlock. Religion could also play its part. The puritan Martindale family were horrified when Hugh Martindale 'growing wild and unmanageable, did to all our griefes marrie a papist'. Hugh's action showed that it could be done, but he had to remove to Ireland and had few further dealings with his family. They were much happier when his younger brother Henry chose 'an holy young woman of pious parentage'.[32]

Such qualities of good reputation, religious conformity and an acceptable portion might, of course, be found in many prospective partners, for the pool of eligibles for people of this rank was considerably larger than among their social superiors. What often seems to have clinched the matter and determined the particular choice of where to woo was personal attraction, even full-blown romantic love. A degree of personal and physical compatibility might be implied by the fact that marriage partners were so often close in age, but yet stronger evidence exists in some abundance. Richard Gough's account of the families of Myddle, for example, frequently alleges love as the basis of good marriages, while for explicit demonstration of its influence we can do no better than to point to Roger Lowe's own account of his courtships. Lowe's breast undoubtedly swelled with romantic impulses of just the kind so evident in contemporary love lyrics and romantic ballads. His courtship of Mary Naylor reached a high pitch of drama when the two vowed 'to live privately and love firmely' and 'ingaged to be faithfull till death' and it is hardly surprising that Lowe was somewhat nonplussed when Mary's affection gradually cooled. Mary's friends did not approve and although Roger had some hopes of winning her father's support, it seems likely that the apprentice mercer was considered beneath her. He did better with Emm Potter, whom he approached after conceiving 'a most ardent affection' and tortured by jealousy at seeing her in company with a rival at the alehouse. She turned out to be an excellent match for him in every way.[33]

Love, or at least personal attraction, could be the keystone in the structure of a good match in the eyes of the young people concerned, if not in those of their parents and friends. Nonetheless it is clear that it was not regarded as something which should sweep aside other considerations. The force of physical and personal attraction was recognized, but in conjunction with, rather than in opposition to, other aspects of parity in a good match. There was more to marriage, as the contemporary proverb put it, than 'four bare legs in a bed'.[34] Henry Newcome clearly married for love, but admitted that he had gone about it in a 'rash and inconsiderate' way and thought 'God might have made it sad to me and done me no wrong; but he very mercifully turned it into good for me'. The selfsame attitude, together with a splendid review of the qualities expected in a match, can be found in Adam Martindale's account of his eldest brother's marriage. Martindale's father, a prosperous yeoman–craftsman, was not 'so severe' as to expect a fully equal fortune from his son's bride, but hoped for a prudent settlement and was well pleased when a match got under way to a young woman 'of suitable yeares' and good character who had a portion of £140. To the grief of the family, the son suddenly threw over the match when he fell in love with 'a young, wild, airy girle betweene fifteen and sixteen yeares of age; an huge lover and frequenter of wakes, greenes and merrie-nights where musick and dancing abounded. And as for her portion it was onely forty pounds'. The family urgently tried to dissuade him, but 'say and do what we could, he was uncounsellable, have her he would' and at last he won his father's grudging consent and married her in 1632. ''Tis true,' Martindale crustily admitted, 'she proved above all just expectation not onely civill, but religious and an exceeding good wife . . . but that was the effect of God's great and undeserved goodnesse, not any prudent choice of his, and the smallnesse of her portion was a great prejudice to our family.' Love, in short, was a good thing in its place, but one should love prudently.[35]

One of the most significant elements in Martindale's rendering of this story is his comment that, although only 10 years of age at the time, even he was conscious of 'the difference of these two matches'. Children learned early to share the values underlying the complexities of matchmaking and to judge accordingly, of their own volition. Thus Ralph Josselin had nothing to fear when his daughter Jane was courted by Jonathan Woodthorp, 'a sober hopefull man his estate about £500'. Jane liked him too, it was an excellent match and matters proceeded swiftly. Josselin was grieved when his daughter Mary decided against Mr Rhea, a neighbouring clergyman, but had to recognize the force of her list of 'exceptions' to the match: 'his age being 14 yeares older shee might bee left a widow with children'; 'his estate being not suitable to her porcon'; and finally, 'he seemed to her not loving'. This was hard-headed judgement, balancing practical and emotional considerations, with perhaps a final sway towards the latter, as is suggested by Josselin's reflection, 'I could not desire it when shee said it would make both their lives miserable.'[36]

Among the landed élite, a variety of criteria governed matchmaking, but considerations of rank and estate necessarily took first place in determining eligibles. For the 'middling sort' parity of wealth and status was an important matter, but their less elevated social position, together with the greater freedom allowed young people in seeking prospective partners, gave enhanced significance to the element of personal attraction, which could, in the final analysis, prove decisive. Of the propertyless we know much less. For many of them, as was recognized by Richard Baxter and others, the decision to leave service and marry, might mean a marked deterioration in their standards of living.[37] It is to be expected, then, that a girl might favour a man who looked likely to be a good provider, while men would look for girls who could run a careful household and contribute to family income. Friends, as we know, would advise on the reputation and likeliness of prospective partners, but they had little occasion to worry about wealth. 'They value not portions,' wrote Carew Reynel of the poor, 'so [long as] they are able to serve, work, or any way earn their living.'[38] Instead, it seems probable that more attention was paid to personal qualities and individual attraction. Given the material disincentives to marriage, it seems likely that its principal attractions were the desire for independence and for the companionship and emotional and physical gratification which spouses could find in one another, together with the satisfaction of raising their own families.

This situation is borne out by the evidence of illegitimacy cases which provide one of our few opportunities to investigate the courtships of the poor. Illegitimacy was comparatively infrequent in this period as compared with its incidence in the early nineteenth century, though it was more common in England than in seventeenth-century France. For a brief period at the turn of the sixteenth and seventeenth centuries, the illegitimacy ratio calculated by demographers (the proportion illegitimate of all known births) reached a temporary peak, for reasons to be discussed in Chapter 4. In the main, however, the average parish saw an irregular trickle of illegitimate births. The circumstances underlying these births cannot always be explored, but where additional evidence is available, in the form of court proceedings, the results are highly revealing.

To the religious moralists of the period, illegitimacy was merely a sub-category of the general and perennial problem of 'whoredom', a sexual laxity allegedly produced by a population which regarded sexual transgressions as merely the 'tricke of youth'. In fact the problem was far more complex. English villages did indeed have individuals who regularly bore or fathered bastard children, and even illegitimacy-prone families, though whether they represented a deviant sub-culture or simply a vulnerable, exploited, even demoralized, element among the rural poor, is a matter open to debate. Again, a number of illegitimate births resulted from the classical circumstances of the sexual exploitation by masters or gentlemen of servants or social inferiors. For the most part, however, illegitimate children appear to have been conceived by couples of similar social position, very commonly servants in husbandry, who intended to marry, yet whose marital plans were dislocated.[39]

The association of illegitimacy with marital opportunity is strongly suggested by the fact that close studies of particular parishes have revealed that the age of women bearing their first illegitimate child was almost identical to the average age at which more fortunate women bore their first child in wedlock. It is confirmed by the evidence of depositions and examinations in the courts. In 1602, for example, Grace Burles of Terling in Essex bore a child to Edward Shipman. It was declared in court that Shipman 'mindeth shortlye to marye her' but that he had been 'prest for a soldier'. In this case, as in quite a number of others, the intended wedding did eventually take place. Other girls were less fortunate. Mary Foster and Edward Alexander were fellow servants in the Essex town of Witham and planned to marry. However, they broke up. He had moved on to service elsewhere by the time she discovered her pregnancy. Or again, Alice Jackson was a Worcestershire servant girl who had 'behaved herself very honestly' until in 1617 she was courted by a fellow servant who 'did make great protestations of love . . . promising by many great vows to marry her'. When she was pregnant he proved less ardent and fled the county.[40]

In cases such as that of Alice Jackson the girl was doubtless deliberately deceived by her suitor. But many others show clearly that a genuine 'motion of marriage' was underway: friends had been consulted, parents informed, even banns called, before circumstances frustrated the wedding. Whatever the particular case, these tragic stories reveal a great deal about courtship in the lower reaches of the social scale. They confirm the relative freedom of choice of the young people concerned – and the dangers which that freedom entailed. They further make clear the significance of personal and sexual attraction in courtship. Again, they reveal how the restraints upon sexual activity imposed by the realities of a pre-contraceptive age in which sexual activity led almost inevitably to conception, crumbled once marriage was in sight. In this, the parents of illegitimate children were not unusual. Demographers tracing brides to the birth of their first child in parish registers have revealed that English brides were very commonly pregnant in this period – generally between 10 per cent and 30 per cent in different parishes.[41] In some areas this may have been the result of a formally recognized right to commence sexual intercourse after betrothal – for in canon law a public promise to marry followed by sexual intercourse constituted a valid, though irregular marriage. The church, however, frowned upon this practice and the ecclesiastical courts punished it with public penance. What seems most likely is that popular attitudes, though far from loose, were simply more flexible than those of society's professional moralists. When marriage was, or seemed, assured, couples whose attraction for one another was a prime reason for their courtship, commenced sexual relations. Indeed, it may even be possible that for those in service, whose marriage plans were well advanced, but who had good reason to stay under their masters' roofs where they were better housed and fed and could save money, pregnancy was the signal to actually leave service, get married and set up together. Whatever the case, it is clear that bridal pregnancy was widely tolerated.

Some girls, however, became not pregnant brides, but the mothers of bastards. There tolerance ended. They were likely to be brought before the church courts, questioned and ordered to do penance in public. If there was a danger that their children would fall upon the parish poor rates, they might be brought before the Justices of the Peace, and perhaps committed to a house of correction. Dismissal of pregnant girls from service and callous hustling from parish to parish of those whose place of settlement was questionable were not uncommon. Finally, in childbed they found themselves surrounded by midwives charged to refuse to assist them until they declared, often with the accompaniment of bloodcurdling oaths – 'that the childe should sticke to me as the barke to the tree' being but one example – the name of the father of the child. It is scarcely surprising that some girls faced with these terrors concealed their pregnancies, bore their children alone and then exposed, abandoned or deliberately killed them.[42]

Such harrying of these wretched girls – for it was they who suffered, the father rarely receiving worse punishment than penance and a maintenance order if he could be found – might be seen as a necessary defence of the implicit principle of England's marriage pattern: that children should not be born save within economically independent nuclear families. Be that as it may, the whole question of illegitimacy reveals something of the human cost of that system. For illegitimacy may provide a fair indication of the disjunction which could exist between marital hopes and marital opportunities. Marriage and family formation might be free to all, as Perkins opined, but they were not easily attainable by all. For the poor, and in particular for poor women, marriage was not secure until it was accomplished. Accordingly many, perhaps most, were cautious, like the Somerset servant who told her eager lover, 'No, truly you shall not lye with me till we be married, for you see how many do falsify their promises. . . . I am but a servant and if your friends should not consent to our marriage we are undone.' Others gambled: some won, some lost.[43]

Conclusion

To draw to a conclusion, it is evident that in the selection of marriage partners the notion of parity in a match, so much stressed by contemporary moralists, did indeed deeply influence choice, whether that choice lay entirely with the individuals concerned, or was subject to the direction or consent of others. Of the various criteria in which parity was sought, however, there were variations in the relative weight placed upon particular factors. At the top of the social scale, personal attraction might be outweighed – *if* the conflict arose – by material and social considerations. As the social scale was descended, personal preference became subject to less severe constraints. It would be unwise, however, to argue too rigid a distinction between material, social and emotional factors in matchmaking, or to rush too readily to conclusions about shifts from one principal criterion to another over time. They ran together. It is clear that a degree of economic calculation was always necessary and its prominence in the marriages of the propertied, highlighted as it is in the surviving documentation, for they had most reason to set it down carefully, should not be too bluntly interpreted. Much may have gone unrecorded. Again, an apparently greater emphasis on emotional considerations towards the end of our period might be in part an illusion created by better documentation in the form of diaries and letters. In any case, it must be remembered that emotions are not generated in a social vacuum. They could be aroused where an individual had, as it were, *learned* to love, in accordance with the values of his or her day and station in life. However analytically distinguishable they might appear, material, social and emotional elements in marriage were in practice hopelessly intermingled.

The result, as might be expected, was a great deal of demonstrable 'homogamy' in marriage: like married like. All of the principal social groups were essentially endogamous, marrying within their own ranks. Where they made exogamous marriages, often in the case of younger children, they rarely strayed far in terms of social and economic parity, forming instead what might be called clusters of intermarrying social groups.[44] The peerage might intermarry to some degree with the upper gentry, with wealthy merchants and lawyers, the gentry with mercantile, legal and clerical families, and sometimes with wealthy yeomen. So we might continue down the social scale. As in social distance, so also in physical distance, for the geography of marriage partner selection reflected the spatial dimensions of the world within which families of different rank moved. For the aristocrats and greater gentry who visited court or took part in the London season, marriage alliances might be national in scope. The gentry married for the most part within the gentle society of their counties, though the proportion of gentry marriages thus circumscribed could vary with the size and geographical location of a county, from the 82 per cent of large, peninsular Kent, to the 37 per cent of small, easily accessible Hertfordshire. Humbler people married within the social area in which they moved for various purposes – generally within their parishes of residence (as distinct from their parishes of birth) and neighbouring settlements.[45]

In marriage, as in other respects, social groups frayed and became blurred at the edges and marriage might promote a degree of both social and physical mobility. This should not be exaggerated however. In general marriage confirmed social distinctions, and the process of family formation both faithfully reflected, and served to perpetuate the social order: its privileges, its obligations, its opportunities, its constraints and its injustices.

4 *Husbands and wives, parents and children*

On 11 December 1644, Ralph Josselin attended the wedding of one of his less prosperous parishioners. 'Dind at a strange vaine wedding,' he noted in his diary, 'a poore man gave curious ribbands to all, gloves to the women and to the ringers, yett there was very good company.' The celebration of marriage in the later sixteenth and the seventeenth centuries was a very public and joyous occasion. Even the relatively poor, as Josselin recognized with a mixture of disapproval and surprise, put on some show, with ribbons, gloves, bell-ringing and a dinner. Elsewhere, they might have held a bride-ale towards which the guests themselves contributed money and foodstuffs, or at least a drinking and dancing in the alehouse. Among the yeomanry it was an even grander occasion – one Staffordshire man spent 31s. for his daughter's gown cloth in 1601, with a further 7s. 6d. for bones to line the gown, 16s. for trimmings and 8s. 6d. for her hat, while at a yeoman wedding in Suffolk in 1589 a bullock and seven sheep were consumed by the guests, not to mention prodigious quantities of bread and beer. Gentry weddings were splendid spectacles. When squire Harlackenden's daughter was married at Earles Colne in 1656, the expenses shocked both him and his friend Josselin, but the indulgent father swallowed his puritan dislike of such vanity and paid up; while the wedding of Sir Thomas Mildmay in another Essex village in 1589 was an event which drew spectators from nearby parishes just to witness the ceremony.[1]

Pomp and circumstance according to means, full bellies, muddled heads and neighbourly jollity thus marked the formal end of parental obligation for a child and the recognition of the formation of a new family. The celebration over, the new couple were left to find their own way and to begin the working out of their marital roles. They might expect a little help and doubtless received a good deal of free advice – as at the handfasting of Martin High and Janet Ferry at Croxdale in County

Durham, when Janet's grandfather, 'standing against the barn wall' before the assembled neighbours, gave his blessing to the couple 'and sayd so much to them there', as one witness ruefully recalled, 'that one might have goon a mile in the spac'[2] – but from this time on it was up to them.

Marital relationships

The ideal

It might be assumed that the establishment of the 'conjugal role relationships' of each new couple was a fairly unproblematic matter in this period – that husband and wife would slot easily into the well-established roles defined by a traditional culture. Certainly conventional moralistic thought held this to be true. To the authors of the conduct books, conjugal relationships should be conducted according to a pattern which was both natural and divinely ordained. Its most essential element was the recognition of the supreme authority of the husband.

To William Perkins, writing in 1590, the husband could be defined as 'he that hath authority over the wife'. To William Whately, writing in 1617, the husband was God's officer and king in his own house, while five years later William Gouge asserted that the husband was 'as a Priest unto his wife. . . . He is the highest in the family, and hath both authority over all and the charge of all is committed to his charge; he is as a king in his owne house'. As might be expected in the light of these high claims, the principal duty of the wife was simply to obey. Perkins summed it up when he defined a wife as 'the other married person, who being subject to her husband yieldeth obedience to him'. She should acknowledge him in all things and render full obedience, 'that is wholly to depend upon him, both in judgement and will'.[3]

Given these central assumptions, it is hardly surprising to find that the qualities conventionally ascribed to a good wife were essentially submissive. She should be patient, loving, sweet, modest, quiet and obedient. A bad wife, on the other hand, was assertive, capricious, quarrelsome, scolding, inconstant, foolish and extravagant in dress. That women were prone to these faults was generally acknowledged and the literature of the period provides many examples of a conventionalized misogyny which was in its way the mirror image of the courtly cult of female excellence affected by sonnet writers: John Donne, for example, could write in both modes. Literary exaggeration of both extremes apart, however, there is no doubt that woman's alleged inferiority, mental, physical and moral, was generally accepted by the male moralists of the day, and justified by the scriptural authority of the creation myth, Eve's role in the fall of man, and the opinions of St Peter and St Paul. The husband's duty was to 'mould' his wife in such a way as to bring out the good in her and render her serviceable.[4]

This aspect of attitudes towards women is well known and justly notorious. It is very far from being the whole story, however, and we must be careful to avoid the painting of too black a picture. Woman's subordination was axiomatic, and was enshrined in legal disabilities, particularly with regard to property rights. Nevertheless it was also commonly agreed that the husband had duties towards, as well as privileges and authority over, the 'weaker vessell'. If these were in part a further instance of the officially patronizing attitude towards women, they also had much more positive elements. The husband was charged with the duties of providing for his wife, of protecting and maintaining her, and of bearing with her infirmities. But the element of partnership in marriage was not forgotten. The husband should be not only his wife's guide, but also her friend. To Whately the roles of husband and wife were complementary, the wife being not only his 'subordinate' and 'deputie', but also his 'associate'. Perkins saw husband and wife as 'yokefellows' and insisted that husbands should honour their wives and even suffer their admonishment as well as taking their advice. This element of the moralistic conception of the ideal marriage was encapsulated in the frequently repeated point that woman had been created neither from the head nor the foot of the man, but from his side, 'that shee might walke joyntly with him, under the conduct and government of her head', as 'R. C.' put it in 1598. The mutual duties of marriage extended, in Perkins's formulation, beyond mere cohabitation to what he called 'communion', a condition which ranged from the 'right and lawful use of their bodies or of the marriage bed', through 'cherishing one another' with goods, labour and counsel, to 'an holy kind of rejoicing and solacing themselves each with other in a mutual declaration of the signs and tokens of love and kindness'.[5] This mutuality in marriage is a less dramatic aspect of moralistic advice than their assertions of male authority, but it was of equal importance to the writers of the conduct books and it should never be ignored. Nor was the stress on mutuality within marriage a novel development of this period. For though it has been argued in the past that this aspect of marital advice originated with the English puritans, it has been conclusively shown by Powell and Davies that the puritan authors of conduct books were merely the principal practitioners of an old-established genre and that (exceptional radicals and sectarian teachers apart) they added little that was distinctive to their teachings on marriage. They were part of the Christian mainstream.

Indeed, the popular 'proof' of their teachings on mutuality, that Eve was made from Adam's side, originated with St Jerome.[6]

The reality

Male authority, tempered by the mutual duties of Christian marriage, seems a clear enough guide to the roles of man and wife within marriage in this period. It would be unwise, however, simply to accept it at face value. Conventional definition of roles and the actual performance of them in everyday life can be quite different things, and as Powell argued long ago about the problem of women's place in society in general, 'we should get a fairer and more fundamental view by examining historical and biographical facts, rather than by studying the writing of moralists, lovers and satirists'.[7] In practice, of course, marital roles must have varied in some degree. Unfortunately the surviving documentary evidence of marital relationships is sparse and the best of it (in the form of diaries) is biased in several respects: socially (towards the middling and upper ranks of society), ideologically (towards the deeply religious, especially ministers), and by sex (towards men). Nevertheless the evidence of diaries can be used and filled out sufficiently from other evidence (especially wills) to modify in some degree the stereotype of marital relations. The picture which emerges indicates the *private* existence of a strong complementary and companionate ethos, side by side with, and often overshadowing, theoretical adherence to the doctrine of male authority and *public* female subordination.

That the balance of these elements varied from marriage to marriage is itself an indication of the fact that each couple needed to work out for themselves their marital roles within the context of their general expectations of marriage: in a sense each couple evolved a *modus vivendi* of their own. It was a process which had its ups and downs, as is admirably illustrated by Henry Newcome's diary entries during the first year or so of his marriage. On Saturday 12 May 1649, he was deeply upset by one of their early quarrels and wrote: 'I studied for Sunday with a great deal of distraction by reason of some very idle and frivolous passages 'twixt my wife and me which (to show the fickleness of any content of this life) arose out of nothing and grew to that height as never any grief reached upon us yet.' Two months later things were much better and the Newcomes 'spent this morning very idly, in throwing water one at other', a kind of playfulness which Henry's puritanism did not preclude, though he added in the margin, 'What a strange toy and vanity'. It was not long, however, before he had occasion to 'bless God for comfort and quiet restored with my wife'.[8] The Newcomes were learning to live together; not without friction, not without fun.

It is important to recognize this element of individual evolution in marriage, allowing for the play of particular personalities, as a counterbalance to the simple moralistic-legal stereotype of marital relations. It was a process which took place in the context of a good deal of practical co-operation of man and wife, since marriage was emphatically an economic partnership. This reality was perhaps clearest cut among the 'middling sort' of small farmers and independent craftsmen and tradesmen. William Stout's father, for example, farmed twenty-four acres on the edge of the Lake District and his mother was 'not onely fully imployed in housewifry but in dressing their corn for the market, and also in the fields in hay and corn harvests, along with our father and the servants'. Urban wives of craftsmen and tradesmen were busy in the shop as well as above it. What was true of the 'middling sort' was equally true of the labouring poor. The wives of weavers working at piece rates in the cloth townships of the north, the west country and East Anglia were commonly engaged in spinning for their husbands' employers, as indeed were the wives of many agricultural labourers in these districts – in Essex female involvement in spinning for the looms of the cloth towns was widespread throughout the north and centre of the county. If no such opportunities existed locally, then there was casual labour in weeding, haymaking and harvest time, stone-picking, gleaning, washing, perhaps keeping an alehouse and many another way of earning a penny or two towards the family's subsistence. Indeed, for many of the poorest villagers and townspeople the joint endeavour of feeding, clothing and housing themselves and their children may well have dominated the marital relationship, though this is not to suggest that marriage for the poor did not have other satisfactions.[9]

In the highest ranks of society wives might be less active in economic matters, more ornamental and idle – more possessions to be displayed than partners. Grace, Lady Mildmay described herself as having 'spent the best part of my youth in solitariness', consoling herself with reading, music and needlework during her husband's frequent absences. Similarly, Ann Clifford, a woman later to prove herself of signal ability, was deeply frustrated by her relative seclusion and impotence during her marriages to the Earl of Dorset and the Earl of Pembroke, later recalling that 'the marble pillars of Knole in Kent and of Wilton in Wiltshire were to me oftentimes but the gay arbours of anguish'. Such a situation might have been all too often the outcome of marriages in which the parties had exercised little personal choice and had less practical need to develop a personal accommodation of marital roles. But this should not be exaggerated. The wives of the gentry were still crucial in the running of their households and this was a full-time job in such extensive establishments. Sir John Oglander was proud indeed of his diligent wife who 'never wore a silk gown but for her credit when she went abroad': 'she was up every day before me and oversaw all the outhouses: she would not trust her maid with directions, but would wet her shoes to see it done herself'. Many a gentry estate was under the temporary management of wives during their husbands' necessary absences and they could thrive under considerable periods of such supervision, as the civil war years were to witness. If there was a norm at most social levels, then it was perhaps that of complementary activity in day-to-day affairs. Indeed, no clearer tribute to the practical experience and economic competence of women and to the trust placed in them by their husbands exists than the terms of their husbands' wills. The naming of a wife as executor and the granting to her of full control of the family patrimony and the responsibilities of maintaining and bringing up under-age children, was not merely frequent in the wills of the period, it was normal.[10]

Behind the plain legal formality of such wills must have lain a strong bond of mutual respect, and the existence of such sentiments is hinted at in other ways. Decision-making, for example, lay officially with the husband, but it was frequently based upon prior discussion between husband and wife. Effectively, then, it was shared. During the period of her diary, 1599–1605, Lady Margaret Hoby frequently discussed business affairs with her husband, Sir Thomas. Henry Newcome talked over 'matters of greatest concernment' (namely his future career) with his wife and found her ready 'to further me therein all that she could'. Such agreement and support was clearly important to him, as it was also to the diarists Ralph Josselin and Adam Eyre.[11] Of course, such discussions did not always end in ready agreement, but the very existence of expressed disagreement tells us something about the actual nature of the relationship. Indeed, the examination of marital conflict and its resolution can provide very revealing insights into those few marriages of which we have accounts in any detail.

Wives, as we have seen, were enjoined to be obedient and to avoid contention. It was advice often repeated as when one Sussex gentlewoman was counselled to 'endeavour to please' her husband and to 'dwell with him in an amiable meekness of minde and doe not greeve his spirit with the least frowardness'. Perhaps it was often so among the gentry, for it has been alleged that the letters of gentlewomen reveal a pervasive anxiety to please their husbands coupled with an implicit fear of their displeasure.

Formality of style may conceal much, of course, but the possibility of a more submissive relationship can at least be raised. Wives of the aristocracy and upper gentry were more often significantly younger than their husbands than was the case in the population at large, and their marriages were subject to greater parental influence; both factors may have had their effects. Lady Mildmay, in her 'meditation on the corps of my husband' of 1617, recalled: 'I carryed alwayes that reverent respect towards him in regard of my good conceipt which I had of the good partes I knew to be in him, that I could not fynde it in my heart to challenge him for the worst word or deede which ever he offered me . . . but in silence passed over all such matters betwixt us.' Ann Clifford had the spirit to resist both King James I and her husband, the Earl of Dorset, over the question of giving up her claim to her father's lands, yet she appears to have accepted meekly the unkind treatment meted out to her for her resistance. 'Sometimes I had fair words from him and sometimes foul,' she remembered, 'but I took all patiently and did strive to give him as much content and assurance of my love as I could possibly.'[12]

If submissiveness characterized the marital relations of great gentlewomen, however, they were sharply distinguished in this respect from their social inferiors, for the diaries of the middling sort contain quarrels enough. Of these we have only the husband's view, but it seems significant that quarrels were not uncommon, that the wife very often seems to have taken the initiative in asserting herself, and that marital bickering was not usually cut short promptly by assertions of the husband's patriarchal authority.

Henry Newcome's distress when experiencing for the first time the combative aspect of marital relations has already been seen. By 14 July 1652, he was thoroughly exasperated. 'I was exceedingly perplexed about my wife,' he recorded. 'God knows what I should do. These four years have I now lived with her, and do not know how to humour her. When she is angry, I do aggravate her passion by saying anything. . . . When she is patient, peace is so sweet to me that I dare not speak lest I should lose it.' The occasion of this confession was his wife's angry complaint that she was overworked and badly needed another servant in the household. It is perhaps significant of male authority, even within what began as a love match and seems to have been a very companionate marriage, that Elizabeth Newcome had to raise trouble in order to get her point over. But neither Newcome's emotional reaction, nor his response shows him wielding his authority. Having recorded his confusion of mind he began to consider whether he was indeed in the wrong: 'it may be the devil would scandalize me by her pains, and that I enslave her. . . . But God knows it is not in my mind'. In the end he gave way to her demands, though he continued to maintain a theoretical male superiority by consoling himself, 'I must confess I think all women to be thus weak. I believe they have much to do any of them. A lamentable weak creature.'[13]

Of particular interest in this respect is the case of Adam Eyre, a Yorkshire yeoman and an ex-captain in the army of Parliament. Whereas Newcome was simply contending with inevitable domestic disagreements, Eyre's marriage seems to have been in real trouble in the summer and autumn of 1647. We do not know why this was the case, though a few clues exist. Eyre was undergoing severe financial difficulties, partly as a result of his war service, partly through his own mismanagement, and his wife seems to have been anxious to preserve some property which was in her own name. Susan Eyre had very poor health and was in frequent pain. On top of this she does not seem to have wholly shared her husband's religious radicalism, while she clearly disapproved of his over-enjoyment of alehouse company. The fact that he had only recently returned from military service and that he was still preoccupied with, and not infrequently absent upon, official business, may not have helped. The record of how they handled their difficulties is invaluable.

On 26 May, Eyre recorded resignedly that his wife 'was very extravagant after her old humourous way', suggesting a previous acquaintance with her temper, and this was confirmed a fortnight later when he was foolish enough to criticize her way of dressing. 'My wife began, after her old manner, to braule me and revile me for wishing her only to weare such apparrell as was decent and comly, and accused mee of treading on her sore foote, with curses and othes; which to my knowledge I touched not; neverthelesse she continued in that extacy til noone.' After an afternoon's brooding on the matter he decided to assert his authority, though he chose an unusual manner: 'at diner I told her I purposed never to com in bed with her til she tooke more notice of what I formerly had sayd to her'. He was not sure he could keep this resolve, adding 'which I pray God give mee grace to observe; that the folly of myne owne corrupt nature deceive mee not'. How long he kept this up, it is hard to say, but things seem to have normalized in the ensuing weeks, despite references to friction on 23 June – 'This night my wife was worse in words than ever' – and on 30 July – 'This day I stayd at home all day, by reason my wife was not willing to let mee goe to bowles to Bolsterstone.'

The Eyres were certainly sharing their bed again by 6 August when her sore foot gave her a restless night and 'sleepe went from' him. His reflections that night, however, reveal just how bad things were: 'sundry wicked worldly thoughts came in my head, and, namely, a question whether I should live with my wife or no, if she continued so wicked as shee is'. This was the crisis point for him and he was so distressed by his thoughts that he rose, prayed, consulted a devotional book and prayed again before finding his peace of mind and sleep. Quite what he decided we can never know. He referred cryptically to his 'sore temptation' some days later but did not broach the subject with his wife. In September she accompanied him on a journey to London, and though discord revived on their return, he bore with it stoically, as he did on two days in October when she was 'very angry' and 'very angry all day', on 20 November when she was 'exceeding angry' and then on 19 December when she was 'very unquiet and uncharitable . . . God forgive her'.

Meanwhile Adam seems to have been silently coming to terms with his position in several respects. In early December, a number of entries of unusual intensity suggest that he had reached a crisis point in his religious development – a major spiritual landmark for a tortured Puritan like Eyre. Certainly from this time on he wrote more frequently and with more assurance on spiritual matters. The inconsistency between his rigorous beliefs and his self-indulgent life-style seems also to have demanded resolution, and on 22 December he cast up his accounts and decided 'hereafter never to pay for anybody in the alehouse, nor never to entangle myselfe in company so much again as I have done; and I pray God give mee grace that, sleighting the things of this life, I may looke up to Him'. Finally on 1 January 1648, after a stormy night when the kitchen chimney collapsed, yet did no great damage – something Eyre interpreted as a special providence – he approached his wife to settle matters. In doing so, it is notable that he turned neither to his authority, nor to the expedient of a legal separation, but rather attempted a compromise, bolstered by religious resolution and an explicit appeal to the ideal of mutuality in marriage. The passage deserves quotation in full:

> This morne I used some words of persuasion to my wife to forbeare to tell mee of what is past, and promised her to become a good husband to her for ye tyme to come, and shee promised me likewise shee would doe what I wished her in anything, save in setting her hand to papers; and I promised her never to wish her thereunto. Now I pray God that both shee and I may leave of all our old and foolish contentions, and joyne together in His service without all fraud, malice, or hypocrisye; and that Hee will for ye same purpose illuminate our understandings with His Holy Spirit, Which in the midst of worldly cares and cumbrances may be our guide and direction, and from all temptacions and perills our perpetuall protection, to the glory and praise of His great and glorious name. Amen.

For the remaining year of the diary they seem to have kept this resolution. There is only one more reference to a quarrel, while Adam clearly tried hard to modify his conduct, bolstered by religious fortitude and deeply sorry for occasional lapses of temper and sobriety. He also kept his promise to his wife over the inviolability of her property.[14]

Clearly this was a marriage which came dangerously close to breakdown. Nevertheless both Eyre's response to the problem and the manner in which he sought its resolution seem highly significant. His expectations of his marriage were high and its failures deeply distressed him. In this, his reactions were similar to Henry Newcome's and to those of an earlier puritan diarist, Richard Rogers, who in 1588 and 1589 recorded his regret at occasions of 'roughness', 'sharpness' and 'waspishness' in his speech with his wife, and regretted his slowness in patching up these quarrels. Unlike Rogers, Eyre was initially inclined to blame these marital turmoils on his wife and to assert his authority. Susan Eyre however would not accept this, and gradually he came to recognize his own share of responsibility. Accordingly, his solution was to start again on the basis of mutual understanding. Although there was verbal violence enough, it never broke down into physical violence – the nearest it came to that was when Adam broke his wife's spinning wheel in a fit of temper, and even then he promptly and remorsefully set about repairing it.[15] In fact none of the contemporary diaries known to me provides evidence of wife-beating as a response to domestic conflict. Undoubtedly it was allowed (in 'moderation') by English law, but it seems likely that the religious moralists were as much reflecting as shaping the opinions of their audience when they unanimously opposed it. As 'R. C.' wrote in one of the most popular conduct books, a husband should observe three rules in dealing with his wife's faults: 'often to admonish; seldome to reprove; and never to smite her'.[16]

Whatever the evidence of the diaries of the 'middling sort', however, it is not uncommonly assumed that wife-beating was a characteristic aspect of domestic conflict in the marriages of the poor. Here, if anywhere, it might be supposed, could be found nakedly displayed the authoritarianism of the seventeenth-century marriage. Certainly instances of husbandly brutality can be recovered from the court records of the period, but such evidence must be handled with caution. Take, for example, the case of John Barnes, heard at Ely assizes in 1652. Returning from the alehouse 'somewhat hott with beere' and being told by his wife that 'hee was a Rogue and that ther was many a Truer man Hanged', he beat and kicked her so severely, 'out of a hastie collericke humour', that she died of her injuries. This case may seem classical. The fact remains, however, that his neighbours strongly disapproved of his persistent abuse of his wife and they readily came forward to give evidence against him.[17] In the seventeenth as in the twentieth century it may have been that wife-battering was considered reprehensible but that neighbours felt unwilling to interfere unless matters were carried to extremes, as is further suggested by a petition of the villagers of Yardley to the Worcestershire justices in 1617. They complained of one householder who 'did beat his wife most cruellie' as part of a general rehearsal of his manifold disorders. Clearly they held this against him, but might not have acted had he not exhausted local tolerance by other acts of more public concern. Wife-battering, then, was certainly known (and homicides within the family made up a substantial proportion of all killings) but this is not something which can be held to demonstrate that physical violence was an accepted feature of lower-class marriages. If anything, the evidence of popular attitudes points rather to the reverse. Both the violent husband and the scolding, domineering wife were the objects of popular disapproval and both might be subject to informal and on occasion, formal community sanctions. The ideal was to avoid either extreme in marital relations.[18]

Cautious interpretation is also required in discussing another much publicized negative aspect of conjugal relations: the sexual double standard. There is much evidence to suggest that the sexual misdemeanours of men were regarded with less hostility than those of women and that wives, particularly in the highest reaches of society, were often expected to tolerate the infidelities of their husbands. But again, this should not be exaggerated. Contemporary moralists were united in their condemnation of both sexual infidelity and the double standard, even though they might emphasize the social consequences of a wife's infidelity more strongly than they did the evils of a husband's resort to whores or exploitation of servant girls. Of course, the brothels of the towns had customers enough and the philandering of adulterous husbands made a steady contribution to the incidence of illegitimacy. However there is evidence of popular disapproval of adultery by either party and, though the gentry were generally immune from such sanctions, blatant or 'scandalous' adultery in village communities was liable to lead to the presentment of offenders of either sex to the church courts. An unblemished reputation for sexual probity was of particular importance for women, but it was also something to be valued by both partners to a marriage – as witnessed by the fact that it was often enough defended from slanderous reproaches in expensive church court actions for defamation. These facts serve as a further reminder that marital relations were conducted within the broader context of the neighbourhood and that, in areas of nucleated settlement at least, the conduct of both husband and wife could be subjected to the sanctions of neighbourhood opinion. The evidence of public presentments to the courts suggests that village officers were less willing to prosecute married members of the community for sexual misdemeanours than single people. Nevertheless such restraint had its limits, while the powerful informal sanction of gossip existed to subject domestic conduct to constant scrutiny and evaluation. In a society in which personal reputation could be a matter of considerable practical significance, such sanctions could not lightly be ignored.[19] The double standard existed; 'moderate' wife-beating was legal. Both facts may reveal much about fundamental attitudes towards women, but both practices were also clearly disapproved of and neither can justly be held to have been characteristic of marital relations.

In the domestic economy, decision-making, conflict resolution and sexual behaviour, mutuality in marriage, within a context of ultimate male authority, may well have been not only the conjugal ideal, but also the common practice among the English people as a whole. We cannot, of course, expect it to have been either constant or universal. Persistent dissension, cruelty and infidelity could result in the effective breakdown of marriage, and where this happened there was little hope of divorce as we understand it. The ecclesiastical courts had the power to nullify unconsummated or legally invalid marriages, or to order judicial separations on the grounds of adultery, apostasy or cruelty, but such research as has been done suggests that such cases were very rare indeed. Only a private Act of Parliament could secure a divorce proper and this was rarer still.[20]

Among the poor, there is evidence to suggest that the breakdown of marriages might lead to informal separations or simple desertion of one spouse by the other. The church courts not uncommonly heard presentments of couples who were living apart from one another without formal licence, some by choice, more because they had found it impossible to sustain an independent household, while the records of poor law administration provide further examples of simple desertion. Richard Elings of Feckenham in Worcestershire, for example, deserted his wife in 1619 and went off to Oxfordshire where he took up with another woman, claiming that his first wife was dead.[21] Given the inadequacies of communication in the period and the great difficulties involved in identifying individuals, it was easy enough to disappear completely if the need was felt strongly enough. This was no way out, however, for those whose property and obligations kept them tied to a particular locality. If their marriages were unsuccessful, then they had to be endured. Richard Gough knew of several such cases in Myddle, while Henry Newcome also cites a number of unhappy marriages. On one occasion he was called in to counsel one of his cousins on how to revive a failed marriage, but concluded that things had so far deteriorated through 'jealousy' and 'want of affection' that 'nothing but the power of religion could make them live like man and wife'. Elsewhere, he observed of a leading gentleman, Mr Wrigley, and his wife, that despite her religious faith and his intelligence they 'could not hit it to live quietly and comfortably together, but lived in perpetual secret unkindness'. In the reckoning of marital failure, such couples must be considered alongside the more dramatic instances of negligent, drunken, violent and improvident husbands and shrewish, domineering wives, which stand out in the court records. For such couples, marriage was a cross to bear and release came only with the death of a spouse – though it can be remarked that death rates were such that it has been suggested that a greater proportion of marriages were prematurely broken by death in the seventeenth century than by divorce in mid twentieth-century America.[22]

A degree of marital failure is to be expected in any society, of course, but there is no reason why a realistic acknowledgement of the pathological side of marital relations, should lead us to conclude that in general they were cold, authoritarian and characterized by low expectations. After all, a great majority of spouses had exercised personal choice in their selection of marriage partners and this was a good basis for the working out of a strong mutual affection and respect. Indeed the strongest surviving evidence suggests that this, if anything, was the norm. Despite her stress on the degree of calculating arrangement which went into the marriages of the Verneys, Miriam Slater does not preclude 'the development of an affectionate and enduring relationship' and allows that, even though Sir Ralph Verney's love and concern for his wife were somewhat formal and expressed in his letters 'in the manner of a worried parent to a rather frivolous adolescent', Lady Verney nonetheless loved him in the full romantic sense and saw no incongruity in the expression of such affection. Other evidence is much less qualified. The diary of Lady Margaret Hoby reveals that this Yorkshire gentlewoman and her husband regularly set aside time from a busy life to walk and talk together. They kept one another company when sick, discussed business and performed their religious duties together. In the evenings he read aloud to her and when separated they exchanged frequent letters. The independent evidence of a Star Chamber deposition shows Sir Thomas anxiously visiting his wife when she was sick and defending her from the disturbance occasioned by a troop of drunken hunting gentry. Moreover, he wore her picture in a bracelet on his arm until the hour of his death and testified in his will to the 'extraordinary affection that was betweene her and myselfe'. Lower in the social scale, William Gouge thought it necessary to warn his congregation of London citizens against unseemly displays of affection, including the public employment of Christian names and such pet names as 'duck', 'chick' and 'pigsnie'. Richard Gough's account of the families of Myddle provides ample examples, approvingly cited, of loving couples whose marriages were eminently successful partnerships in both practical and emotional terms. Alan Macfarlane, in his thorough analysis of Ralph Josselin's diary, has provided a picture of a marriage in which the bond with his wife was the most significant relationship in Josselin's life. The couple were rarely apart and when circumstances necessitated separation they missed one another badly. They were tender and anxious to one another in times of illness, were upset by the inevitable domestic quarrels, shared the duties of housekeeping, decision-making, and child-rearing, and also their interests, friends and leisure time.[23]

Such a detailed record of a married life of over forty years is unique for this period. Our more fragmentary glimpses of other marriages, however, do not suggest that the Josselins were in any way abnormal. How often similarly satisfactory marriages lay behind the necessarily plain and formal terms of the wills, which provide our only insight into many thousands of marriages, is a matter for conjecture. Certainly, as we have seen, testators showed a generally high degree of respect for the capacities of their widows to provide for and raise young children. Moreover, where child-rearing was already accomplished, they commonly provided carefully for the future well-being of surviving spouses. Gentlewomen had their jointures, carefully negotiated at the time of their betrothal, while customary law usually provided a third of the family property for the maintenance of the widows of manorial tenants. Yet most testators went well beyond this in their provision – a straightforward life interest in the farm or family house being the norm. In other cases very specific arrangements for a widow's well-being might be laid down, as in the case of Grace Meade of Orwell in Cambridgeshire. In her husband's will of 1585 she was to have the parlour of the family house together with its furnishings, in addition to which she was left sheep, cows, a plough team and four acres of land, which her son was to plough for her as well as providing his mother with a load of hay a year. Such practical foresight bespeaks at least a degree of consideration for a widow's welfare. Some wills suggest still more. Those of the Sussex gentry are couched in terms indicative of domestic tenderness sufficiently often for Anthony Fletcher to conclude that 'marriage seems to have brought deep and lasting fulfilment to many'. Nor is this a feature only of gentry wills. References in the wills of the common people to 'my loving wife', 'my loveing deare wife' or 'my beloved wife' might be dismissed as mere convention, but the very existence of such a convention is of some significance, while it is probable that these phrases were often heartfelt. Some testators went further still, like Jane Salter of Terling in Essex, who asked to be buried 'by my late husband', or Edmund Hodgson of Darlington, who wished to be interred 'so nighe the corps of my wyffe as may be'.[24]

In at least one respect the marriage of Ralph and Jane Josselin *was* unusual – it lasted over forty years. Many marriages were broken after only a few years by the early death of one of the partners and where this was so, remarriage was common. It could also be very swift – often within a year of a spouse's death.[25] For many a young widow or widower, remarriage was virtually a necessity and this fact explains the swiftness with which it could be undertaken, though it would be arbitrary to assume that practicalities dominated the selection of second marriage partners to any greater degree than they did the choice of a first husband or wife. In some cases the reverse might equally well be true. Again, it is possible that the quality of marital relations may have differed in second or subsequent marriages, especially perhaps where these involved a greater than usual age-gap between spouses, or where they tilted the balance of domestic authority towards the wife. Of these matters we know little with any certainty, but no simple inference can be made from the demographic fact of remarriage, either about second marriages or about the unions which they succeeded. The premature death of a spouse was a possibility of which husbands and wives in this period were demonstrably aware, but this is not to say that it coloured their whole attitude to marriage. Many had to adjust to it but to some the loss was shattering. Henry Newcome's mother died of grief and was buried together with her husband. William Stout recalled how 'the loss of soe loving, industrious and provident a husband and partner much affected my mother with sorrow'. Adam Martindale's son was so affected by his wife's dangerous illness that 'much desiring her life and fearing her death' he 'begged of God that he might die in her stead'. For all of these and many more the death of a spouse was no release, but a deeply felt personal tragedy.[26]

Of marital relations in late sixteenth- and seventeenth-century England, much remains obscure. The weight of the evidence reviewed here, however, suggests that, despite the inevitable counter-examples and the individual and social variation which is to be expected, there is little reason to follow Professor Stone in regarding the rise of the companionate marriage as a new phenomenon of the later seventeenth and eighteenth centuries.[27] It seems to have been already well established. It is true that the best of our evidence is derived from the diaries of deeply religious people, puritans who had especial cause to follow the advice of moral teachers on the subject of mutuality. Yet such supplementary evidence as can be gathered does not suggest that they were unusual in their marital relations, while the teachings of the moralists themselves were neither new, nor distinctively Puritan. They represented for the most part the mainstream of opinion on the best practice in marriage. In the present state of our knowledge it would seem unwise to make too sharp a dichotomy between the 'patriarchal' and the 'companionate' marriage, and to erect these qualities into a typology of successive stages of family development. It may well be that these are less evolutionary stages of familial progress, than the poles of an enduring continuum in marital relations in a society which accepted both the primacy of male authority and the ideal of marriage as a practical and emotional partnership. Most people established their roles within marriage somewhere between the two, with the emphasis, for the most part, on the latter.

Childbirth and childhood

As each newly married couple gradually established their individual roles within marriage, the situation would rapidly have been complicated by the arrival of children. Of those brides traceable from their marriages to the baptism of their first child in the parishes of Orwell (Cambridgeshire), Wimbledon (Surrey), Cuckfield (Sussex) and Kirkham (Lancashire), P. E. H. Hair found that over a third bore their first child within twelve months of marriage, while between two-thirds and four-fifths had done so within two years.[28]

Such rapid parenthood reflects the fact that in an age without efficient contraceptive methods children were the almost inevitable result of a sexual union at marriage. But they were also valued in themselves – as the blessing of God to those influenced by religious teachings, as guarantees of the perpetuation of the family line to those concerned with their lineage, as a source of personal pleasure and emotional satisfaction to all. Infertility was not regarded in England as a particular stigma and it did not provide grounds for a divorce or legal separation. It was, however, a personal tragedy, for children were clearly desired. Ralph Josselin, married in October 1640, happily entered in his diary for July 1641, 'I began to have some hopes of my wives breeding, which proved so indeed to our great joy and comfort.' His pleasure when his first daughter was born on 12 April 1642 was amply demonstrated by the fact that he spent the substantial sum of £6 13s. 4d. on her christening celebrations and confirmed by his comment that even in infancy the child proved 'a pleasant comfort' to both him and his wife.[29]

Thereafter, childbirth was frequent, in Josselin's family as in most others, and a time of considerable anxiety, for death in childbed was common enough. Quite apart from the risk of death, suffering in childbirth could be appalling in an age lacking either anaesthetics or gynaecological sophistication, and in which the aid of the village midwives could be as much an additional danger as a help – as is only too apparent in the gruesome casebook compiled by Percival Willughby, one of the few medically trained 'midwives' of the period. Henry Newcome had good cause to pray earnestly for his wife's safe delivery during her confinements, and as parish minister he was often called to do the same for parishioners of all social ranks. Given the comparative frequency of confinements and the dangers attending childbirth, it is scarcely surprising that the diary of Ralph Josselin contains some suggestions that, as his family grew, anxiety for his wife's safety, coupled with the economic costs of raising his children, led Ralph to regard new pregnancies with diminishing enthusiasm.[30] That others probably felt the same is strongly suggested by demographic statistics produced by 'family reconstitution' which provide clear evidence that some form of family limitation was practised in many families in the seventeenth century, probably by the use of prolonged lactation to inhibit new conceptions or by the practice of *coitus interruptus*.[31] However it was achieved, such fertility restriction did not, of course, amount to family planning. There was no contraceptive method adequate to that task. Nor is 'family planning' a concept appropriate to the demographic realities of the day. Rather, efforts were made to limit family size once a sufficient number of surviving children had been born to a couple, and once it had become apparent that further births might prejudice the well-being of the existing family.

In that calculation the principal factor was the number of surviving children. Many did not survive. In the model population constructed for pre-industrial England by the demographers Wrigley and Schofield, they estimate that 34.4 per cent of all deaths would have been deaths of children under 10 years old, and only 6.7 per cent those of adults aged 80 or more, as compared with 2.4 per cent of deaths among the under-10s and 48.4 per cent of deaths among the over-80s in a model population constructed for contemporary England. Although infant and child mortality in late sixteenth- and seventeenth-century England was actually rather low by the standards of some other European populations of the time, it was nonetheless bad enough. In a study of the actual records of eight parishes in the period 1550–1649, Wrigley and Schofield established that something like a quarter of all children born would fail to live to the age of 10, the heaviest mortality being within the vulnerable first year of life.[32]

Despite these stark facts, the relatively high birth rate meant that a substantial part of the English population – probably something in the region of 40 per cent – consisted of dependent children living at home with their parents. Children, as Peter Laslett has observed, were everywhere; and those who had survived infancy had to be reared.[33]

It is at this point, however, that our evidence becomes exceedingly thin. Even such a remarkable document as Josselin's diary provides relatively little information on the actual rearing of small children, as compared with its richness on the subject of their subsequent development and eventual marriages. Again, of those sources available very few provide us with a woman's perspective on the process of child-rearing. The moralistic conduct books, of course, laid down general principles for the 'bringing up' and the 'bestowing' of children (the two principal duties of parents), but for the most part they are lamentably unspecific. A number of contemporary medical manuals provide examples of advice on the swaddling (generally for a month or more), feeding (on demand and preferably by the mother) and weaning (at between 1 and 3 years) of infants.[34] But they too give little information on child-training. Moreover it is highly unlikely that these works were widely known and used and we have no real justification for assuming, without independent evidence, that the advice given was followed by most young mothers, who are more likely to have learned how to rear children from their own mothers or their neighbours. All in all, it seems likely that there was some variation in the upbringing of children between social groups, between regions and indeed between families. The problem is that of approaching these matters in any adequate way.

Given this problem it may well seem surprising that a number of historians have written with great confidence on the characteristics of childhood in this period. We have a history of childhood of sorts, though it might be said with some justice that it is less a history than a pathology, distinguished above all by its extreme pessimism. Childhood, we are told, was at best a period of misdirected, essentially repressive, parental 'care', 'to be endured rather than enjoyed'. At worst it was a nightmare of abuse and neglect. High rates of infant mortality entailed an emotional coolness towards, even a disinterest in, small children. As children grew, great distance was maintained between parent and child and there was a lack of strong emotional bonding. Emphasis was firmly placed on the rights of the parent over the child (which was regarded as a species of property) rather than upon the duty of the parent to the child. The developmental problems of children and their special needs were scarcely recognized, let alone understood. Child discipline was extremely severe, both physically and in terms of psychological repression, the object being to 'break the will' of the child. The individuality of the child was disregarded and near absolute parental control was exerted over both the choice of occupation and the marriages of children. As a result, children grew into emotionally crippled adults, who in turn wreaked havoc on their own children.[35]

Accounts of this kind have a certain superficial plausibility as interpretations of what little is actually known of childhood in this period. On closer examination, however, it rapidly becomes apparent that in certain key respects, they are based to a disturbingly large extent upon unwarranted presumption and dubious inferences. It is true, for example, that children often died young; yet this fact does not in itself justify the assumption that parents responded by maintaining an emotional coolness towards young children. There can be no denying that the authors of conduct books laid considerable emphasis upon the authority of parents and upon the duty of children to honour and obey their fathers and mothers. They also, however, stressed the obligations of parents towards their children and gave advice which was much less harsh and much more aware of the needs of children than is commonly alleged. Again, it cannot be denied that children were little protected by law, that the rod was frequently used in schools and that some children, most often orphans, illegitimate children and pauper apprentices, lacking the protection of their parents, were grievously neglected and abused. However the only really thorough study yet available of relations between parents and children in the family – Alan Macfarlane's analysis of the family life of Ralph Josselin – presents an utterly contrasting picture of great parental care and warm emotional bonding. In the history of childhood, more than in any other area of social history, it may well appear that interpretive fertility has far outrun its empirical support. Questionable and basically unsubstantiated hypothesis has gained the status of accepted fact. If this is to be overcome, it can be done only with the aid of further close studies of particular families, though even so the evidence upon which such studies can be based comes late in time and is socially and ideologically biased. Of childhood among the mass of the population we have fewer glimpses, though wills are of some assistance and further imaginative research such as that of Barbara Hanawalt on medieval coroners' inquests (which revealed the stages of development of small children through examination of the circumstances of their accidental deaths) may provide further help.[36] As matters stand, an adequate history of childhood remains an aspiration. Nevertheless something can be done, with the aid of a number of diaries and autobiographies, of wills and other supporting evidence, to probe a little further the question of relations between parents and children and provide at least a counter-argument to set against the black legend of childhood.

Parent–child relationships

Parents, according to William Perkins, could be defined as 'they which have power and authority over children'. This power and authority, however, was not accorded unconditionally, for parents also had two great duties: 'to bring up their children' and 'to bestow them when they have brought them up'.[37] How, in so far as we can determine, did parents discharge these duties?

In the first place, most parents appear to have done their utmost to provide for their children's physical welfare, to feed and clothe them while still in their charge and to provide for their maintenance when possible long afterwards. Among a minority of the gentry and urban tradesmen infants were sometimes placed in the keeping of wet nurses, a practice which has been too readily seized upon as evidence of a general lack of parental care. Such an inference is unjustified. Among the gentry care was often taken in the selection of nurses, who sometimes lived in under the supervision of their employers, and commonly lived nearby. As for the urban 'middling sort', the actual extent of the practice remains obscure, though it seems unlikely to have involved more than a tiny minority of urban infants. Indeed, we know all too little of nursing in general, far too little to support the weight of inferential interpretation which has been placed upon the practice. That it continued is evidence only of the inertia of custom among an untypical minority of families. Interpretations of its significance have been too much influenced by our knowledge of the callous neglect sometimes shown in the placing of pauper children, commonly orphans or illegitimate, in the hands of nurses who did little to ensure their survival. This was a shocking practice, but it was one which also shocked many contemporaries and we know about it largely because of their attempts to draw attention to the abuse, or to punish it in the courts. Given the inadequate policing of the day, especially in great cities, it persisted, but it cannot be held to have been indicative of general attitudes towards infants. Most infants were nursed at home, and by their mothers. The moralists and doctors of the period advised it and most mothers probably never considered any alternative.[38]

As children grew, there is abundant evidence that parents made every effort to maintain them properly. It has been estimated, for example, that between the ages of 35 and 55 Ralph Josselin spent between a quarter and a third of his total income from all sources on his children. He was deeply worried in September 1648 when financial difficulties in a bad harvest year weakened his ability to provide for them as well as he would have liked. What was true of the 'middling sort' was equally true of the poor. The preachers of the period inveighed long and loud against poor men who drank their wages at the alehouse while their wives and children cried at home for bread. It was a popular theme with professional moralists and not without some foundation; but there is evidence enough to tell a different story. Given an annual income of between £10 and £15, at a time when, to judge by poor law accounts, the adequate feeding and clothing of a child cost a minimum of something in the region of £2 a year, a labouring couple with several dependent children probably spent an even larger proportion of their income on their children than did Ralph Josselin. It was said of the farm labourers of Essex that they were 'so extream poor that they are scarcely able to put bread in their childrens bellys'. Yet they tried. Henry Newcome recorded several cases of mothers who struggled to maintain their children in conditions of the greatest adversity – women like 'Aunt Key' of Bury who, in the famine of 1598, confronted with the symptoms of malnutrition in her children, tramped across the moors of Lancashire in search of food until she had provided for them, or Anne Haslom of the same town who, neglected by her husband, managed to earn enough with her own spinning to provide for the children, though sparsely at best.[39] Thousands of poor law petitions in the files of county quarter sessions records testify to the efforts of the poor to maintain their families. Indeed the records of the same courts provide more than a few examples of parents who were prepared to risk hanging by stealing to feed their children during times of particular hardship.

There was more to the bringing up of children, of course, than simply material provision, important and revealing though it is. Parents made a heavy financial investment in their children, but they also made a considerable emotional investment. This stands revealed in many ways. Parents, as we have seen, were very conscious of their children's mortality and it is often assumed that this bred a degree of resignation, even a general indifference to children's deaths. There is much evidence, however, to suggest that it led not to indifference but to a persistent anxiety for their children in the face of the hazards of illness and accident. Ralph Josselin was extremely concerned about his children's illnesses and recorded in his diary successful remedies for childhood ailments, presumably with a view to future use. When his children died, he recorded the fact in diary entries which reveal profound grief and a sense of loss which was as bitter in the case of 10-day-old Ralph as in that of 8-year-old Mary. Adam Martindale, blunt and materialistic though he often was, was so tortured with anxiety during his son John's last illness that he broke off urgent business in Chester and rushed home a day early only to find his family 'distracted' by the boy's death and in need of 'much consolation'. Similarly Henry Newcome and his wife searched diligently for a remedy when their son Henry was sick with the worms, and having discovered one, had occasion to recommend it later to many other anxious parents in Manchester. Like Josselin and Martindale, Newcome also recorded his children's preservations from accidents – as when Daniel narrowly escaped drowning on a fishing expedition in 1659, or on another occasion had an arrow shot through his hat during archery practice – and attributed their deliverance gratefully to a benign providence. After one of these adventures he wrote with evident feeling, 'I consider the sad things that befal parents about children. May not one beg of God, that if it be his will, he will save us from such afflictions, and if he sees it good, 1. That my children may be kept in health, or from sad and grievous distempers. 2. However not to die immaturely, if God see it good, especially not untimely deaths.'[40]

Frequent anxiety did not end with early childhood, nor was it confined to the problems of illness and accidents. It accompanied the schooling of children, the development of their characters, the 'putting out' of children as servants and apprentices and the selection of marriage partners. Nor indeed did it cease to afflict parents when their children had left home, for it could continue as long as parent and child lived. Henry Newcome's detailed account of his worries over his son Daniel may serve as an example. In December 1660 when the child was 8 years old Newcome was concerned by the fact that Daniel was 'untoward in his learning' and prayed for him. Four years later he was worried by Daniel's persistent misbehaviour. In 1668 he was at great pains to get the boy apprenticed to a good master in London, a matter which involved considerable heartache for all concerned. But this was not the end of the Newcomes' concern for Daniel. Within a year there was worry over his misbehaviour in London, followed by acute anxiety when he ran away from his master. Arrangements were made for the boy to go on a trading voyage to Tangier and Jamaica in 1670, itself a cause of sleepless nights and anxious inquiries when rumours reached the Newcomes that some English ships had been taken by Barbary corsairs. Daniel, in fact, was safe and returned in 1672 to live at home while Newcome anxiously did what he could to settle him in some new employment. Then in 1674 he married, without his parents' knowledge, an under-age girl and Newcome was confronted with the problems of helping him set up home for himself. Nor did concern end there, for anxiety on Daniel's behalf recurred intermittently – on the death of his wife, his remarriage, his mistreatment of his daughter, his general style of life and failure to settle himself – right through until his death at the age of 31 in 1684.[41]

Such prolonged parental anxiety for the physical, material and moral well-being of children was by no means unique. Ralph Josselin felt it for most of his children, though particularly for the prodigal of his family, John: 'my soule yearned over John', as he put it.[42] Such detail is usually beyond us. Yet the same spirit can be detected very frequently in the wills of the period. Sometimes these may include an explicit statement of a testator's general concern for a child, as when Ralph Dennis of Ancroft parish in Northumberland asked his son-in-law in a will of 1612 'to have a speciall care that my sonne Edmund being now an infant be not wronged so farr as he may be able to procure help for him', or when William Scurfield, yeoman, of Great Stainton in County Durham, asked two friends in 1626 to see his children 'brought up in the feare of god and other good employments according to their opportunytes that they may be better enabled to govern themselves and their estates when they shall come of age'.[43] More often, however, concern was implicit in the terms of the wills, though none the less real for that. Testators leaving behind them several young children not infrequently laid down instructions of quite extraordinary complexity for their executors, specifying the legacy which was to go to each child at a stated age and laying down alternatives which were to be followed in the event of the premature death of any of the children. Clearly they were determined to do their best to ensure their children's well-being in all eventualities, some even going so far as to make provision for unborn children still in the mother's womb. Moreover, in their apportionment of the legacies of their children, the guiding principle of testators would appear to have been a determination to provide as well as they could for all their children. Here was no rigid adherence to traditional inheritance customs, but rather the flexible adoption of whatever strategy seemed the best means of advantaging each child when it came to make its transition into the adult world. Where land was involved there was a clear bias towards primogeniture in inheritance throughout most of England, though this, it seems, was less the dictate of custom than the realistic recognition of the need to keep together the estate upon which the standing of gentry families depended, or, lower in the social scale, a viable family farm. Even where partible inheritance was customary, as in Kent and parts of the northern uplands, arrangements were commonly made whereby one child bought back the land left to others, thus preserving the estate while providing for younger children. More generally, younger children were provided for by the allocation of portions of household goods, farm stock or cash legacies (often to be paid out of the profits of the family holding) at such time as they married or came of age, while in the most prosperous families additional houses or outlying parcels of land, accumulated during the testator's lifetime, might be bequeathed to young children. William Stout's father, for example, left his 'antient estate' of sixteen acres to his eldest son Josias. He left his other four sons parcels of land specially bought for the purpose, together with cash sums, while £80 was reserved for the dowry of his daughter Ellin.[44]

Wills were produced for the most part by the more substantial members of village communities, by yeomen, husbandmen and prosperous craftsmen; those who had most to leave. It seems no accident, however, that when the less prosperous made wills it was very often the case that they were still at the child-rearing stage of the family cycle. It was probably this fact which persuaded them to take the unusual step of making a formal will. The case of Priscilla Sizer of Terling in Essex can provide an example. She was a poor widow with two small sons. In her will she specified that her few pathetic possessions were to be sold and the money given to the overseers of the poor. She knew that it was inevitable that her children would fall on the poor rate, but she hoped that what little she had might provide a stock sufficient to apprentice them when they came of age. Had she lived longer it is unlikely that she would have made a will, for she would have done what she could for her children already. The transfer of property from generation to generation was not a single event precipitated by parental death, but, for those parents who lived to see their children grown, a long drawn out process involving (for those who could afford it) the provision of education for a child, the payment of marriage portions and apprenticeship fees, or the gift of goods and money to help children establish themselves independently.[45] Parental provision and aid could extend throughout life, with ultimate inheritance often involving simply the distribution of the residue of parental property, with due allowance made in its apportionment for what each child had already received. The method and the timing varied, as did the degree of provision that parents could afford. The ideal remained the same: to bring children up and to bestow each of them as well as possible.

Parents, then, made a material and an emotional investment in their children which was both considerable and prolonged. We might well ask what they expected in return. The answer would seem to be, very little. Certainly parents did not seem to have regarded their children as a source of labour to any significant extent. Among those who could afford it, the education of their children appears to have filled in the years between small childhood and their eventual departure from the family home into apprenticeship or service. None of Ralph Josselin's children, for example, was economically productive before leaving home, which for all the girls was before the age of 14½ and for the boys at something over 15.[46] Where parents could not afford such education, of course, children were expected to play their part in the family economy. From her examination of the autobiographies of a number of humbly born nonconformists, Margaret Spufford has concluded that most children were probably regularly engaged in some kind of work by the age of 7, and that they could often earn 2d. or 3d. a day by their labours. Thomas Tryon, son of an Oxfordshire craftsman, for example, began carding and spinning wool at about that age and 'was so Industrious and grew so expert that at Eight Years of Age I could spin Four Pound a day which came to Two Shillings a Week', as he proudly recalled.[47]

Such earnings were doubtless of the greatest assistance to poor families, but they should not be seen crudely in terms of the exploitation of child labour. Children were asked to perform only 'such work and service as was suitable for [their] age and capacity', as Thomas Chubb, the son of a Wiltshire maltster, put it. Moreover, the work might often be a necessary part of the child's education for the future. Josiah Langdale of Nafferton in the East Riding, for example, was spared from work until the age of 9 when his father died. Thereafter, 'being a strong boy', he 'was put to lead Harrows and learn to Plow', while in summer time 'I kept Cattel . . . and moved them when there was Occasion with much Care'. By the age of 13 he could plough alone and was an experienced stockman. In general the most that could be expected of a child's labour was that he might gain 'his lyvinge and some thing besides', as Thomas Wilson said of the children of Norwich. They might, if their father had a farm, reduce the costs of labour, as was the case with William Stout and his brothers whose schooling was interrupted at peak times of the agricultural year, 'two of us at 13 or 14 years of age being equal to one man shearer'. But the limited degree of children's economic role is well demonstrated by the fact that in their early to mid teens, the very point at which their contribution might be expected to have become truly significant, they left home to enter service or apprenticeship and were replaced, if their parents could afford it, by servants working for hire.[48]

Once placed in service, some children may have remitted part of their wages to their parents, perhaps on their periodic visits home between employers, but of this we have no firm evidence. What is much clearer is that service, like apprenticeship, was part of the child's preparation for an independent existence in the adult world. Servants gained valuable working experience, enjoyed opportunities to save which might never come again, and as they reached their 20s had the chance to look out for opportunities for permanent settlement and marriage.[49] That achieved, they were rarely expected to contribute to the maintenance of their parents in their old age – even if parents had survived. Some fathers of advanced age handed over their farms or workshops to their sons, retiring to the parlour or a cottage. Some worked till death themselves, but required inheriting sons to care for their widowed mothers.[50] Such cases, however, were exceptional. The evidence of wills makes it clear enough that though parents invariably helped children into adult life, they rarely expected economic aid in their turn.

Children, then, were not regarded as either a potential labour force or a form of insurance against old age. This is not to say that their parents expected nothing of them. Parental expectations, however, were less economic than emotional. On the evidence of the diaries and autobiographies of the period it would appear that they wished their children to be what Henry Newcome called 'comforts'. What did he mean by that?

In the first place he meant that parents found in their children a source of emotional satisfaction. Ralph Josselin, it may be recalled, found his first daughter 'a pleasant comfort'. Adam Martindale found his baby son 'sweet company to his poore mother in mine absence and a refreshing to me at my returne'. Children were a source of delight; 'pretty things to play withall' as one observer put it. As they developed, parents took much satisfaction and quickly noticed and recorded their latest accomplishments. 'My boy is now lively, somewhat fuller of spirit, of a good memory, a good speller apt to learne', wrote Josselin of his son Thomas, then aged almost 6, in 1649. There is little to suggest that children were forced in their development. Their childishness was both recognized and indulged, but each new achievement or indication of character was greeted with pride. Witness Adam Martindale's evident delight at the sight of his 2-year-old child at play and his pride at the boy's daring:

> We had a wanton tearing calfe, that would runne at children to beare them over. This calfe he would encounter with a sticke in his hand . . . stand his ground stoutly, beat it back, and triumph over it, crying *caw, caw*, meaning he had beaten the calfe. I doe not think one child of 100 of his age durst doe so much.[51]

Development into adolescence and adulthood might bring further satisfaction to the parent, but it could also, as we have seen, bring new anxieties. Henry Newcome, whose problems with his son Daniel we have already examined, was acutely aware of this. Indeed, he became preoccupied with the problem and frequently recorded instances of conflict between parents and children (especially fathers and sons) as well as taking the opportunity to discuss the matter with other parents. 'Mr Samuel Leech of Warrington I was with at the fair', he wrote on 6 November 1680. 'His children are all comforts. Poor Richard Nichol's are all discomforts. If most of mine be comforts, how kindly I am dealt with!'[52]

To be a 'discomfort', or a 'cross', to use another common expression of aggrieved parents, meant above all the exhibition by a child of what Newcome called elsewhere 'rebellious untowardness' – disobedience and a lack of respect for the parents' values. Parents hoped for respect, gratitude and obedience from their children and they did their best to instil these qualities in them. Where they succeeded, respect and subordination could be very formally displayed. Children of the gentry stood bareheaded before their parents and knelt for their blessing, and at least some such formality seems also to have been displayed in families lower in the social scale, at least among the 'middling sort'. Obedience was regarded as the principal duty of a child, instilled by precept and catechism, and enforced by both emotional pressure and, on occasion, physical punishment.[53]

These aspects of the relationships of parents and children have been frequently stressed by historians of childhood, and with some justice. Yet for this very reason it is important to recognize that these parental requirements seem to have been exacted within undefined, but nonetheless real limitations. Obedience, for example, frequently meant in practice, not total adherence to parental dictates, but rather a due respect for the feelings and advice of a parent. We have already seen how insubstantial is the myth of parental despotism in the selection of marriage partners. Much the same can be said of parental control of their children's choice of occupation. William Perkins in his advice to parents urged that they take account of their children's individual aptitudes before bestowing them and this does indeed appear to have been the general practice. Thomas Tryon's father wished Thomas to follow his own trade as a tiler and plasterer, but when the boy found it tedious work allowed him to follow his desire to be a shepherd. William Stout's father bought a small farm for William, but finding the boy's disposition to be different, 'minded to get me constantly to schoole to get learning in order to be placed in some trade', while land was bought for a younger brother Leonard 'who very early appeared inclined and active about husbandry and cattel and follow[ing] the plough'. Adam Martindale's spirited and ambitious sister was able to win her parents' consent to let her go to London to seek a place as a lady's maid, despite their justified misgivings, while Adam's own case was not dissimilar. At 14, his father set Adam to learn his own trade, on the advice of relatives who 'were very importunate with him to take me off learning, and set me to somewhat that might be me a subsistence'. Adam dutifully, though regretfully, obeyed. Before long, however, his father 'guessed right which way my mind still went, and . . . he frankely put it to my choice, whether I would go on as I did at present, or returne to schoole againe'. 'I never stood considering the matter,' recalled Adam, 'but thankfully embracing his offer, repaired to mine old master.'[54] In this as in so much else, parents advised and proposed, rather than dictated, while obedience could mean biding one's time pending the winning of parental consent rather than unconditional submission.

Children, of course, were not always obedient or respectful and at such times they were punished. Yet the severity of child discipline is too often exaggerated. The moralists of the period insisted that admonition should come first and that the rod should be used only as a last resort, and even then in moderation, and accompanied by an explanation to the child of the reasons for its use. Henry Newcome, who was conscious of his need 'to look after my children, that they may be well bent when young', followed the first part of this advice too thoroughly. His frequent admonitions were noted by one of his colleagues, who criticized his tendency to 'hang all on their backs'. Nevertheless he disliked intensely the need to exercise what he called 'my duty of correction' and when he punished Daniel in 1664, he 'prayed with him after, entreating the Lord that it might be the last correction . . . that he should need'.[55] There can be no doubt that corporal punishment was commonplace in the grammar schools of the period. References to physical punishment in the home, however, are sparse and tend to suggest that it was employed occasionally, reluctantly and in moderation. Nor is there any need to believe that the disciplining of children was more severe in families of lower rank. Indeed if William Harrison is to be believed, the reverse was true among those whose resolve was not stiffened by consciousness of their parental duties. Harrison, who freely admitted that he sometimes beat his children, agreed with many other moralists that children were too often spoiled for want of correction and alleged that this was particularly so with mothers of 'the poorer sort'. 'Being of themselves without competent wit,' he explained,

> they are so carelesse of their children (wherein their husbands also are to be blamed) by meanes whereof verie manie of them neither fearing God, neither regarding either manners or obedience, doo oftentimes come to confusion, which (if anie correction or discipline had been used toward them in youth) might have proved good members of their commonwealth and countrie.[56]

Admonition, followed if necessary by moderate 'correction', was the contemporary ideal and seems on the whole to have been the norm. The seventeenth century, like the twentieth, had its child-batterers and its sadists, but the people of the day recognized the distinction between punishment and abuse. Newcome was deeply shocked when he learned that Daniel and his wife had so abused their child that a friend had taken her away from them: 'it is an affliction and shame to me', he commented, and took the child into his own care.[57]

If parents lived to see their children attain adulthood the success or failure of their efforts to bring them up became apparent, and where children failed to conform to parental hopes and values they could be a source of real grief. Yet even so, they seem rarely to have been rejected. Despite his disappointment in Daniel, Newcome repeatedly forgave him, worried about him and tried to help him, until eventually he sat by his son's deathbed, blaming himself that he had 'desired the world for him' but had failed to be 'so concerned for his eternal state as I should have been'. When Adam Martindale's son married against his father's advice he dared not face his father, but Adam welcomed him and his wife, housed, fed and clothed them, helped him to find work and set himself up and later provided him with household goods and money. Ralph Josselin put up with the bad behaviour and debauchery of his son John for years in hope of his reform until, in October 1674, before the assembled family, he offered him a fine inheritance if he reformed himself, but only a basic provision for his livelihood if he continued his disorders. John went his own way and on 24 January 1675 Josselin wrote, 'John declared for his disobedience no son.' Even then, however, he added that if John reformed 'I should yett own him for mine', and in fact, he remained preoccupied with John for the remainder of his life and never totally cast him off. His last mention of him was on 14 May 1682 when John, now married, finally departed the parental home. 'John went to his house,' wrote Josselin, 'god blesse him send peace.'[58]

However much remains obscure of the relations of parents and children in this period, it seems clear that in the main, parents did their utmost both to bring up and bestow their children, following their progress with both anxiety and satisfaction, and that they demanded little in return. Their abilities to provide for their children certainly varied greatly, yet the obligation to do what they could seems to have been accepted equally across the social scale. Their aspirations for their children and the standards of behaviour and achievement which they expected of them again doubtless varied, yet even among parents of rigorously puritan beliefs, these appear to have been contained within the bounds of an implicit acceptance of the ultimate autonomy and individuality of the child.

Indeed, it might be argued that the whole system of child-rearing was directed towards (and well adapted to) the 'putting forth' of children all too soon, into a highly individualistic and competitive social environment in which they would have to stand on their own feet. To that end, parents attempted to protect, prepare, advise, and advantage their children while they could, and if their anxious care could sometimes provoke resentment and conflict, there is evidence enough to show that it could also nurture lasting bonds of affection. Most of Henry Newcome's children, after all, were 'comforts' and most children who left descriptions of their parents seem to have remembered them with gratitude and respect. Their parents would have desired nothing more.

As for the question of change in the relationships of parents and children, it would appear that in this, as in other aspects of the history of the family in this period, interpretations alleging massive shifts in the emotional content of parent–child relations are based on flimsy foundations. In the light of the evidence considered here, there seems no reason to believe that parental attitudes towards or aspirations for their children underwent fundamental change in the course of the seventeenth century. It might, of course, be alleged that the attitudes of men like Newcome, Martindale or Josselin represented novel departures in domestic relations. Such an argument, however, would be an argument from silence, for we know too little of family relations in earlier times to judge. Undoubtedly such early diarists and autobiographers were inspired by a depth of introspective piety which might have affected their attitudes in some degree. Yet the only systematic evidence of attitudes surviving in any quantity from the earlier part of our period – wills – suggests that their feelings towards their children were not dissimilar from those of their fathers and grandfathers. The spiritual diarists and autobiographers had the education, the leisure and the incentive to set these matters down – as a record of divine providence towards them in their daily lives. In the matters of fact recorded and in the basic attitudes displayed, they seem far less unusual.

What undoubtedly did change in the course of our period was not so much the fundamental patterns of attitudes and values within the family, but the broader economic and social context within which parents attempted to raise and to provide for their children and young people set out to establish themselves in the adult world, to marry and to raise families of their own. For some the period provided new opportunities. For others it saw a tightening of the material and social constraints within which they were obliged to act. It is with the nature and effects of these changing circumstances that we must now concern ourselves.

Part Two

The course of social change

5 *Population and resources*

Social change in late sixteenth- and seventeenth-century England was slow. Nevertheless contemporaries knew that they lived in a changing world, however blurred might be their perception of the nature and causes of social change. William Harrison discussed the matter with the greybeards of his home parish of Radwinter in Essex and found that they regarded three things as 'marvellouslie altred' within their lifetimes: the 'multitude of chimnies lately erected'; 'the great (although not generall) amendment of lodging', by which they meant better bedding; the 'exchange of vessell' (that is, tableware) from wood to pewter and even silver. Such evidence of rising living standards seemed to Harrison symptomatic of a new prosperity among the farmers and artisans of rural England. He was aware, however, that it was a prosperity which was limited in its incidence both socially, being largely confined to the upper and middle ranks of society, and geographically, being largely confined to the south of England. Moreover it was counterbalanced by a number of detrimental changes. His informants also picked out three 'very grievous' developments: 'the inhansing of rents'; the 'dailie oppression of copiholders' forced by their landlords to pay increased entry fines or to forfeit their holdings; the spread of usury and charging of interest upon loans.[1]

Such were the matters discussed on the alebench and around the fires of one Essex village in the last quarter of the sixteenth century. As our period advanced other observers of more elevated social position added their comments on the course of change in England. Sir Thomas Wilson, around 1600, observed that gentlemen had 'grown to become good husbands' (that is, husbandmen) and learned 'as well how to improve their lands to the uttermost as the farmer or countryman', taking in their lands as leases expired and either farming them directly or letting them out to the highest bidder. Sir William Coventry, in 1670, remarked upon the great increase in the agricultural output of England and pointed to the causes: fen-drainage and disafforestation schemes, enclosure and improvements in farming technique. Similarly, John Aubrey, writing of Wiltshire and Herefordshire in 1684, described a half-century of agricultural change, listing improvements introduced by enterprising gentlemen and now slowly being generalized among farmers. So much for the positive side. On the negative side, preachers, administrators, Members of Parliament and the officers of towns and villages, throughout the nation, pointed to and grappled with a mounting problem of poverty and distress, their concern often triggered by the emergency of short-term crises, yet held, once awakened, by the enduring reality of this phenomenon.[2]

Agricultural improvement and agrarian distress, increased production and widespread deprivation, undoubted prosperity and equally striking impoverishment: in all these ways contemporaries identified the paradoxical symptoms of a changing socio-economic environment. Of change they were undoubtedly aware, though they found it difficult, in the midst of the process of change and lacking the statistical information to inform their analyses, to explore in any depth either the course or the causes of the developments which forced themselves upon their attention. That task, however, has been more than adequately performed by recent generations of economic and social historians. As a result we have an increasingly clear apprehension of the nature and dynamics of change in a century which saw significant modifications of the economic and social structures of England. Central to that process were the complex socio-economic effects of a slowly shifting balance between population and resources, between production and reproduction. It was a process which had its origins somewhat earlier than our main period of interest, and which was to exert its influence long afterwards, yet which reached its crisis and found its resolution within the century which most concerns us.

Population expansion

In the course of the sixteenth and seventeenth centuries the population of England doubled. National population estimates are difficult to obtain, based as they are upon incomplete taxation, military and ecclesiastical surveys. Nevertheless it seems likely that a population of approximately 2.5 million in the 1520s had risen to one of perhaps 5 million by 1680. This general demographic expansion, however, was uneven both chronologically and regionally. At the national level it would appear that the initial increase of the early sixteenth century was checked in the 1550s, renewed thereafter to reach perhaps 3.5 million in 1580, then continued until the 1620s and 1630s when it began to level off, stabilizing by the mid seventeenth century.[3] Locally, both the relative increase in population and the course of change over time varied. Staffordshire saw the doubling of population between 1563 and the 1660s, while the Forest of Arden in Warwickshire saw only a 50 per cent increase in the period 1570–1650. The population of the fenlands of Cambridgeshire doubled between 1563 and 1670, while in other areas of the same county population rise was much less dramatic – as little as 20 per cent over the same period in the upland parish of Orwell, for example. In Wigston Magna, Leicestershire, population expansion occurred largely in the later decades of the sixteenth century and was largely complete by the 1620s; in Cumbria, after a 43 per cent increase during 1563–1603, population actually fell by some 9 per cent in the period 1603–41, before renewed growth, which somewhat exceeded the 1603 level, by 1680. The Forest of Arden presented yet another variant, with a sharp rise of population in the last quarter of the sixteenth century, a pause in the opening decades of the seventeenth century and then new growth in the second quarter of the new century.[4]

Such local variation makes it clear that any attempt at a general explanation of the causes of the demographic expansion of this period must be sufficiently flexible to make allowances for a considerable variety of experience within the general trend. Of the principal factors in the equation of population growth we may agree: we must look to the vital rates of fertility and mortality, to the marital customs which influenced fertility, to the economic circumstances which affected all three of these variables (though to considerably different degrees) and to the question of migration.[5] Yet little agreement is to be found on the issue of the precise nature of the interaction of all these factors, or on their relative importance, while such interpretations of population growth as have been put forward tend to be limited in their applicability. Until recently, for example, there has been a general tendency to place particular stress upon the influence of changing patterns of mortality. Such explanations have the attraction of relative simplicity, for of all the components of demographic change mortality was that least subject to human influence in this period: the death rate from disease was to a large extent 'autonomous'. Thus, it can be argued, a decline in the incidence and virulence of the bubonic plague in the later fifteenth and early sixteenth centuries may have triggered off the population rise of the sixteenth century by ceasing to cull regularly a prolific population. In the mid sixteenth century, catastrophic though short-lived epidemics of viral diseases, perhaps forms of influenza, checked growth, but a return to relatively better mortality conditions thereafter allowed renewed expansion, halted only in the seventeenth century by a rising death rate caused probably by the introduction of new infectious diseases.[6]

Such an argument contains much that is of value. It cannot, however, provide a complete answer. In the first place, historical demographers have demonstrated that populations in this period were able to recover remarkably rapidly from the effects of mortality crises caused by epidemic diseases. When plague ravaged the parishes of Colyton in Devon in 1645/6 and Eyam in Derbyshire in 1665, for example, only a limited number of families were affected, and of these, few were completely wiped out. Children died most commonly and they could be replaced relatively swiftly by the surviving adult population. Where adults died, their places in society were often quickly filled by young people who might actually be afforded better opportunities to marry as a result of the deaths of their elders. If they married younger than was usual, a temporary boost was given to marital fertility which further helped the process of recovery.[7] All this would occur, however, only where there were general socio-economic conditions favourable to marriage and fertility. The question then arises: why were late medieval populations unable to recover from short-term crises and why were sixteenth- and early seventeenth-century populations so much more resilient? Were there new circumstances more favourable to fertility in the sixteenth century *as well as* a somewhat lower death rate? To come at this problem from another angle, historical demographers have discovered in the behaviour of early modern populations a clear tendency towards 'homeostasis', a tendency, that is, to behave in a manner which aimed at producing a rough equilibrium between fertility and mortality. Where death rates were high, fertility was often high. When death rates were lower, fertility was often restrained somewhat – generally through the mechanism of later marriage for those young people waiting to take their place in adult society.[8] Given such a broad situation, it seems worthy of note that the undeniably better mortality conditions of the sixteenth century did *not* produce a compensating reining in of fertility. Again we have the question: did conditions exist which encouraged continued fertility?

Some contemporaries certainly thought so. The moralist Phillip Stubbes inveighed in 1583 against what he saw as a trend towards younger marriages undertaken 'without any respecte how they may lyve together with sufficient maintenance for their callings and estat'. Sir Anthony Thorold, a Lincolnshire gentleman, complained in a letter to Lord Burghley of a new tendency towards young marriages entered into with 'no regard how to live nor where to dwell'.[9] What we know of marriage in this period suggests that such comments were exaggerated. Yet they may also represent a confused perception of a trend towards younger marriage (and enhanced fertility) in response to economic conditions which rendered marriage somewhat easier and undermined to some degree the rationale of delaying marriage. Stubbes and Thorold were traditionalists thinking in terms of an agricultural holding as a prerequisite for marriage. As we shall see, this period offered in some areas growing opportunities of a different type for work in domestic industry or as agricultural labour on more intensively cultivated farms, and these developments may have had their impact.

The causes of the population rise which began early in the sixteenth century remain a subject for speculation, especially as compared with our sounder knowledge of the reasons for the stabilization of population in the mid to late seventeenth century. The fact remains that the first half of our period was a time of demographic growth. It should not be exaggerated for it was a slow expansion as compared with the experience of the developing nations of the later twentieth century – the increase rarely amounted to more than 1 per cent per annum.[10] Yet it was significant enough in a society which had a limited capacity either to absorb increased numbers or to respond to the problems which population rise ultimately engendered.

Redistribution of population and internal trade

Demographic expansion brought many problems in its wake. Of these perhaps the most pervasive in its influence was inflation. The average prices of foodstuffs in southern England, which had remained fairly stable throughout the later fifteenth century, had trebled by the 1570s, and by the early decades of the seventeenth century they had risen sixfold, stabilizing only after 1630 and falling somewhat thereafter. This general inflationary trend undoubtedly had many contributing causes, but of these the most fundamental is generally agreed to have been the pressure of the demand exerted by a rising population upon relatively inelastic food resources. Significantly, the prices of cheaper foodstuffs rose more swiftly than did those of more expensive foods, while those of manufactured products rose slower still. Again, wages rose less swiftly than prices in an overstocked labour market and real wages steadily declined, reaching their lowest point in the early decades of the seventeenth century (by which time they were half those of a century earlier) and recovering only slowly as the seventeenth century advanced.[11] Like the general expansion of population, the influence of inflation varied both regionally and over time, while the general upward movement of prices was very slow save in periods of acute crisis – notably the short-term crises produced by periodic harvest failures. Nevertheless its long-term effects produced, in the first half of our period, both unprecedented opportunities for profit to those who supplied the market and at the same time the gradual impoverishment of those who depended for their living upon wages or fixed incomes.

Inflation, however, was only one consequence of demographic expansion. Another was a gradual redistribution of the English population. As we have seen, there was much local variation in both the extent and the timing of population expansion. Such differences can be explained in part as the outcome of different rates of natural increase – for rates of mortality and fertility varied a good deal. A further contributing factor to local variations in absolute population increase, however, was a redistribution of population produced above all by the different capacities of different regions to absorb, employ, and maintain an increased population. Given the fact that young people left home early to make their own way in the world, passing from master to master until they found a permanent settlement, and the known realities of population mobility among adults, it is scarcely surprising that people tended to gravitate towards those areas which offered them the best opportunity of finding a home and a living. Orwell in Cambridgeshire, for example, has already been cited as a parish which saw a comparatively small increase in population. Orwell was a grain producing upland parish in which there were limited economic opportunities and in which farms could not easily be divided in order to accommodate increased numbers without rendering them economically unviable. Although the population of the parish regularly produced a surplus of baptisms over burials, it failed to grow significantly for the simple reason that surplus young people were obliged to look elsewhere for a living.[12] Where did such young people go?

Many of them gravitated towards England's regions of pastoral agriculture, the areas with extensive commons, and most notably the fens and the forest areas. In Cambridgeshire, the fenlands in the north of the county became the most densely settled area, whereas earlier they had been comparatively sparsely populated. In the fens large commons could be found, on which animals could be raised, making possible a tolerable subsistence even for those with little or no land, while further opportunities existed in the shape of fishing and wild-fowling. Willingham was only one such parish which could both support its natural increase, by subdividing holdings if necessary, and also absorb newcomers. In the Isle of Axholme in the Lincolnshire fens, poor cottagers enjoyed rights to pasture, fishing, fowling and turf-gathering as well as the possibility of employment in the local sackcloth industry. As a result, the period between 1590 and 1630 saw the building of many new cottages and substantial population increase – Epworth Manor, for example, saw 100 new cottages erected in those four decades. Waves of immigrants also moved into England's extensive surviving woodlands. Rockingham Forest in Northamptonshire witnessed a great expansion of the cottaging population, most of whom lived by pasturing animals and despoiling the woods, while in Gillingham Forest on the borders of Dorset and Wiltshire the late sixteenth and early seventeenth centuries saw much subdivision and subletting of landholdings and the absorption of numerous immigrant cottagers.[13]

As the case of the Isle of Axholme suggests, pastoral areas might offer more than just extensive commons and the freedom of the woods and fens; they were also very often the centres of manufacturing industries, organized on the 'putting-out' system by merchant entrepreneurs who found among the under-employed cottagers of pastoral areas a pool of cheap labour. Such areas saw particularly dramatic population growth. In Norfolk, Suffolk and Essex the weaving districts became the most heavily peopled areas of the county. At Frome in Somerset the cloth industry attracted many people who lived in cottages in the neighbouring forest. In the broadcloth-producing area of Wiltshire an inquiry of 1610 discovered hundreds of cottages erected within the preceding thirty-five years, some of them on subdivided holdings let by landlords, anxious to increase their rent-rolls, yet more put up on unsurveyed royal demesne land in the forest. Nor was cloth the only industry to attract workers. The mining, woodcrafts and iron industry of the Forest of Dean in Gloucestershire had the same magnetic power, as did the growing coal industry of the Tyne valley.[14]

Rural England thus experienced significant shifts in the distribution of population and the emergence of congested areas where poor cottagers eked out a living in good times, yet faced chronic distress in years of industrial depression or harvest failure. Equally significant was a shifting balance between the urban and rural populations of England, for if many people drifted towards those rural areas which retained some capacity to absorb them, as many, if not more, moved into the towns. As a result the populations of many urban centres rose dramatically. The experience of the towns was, of course, no more uniform than was that of rural areas. Some towns, facing peculiar economic difficulties, actually stagnated. Most, however, grew, some of them with alarming speed. The populations of York and Exeter grew by some 50 per cent between the early sixteenth and the later seventeenth centuries, that of Leicester by some two-thirds. Worcester doubled in population between 1563 and 1646.

Above all, London grew with startling speed from a city of perhaps 50,000–60,000 souls in the 1520s, to one of 200,000 in 1600, 400,000 in 1650 and 575,000 by 1700, much of the increased population being crowded into new suburbs such as the east London parishes of Stepney and Whitechapel, which contained 7000 people in the 1570s, 21,800 in the first decade of the seventeenth century and 59,000 in the 1670s.[15]

Much of this urban population growth was the result of immigration. Relatively few towns were able to grow by natural increase, since most urban populations endured exceptionally high mortality rates which ensured a regular surplus of burials over baptisms. Worcester was able to contribute something to its own growth, yet London, according to the calculations of Dr Beier and Dr Wrigley, needed something like 5600 immigrants a year between 1560 and 1625 and 8000 a year between 1650 and 1700 in order to replace its population deficit and continue to grow. Urban mortality was bad at the best of times, but it was made the worse by the fact that the towns were subject to recurrent mortality crises of dreadful proportions, occasioned usually by outbreaks of bubonic plague. Bristol suffered such epidemics in 1575, 1603 and 1643–5, Norwich in 1579, 1585, 1592, 1603 and 1626, Plymouth in 1589, 1626 and 1643–4, while London experienced plagues in 1593, 1603, 1625 and 1665, to count only the major outbreaks. Despite all this, the towns grew as receptacles not only of 'betterment' migrants – apprentices and the like from fairly prosperous backgrounds – but also of a swollen stream of 'subsistence' migrants, driven to the towns by economic necessity, which flowed most strongly in the four decades after 1590. Their different rates of growth at different times reflect the varying extents to which they provided attractive opportunities for migrants in the course of our period, but overall the result was a significant urbanization of the national population, for the urban population grew disproportionately swiftly. Whereas in 1600 some 8 per cent of the English population lived in London and seventeen towns with populations of over 5000 (only three having more than 10,000 people), in 1700, 11 per cent of the enlarged national population lived in London and thirty towns of over 5000 people (seven of them now having populations in excess of 10,000). In addition, something like a further 7 per cent of England's people lived in smaller towns.[16]

The general growth of population and its concentration in the towns and in 'dependent' rural areas unable to supply their own foodstuffs had further economic repercussions – notably by exerting increased demand for both agricultural products and the simple manufactures essential to daily life. The most significant demand, of course, was for foodstuffs and the most important source of this demand was provided by the towns. London in particular needed prodigious quantities of food, and the effects of London's needs were felt throughout southern England. Shipments of grain to London from Kentish ports totalled 12,080 quarters in 1587–8, 41,823 quarters in 1615 and 71,090 quarters in 1680–1, while throughout the Thames valley farmers adjusted themselves to the task of supplying the London markets. Oxfordshire, for example, sent wheat, malt, cheese, sheep and cattle to feed the capital.[17] What was true of London was equally the case, though on a smaller scale, for other towns and cities: Bristol, Newcastle, Preston and Norwich, for example. Urban food markets extended their lines of supply deep into the surrounding countryside, while dependent rural areas exerted further demand on a more localized scale. The weaving districts of Norfolk were supplied with food by the cornmasters of the fielden areas of the county. The growing population of the Durham coalfields along the Tyne and Wear formed an expanding market for the farmers of lowland County Durham.[18] Nor was food all that was needed. Much of the output of the northern collieries was shipped by coastal traffic to maintain the fires of London and other east coast towns, while the general demographic expansion created a larger home market for cloth and the miscellaneous manufactures of the industrial districts and the towns. All this bred both a greater degree of specialized production aimed at particular markets and a greater integration of the English economy as myriad rural communities were drawn more deeply into integrated regional economies centred on the cities. Worcester, with its thrice-weekly markets and four annual fairs served both as the centre of an extensive hinterland of its own and as a link in trade between the north and the south-west, between Bristol and the upper Severn valley, London and the west Midlands, England and Wales. King's Lynn on the Norfolk coast linked both coastal and international trade routes to an extensive system of navigable rivers penetrating deep into the heart of England.[19] What each regional centre did for its own hinterland, London did for the nation as a whole, gradually forging a national market out of the diversified regional economies of provincial England.

In this expansion of internal trade, an important role was played by a swelling army of middlemen who specialized in the supply of particular markets. They were enterprising and sometimes unscrupulous men who sought out opportunities, bought in bulk, and bypassed traditional marketing mechanisms when they could, by direct deals with farmers. They were marginal figures, suspected by the government and the poor alike of profiteering and subject to both official regulation and occasional popular attacks, especially in bad harvest years. Yet they were both products and agents of the increasing interdependence of England's regional economies. Some might have their licences withdrawn in years of dearth when local authorities struggled to regulate local economies in the interests of ensuring that local markets were supplied, but increasingly they could not be done without, as the government well knew.[20] For them this was an age of new opportunities, and the conditions which provided those opportunities also underlay other important changes in English society; changes which were produced above all by the differing extent to which particular social groups in specific local contexts were able either to take advantage of the opportunities or to withstand the pressures of the age.

Economic change

Opportunities and constraints

For England's landlords, the gentry and aristocracy, the demographic and economic trends of the first half of our period presented both a threat and an opportunity. On the one hand, inflation threatened to erode their incomes and undermine their living standards. On the other hand, their control of land presented splendid opportunities for those of them possessed of sufficient initiative to profit from both the land hunger and the rising prices of the time. They responded in several ways.

The most general response was to attempt to raise the rental income derived from their lands. By the later sixteenth century, population expansion had already tilted the balance of power between landlords and tenants in favour of the former. Gentlemen who had earlier been forced to choose between granting long leases and favourable rents or seeing parts of their estates pass out of cultivation, now found themselves able to charge higher entry fines and rents and to insist on shorter leases. This trend continued and was accentuated in the late sixteenth and early seventeenth centuries. The willingness and abilities of landlords to exploit the situation, of course, varied. Some were sufficiently conscious of their traditional social obligations to their tenants to hesitate before tightening up their estate-management policies. Again, some were inhibited by the continued validity of long leases granted by their fathers and grandfathers in the very different economic climate of the later fifteenth and early sixteenth centuries – leases which often remained in being until the turn of the sixteenth and seventeenth centuries. Finally, it must be remembered that the great variety of forms of land tenure prevailing in this period meant that a perfect market in land did not exist. Some tenants enjoyed fixed entry fines or rents for their copyholds, while even where landlords' hands were not completely tied, they were generally regarded as being obliged to charge only 'reasonable' fines and rents for their lands.[21]

Faced with these difficulties, landlords had to be flexible in their approach to the problem of maintaining and expanding their incomes. Many sought to establish the nature of their positions by ordering surveys of their estates, and the period after 1590 in particular saw the making of numerous manorial surveys at which tenants presented themselves to show evidence of their tenures. The suspicion with which tenants regarded such surveys is well demonstrated by the experience of Arnold Child who in 1628–9 undertook the survey of several manors in the north of England recently conveyed by the crown to the Corporation of London. At Leeds, a manor containing numerous small copyholds held by clothworkers, he 'could learn little of the tenants, who generallie as it were in a subtle combination, mixt with feare, would have concealed and obscured even palpable things'. What they did tell him, that their entry fines were fixed, he refused either to believe or formally record, for fear of establishing a precedent. Similarly, in the Barony of Bolbec in Northumberland, the tenants refused to participate in the survey. Their fears were justified enough, for Child's reports show how anxious he was to discover any means of increasing the income of his employers.[22] In this he was entirely in accord with the usual estate-management policy of the day. Fortified with their surveys, most landlords and estate managers took every opportunity to raise income. Where possible, troublesome copyhold tenures were converted into leaseholds, either by agreement with the tenants or by the expedient of buying up the copyhold lands. Once leasehold was established, leases for long periods or for such indefinite terms as 'three lives' were replaced with shorter, more frequently renegotiable leases, with the result that by the mid seventeenth century, despite the continued survival of copyhold tenures on many manors, leases for twenty-one years had become the predominant form of landholding in most parts of England.[23]

With or without such tenurial changes, the general trend of rents was upward. We have already seen how vigilant James Bankes was in his watch for opportunities to enhance his income from the manor of Winstanley, despite his desire to be a good landlord and his willingness to favour particular deserving individuals. In this coupling of traditional paternalism with an eye for profit, he was almost certainly typical of many landlords, though it is the search for increased income which has left most evidence to the historian. On the Petre estate in Essex, properties which had produced rents of £1400 in 1572, brought in £2450 in 1595 and as much as £4200 in 1640. Twelve Yorkshire manors belonging to the Savilles of Thornhill had their rents increased by 400 per cent between

1619 and 1651. The rents of the manor of Stoneleigh in Warwickshire amounted to £418 in 1599 and £1440 in 1640. In Northumberland, rents and fines were increased on the Percy estates in the late sixteenth century, and then in the early seventeenth century tenures were converted to yet more profitable leaseholds. Throughout England rent differentials between good and poor land were narrowed as land hunger pressured prospective tenants into bidding high for lands which once they would have scorned. It was a good time for those who controlled access to the land upon which the livelihoods of the majority of their countrymen depended.[24]

Landlords, however, were not solely dependent upon their incomes from rent and their actions did not simply constitute a 'seigneurial reaction' in the direction of rent exploitation. Many also farmed at least part of their estates and in this sphere of their activities also they were well placed to prosper from the falling real costs of labour and the buoyant prices obtainable for their produce. Some landlords went still further and directly involved themselves as middlemen in the corn trade – those of Norfolk being particularly active in this respect. Where they were involved in direct production for the market, the gentry had both the incentive and the resources to introduce new methods aimed at improving their output. Sir Thomas Pelham of Halland in Sussex, for example, was not only a large-scale rentier, but also a vigorous demesne farmer. He introduced 'denshiring' as a means of increasing the fertility of his land and turned over his demesne lands to 'convertible husbandry', an improved method of alternating grazing and tillage which both increased soil fertility and permitted larger numbers of stock to be supported. He bought up Cheshire cattle for fattening on his lands and then sold them directly to London butchers, while like other gentlemen in areas of industrial activity he also had a stake in the industries of the Sussex Weald. Pelham was doing his best to make the most of the market trends of his day and in this he was by no means unusual. As those trends changed later in the seventeenth century, gentleman farmers had yet further incentives to introduce improved methods – this time in the interests of reducing costs and maintaining competitiveness – and so the tide of technical change continued to advance. John Aubrey, describing the changes in Wiltshire and Herefordshire agriculture in his day, listed numerous improvements brought in, often from abroad or in imitation of other English counties, by enterprising gentry. The key to their effort was profit. Clover grass, for example, was described as having first been introduced to Wiltshire in 1650 by Nicholas Hall of North Wraxhall. 'It turned to great profit to him,' observed Aubrey, 'which hath made his neighbours to imitate him.'[25]

Such innovations could best be carried out, as writers on agricultural improvement generally agreed, on lands farmed in 'severalty' (that is, enclosed fields). Some areas of England, of course, had long been enclosed and indeed may never have known the common field system of agriculture – Kent, and much of Essex, Somerset and Devon, for example. Elsewhere, former common fields had sometimes been enclosed and turned into sheep-runs in the later fifteenth and early sixteenth centuries – principally in the midland counties. Enclosure in the late sixteenth and seventeenth centuries, however, was a rather more complex phenomenon. Sometimes it involved the reorganization of the scattered strips held by tenants in the open fields into compact enclosed farms. This process might proceed piecemeal with the landlord's blessing, as was usual in the west and north-west, or might result from a single dramatic act on the part of the landlord, sometimes accompanied by the eviction of unco-operative tenants, as was sometimes the case in the Midlands and on the coastal plain of Durham and Northumberland. Elsewhere, enclosure might mean the fencing off of former common pasture or waste in areas where such commons were still extensive, or again it might be introduced as part and parcel of drainage and disafforestation schemes in the fens and forests. Whatever its form, enclosure tended increasingly to be the prelude not to depopulation and the giving over of former farmland to sheep, but to the introduction of convertible husbandry. It was frequently undertaken after agreement between a landlord and his leading tenants, while in general those tenants whose rights were affected were compensated. Nevertheless, all enclosure had the effect of extinguishing common rights, the importance of which to small tenants and cottagers might be incalculable. Where extensive commons were lost, or where the number of agricultural holdings in a reorganized manor was reduced, the 'improvement' could constitute a disaster to many. The difficulty, as one report on enclosure put it in 1607, was that of reconciling conflicting interests in such a way that 'the poor man shall be satisfied in his end: habitation; and the gentleman not hindered in his desire: improvement'.[26] Much the same might have been said of tenurial reorganization, rent rises and the rest. The landed gentry were determined to stave off the pressures and to exploit the opportunities of the day. Overall, although some gentle families did badly as a result of bad luck or incompetence, most did well, and as a class they prospered exceedingly, both from their rents and the fruits of their own enterprise. They were well placed to do so, and where their interests came into conflict with those of their inferiors, they had the power and the purses to gain their way. That, in the final analysis, was what mattered.

Landowning gentlemen, however, were not the only social group to prosper in this period, nor were they without allies among their social inferiors in their schemes for agrarian reorganization and improvement. England's small farmers were not, after all, a homogeneous social group and their fortunes were to vary considerably. In their experience, the crucial determining factors were to be their relative responsiveness or vulnerability to the market trends of the period. For they were far from being peasant subsistence farmers concerned only to provide their families' needs from their own holdings. England retained pockets of simple subsistence farming, to be sure, but very few small farmers were isolated from the market, and for most, market opportunities were the first factor to consider in their husbandry. Had matters been otherwise their experience in the course of the late sixteenth and seventeenth centuries would have been quite different. As it was, the period was to reflect in their varying fortunes the extent to which they had already become commercial farmers, and to demonstrate both the benefits and the risks which flowed from that situation.

Those best placed to prosper were the yeomanry, those who farmed considerable acreages, whether they were freeholders owning their own land or substantial tenants. If freeholders, they were immune from the rent increases of the period. If large tenants then the profitability of their farming was commonly such as to enable them to afford rent increases with comparative ease. Like the gentry, they benefited from low labour costs as employers, while as large-scale producers they stood to gain from rising prices. Such was their output that they were well insulated from the effects of poor harvests. At the worst of times they produced enough to feed their families and to have a surplus which could be sold at inflated prices in time of scarcity. Indeed, too abundant a harvest and falling prices presented them with more of a threat than did dearth.[27] Again like the gentry, they took a thoroughly rational and calculating attitude towards profit. The account book of the Berkshire yeoman Robert Loder abundantly demonstrates his economic attitudes. In 1613–14, for example, he worked out the profits yielded by his wheat and his barley crops and decided to grow more wheat in future. He was very conscious of changes in price levels. He estimated the value not only of his grain, but also his straw and chaff, calculated the costs of wintering his cattle and the profits of his orchard and pigeon loft, set the profits made for him by his men and his horses against their costs in fodder, food and wages and made an allowance for losses through petty pilfering by his workers. Here was economic rationality indeed. Nor was Loder alone in this. He was perhaps more articulate than many of his contemporaries and more conscientious in his record keeping, but his attitudes were matched elsewhere. William

Harrison revealed, in a passage which admirably illustrates the mixture of tradition and modernity in the rural economy of England, how commercial attitudes could be expressed in a broad rustic vernacular when he described the 'superstitious' efforts of farmers at divination: laying twelve ears of corn on the hearthstone, observing the moon and the flight of cranes. The object of these practices was that of forecasting market trends in grain prices. Such yeoman farmers, as their leading historian has observed, were not 'a contented peasantry that reaped and sowed as the seasons fell', but often 'ambitious, aggressive, small capitalists . . . determined to take advantage of every opportunity, whatever its origin, for increasing their profits'.[28]

Such opportunities might include the adoption of production-boosting or cost-cutting innovations of the type pioneered by their gentry neighbours and landlords, for these men had the incentive and the means to adopt new methods. As Harrison observed, the farmers of his day were 'growne to be more painfull, skillfull and careful *through recompense of gaine* than heretofore they have beene'. Market-oriented specialization and innovation could be introduced well enough even within the apparently traditional framework of the open field system: Robert Loder held his land in the open fields, while open field farmers in nearby Oxfordshire were perfectly capable of specializing in the production of crops in demand on the London food market. However, yeomen also appreciated the advantages of farming in severalty. In fielden areas they often pushed ahead piecemeal, consolidating groups of strips and enclosing them, creating islands of enclosure within the common fields, while they were often willing to agree to the larger-scale proposals of manorial lords. The loss of traditional common rights meant less to them than to smaller folk and they were generally well compensated for their co-operation.[29]

In all these ways the interests of England's substantial yeomanry commonly went along with those of the gentry and the yeomen, like their social superiors, tended to prosper. Their prosperity, of course, varied according to their particular opportunities and individual skill and initiative. In general, however, they did well, at least until the later seventeenth century, when stable or falling grain prices drove some to the wall in fielden areas, forcing them ultimately to sell their land.[30] Even so, there was a place for them as substantial tenant farmers, and whatever the fortunes of individuals, yeomen prospered as a group. This is best demonstrated in studies of their inventories which show, much as William Harrison's village fathers observed, gradually rising living standards, the rebuilding of farmhouses and their stocking with goods of increasing sophistication and comfort. Such benefits came first to the south-east, but they were generalized to other areas in the course of the seventeenth century – the more so when, in the latter part of our period, stable livestock prices and falling grain prices enhanced the prosperity of the pastoral north and west. The general prosperity of the yeomanry was very visibly displayed in remodelled houses, better clothes, joined tables and chairs and fine shows of pewter and silver, not to mention cash in hand. They also bought up land when they could, spent more on the education of their children and set them forth in the world with larger legacies and portions. Some of them even became gentlemen.[31] All in all, it was a period which had its risks, but these were more than balanced for the yeomanry as a group by the opportunities which it afforded.

Less well-placed to prosper were England's small husbandmen. Though not isolated from the market, these smallholders were less able than their yeoman neighbours to exploit its opportunities to the full. They simply produced too little, and as a result the problem of maintaining their families loomed proportionately larger in their economic calculus. Given these circumstances they were necessarily more cautious, less willing to try new methods or to engage in improvements, for they could afford neither the attendant costs nor the risks involved. Walter Blith, author of *The English Improver Improved*, described them in 1652 as 'mouldy old leavened husbandmen, who themselves and their forefathers have been accustomed to such a course of husbandry as they will practise, and no other, their resolution is so fixed, no issues or events shall change them'. This was unjust, for they were prepared to take up new methods, but only once they were tried and sure. In contrast to the enterprising gentry of Wiltshire, Aubrey found the husbandmen 'very late and unwilling to learn or be brought to new improvements'. 'They go after the fashion,' he observed, 'that is, when the fashion is almost out, they take it up.'[32] From his point of view this was lamentable conservatism. From theirs it was prudent good sense. Nevertheless, few smallholders were insulated from the economic trends of the day; they could not retreat into mere subsistence farming. Even if they were dependent on the market for only part of their necessities, inflation was brought home to them through the medium of their rents and the need to meet high rents might draw them further into the market place than they might ideally have wished. 'If their sow pig or their hens breed chickens,' wrote Richard Baxter of the surviving small tenants of the later seventeenth century, 'they cannot afford to eat them, but must sell them to make their rent. They cannot afford to eat the eggs that their hens lay, nor the apples or pears that grow on their trees (save some that are not vendible) but must make money of all.' At worst it could be so, even in a good year, for an abundant harvest meant low prices. In a bad year they produced too little to be able to benefit from dearth prices. Instead many were forced to sell what they had quickly in order to pay their rents and later to buy at inflated prices in order to feed their families – a situation graphically described by William Harrison.[33]

In these circumstances, the fortunes of the small husbandmen depended to a very large extent upon a variety of factors which might help to spread their risks and lessen their insecurity. Some had the good fortune to enjoy favourable tenures and fixed rents inherited from the past and not yet subject to rationalization by their landlords. Copyhold rents on the manor of Ridley Hall in Essex in 1678, for example, were negligible, while some of the tenants were further liable to provide their lord with nine days work in the course of the year, a hen at Shrovetide and fifteen eggs at Easter. This remarkable survival was only possible because the bulk of the land on the manor was let out in large units at market rates. The landlord could afford to bear with his copyholders; there were only four of them and their holdings were tiny.[34] Proximity to good markets was another factor which could help the small man. Smallholders living near large towns could make better profits than those more distant from the market place and might even specialize in market gardening. 'London is a market which will take up all that they bring,' wrote Baxter of Middlesex husbandmen, '. . . and, by garden stuffs and by peas and beans and turnips, they can make more gain of their grounds, than poor country tenants can do of ten times the same quantity.' Finally, the husbandmen of pastoral areas might have large commons, woodlands and fens to help them augment their living despite their poverty in land, while the presence of industry might offer a further means of adding to family income.[35]

Many smallholders did well enough, and shared in a more modest degree in the prosperity of the yeomanry. For others, however, this was a period of insecurity and decline. In arable areas, enclosure and the extinction of common rights could tip the balance against the small tenant, rendering his smallholding unviable and forcing him ultimately to sell out to more prosperous neighbours, or to fail to renew his tenancy. Inability to meet higher rents could have the same effect for others, while still others might slip slowly into chronic debt – especially in years when the harvest either failed or was too good – and ultimately be squeezed from the land. In fielden England the period saw a general decline in the numbers of small farmers. At Chippenham and Orwell in Cambridgeshire, the early seventeenth century witnessed the disappearance of the middle range of traditional holdings – those of between fifteen and forty-five acres – and the 'engrossing' of these lands by prosperous yeomen. The same picture of gradual consolidation of the land in fewer hands was true of Wigston Magna in Leicestershire and of Crawley in Hampshire and many another lowland village. 'Engrossing' was a general phenomenon in such areas and a more significant element in the eventual demise of the small family farm than the more dramatic evictions by grasping landlords which were once emphasized by historians. Pastoral areas, however (at least those unaffected by drainage, disafforestation and enclosure), saw a different process of change. Here the withholding power of small tenants was greater, and indeed, with population pressure the actual number of smallholdings, subdivided and sublet, increased. Such was the case in Willingham in the Cambridgeshire fens, in Rossendale in Lancashire, where the 200 copyholds of 1608 had become 314 in 1662, or in the Forest of Pendle, which had 55 copyholders in 1608 and 129 in 1662. In such areas the small landholder survived, though sometimes at a lower, more marginal, standard of living.[36]

If the fate of smallholders could thus vary, that of landless or near landless labourers and cottagers was unequivocally bad for most of this period. Population pressure and agrarian change produced both an absolute and a relative increase in the wage-dependent labouring population, while inflation depressed real wages until the modest recovery of the later seventeenth century. Where they enjoyed common rights their situation might be alleviated in some degree, and for this reason enclosure and the extinction of such rights could constitute a real social crisis in areas with a substantial cottaging population. In fielden areas they might find themselves thereafter wholly dependent upon wage labour, while in some pastoral areas the result could be very widespread distress, as 'improvement' undermined the whole basis of the cottaging economy. Little wonder then that they resisted it when they could, though rarely with anything more than temporary success.[37]

Many of these cottagers in pastoral areas were, of course, partly or wholly employed in domestic industries as spinners, carders, weavers, nailmakers, cutlers and the like. Both their wages and the amount of work available for them varied through the period, but the former were generally low, while employment was subject to frequent dislocations, the more so in areas dependent on unstable foreign markets. In Essex, for example, it was reported in 1629 that 40,000–50,000 people were wholly dependent on the manufacture of 'bays and says', the 'New Draperies' which helped English merchants capture southern European markets at the turn of the sixteenth and seventeenth centuries. These workers were described as 'not being able to subsist unless they be continually set on work, and weekly paid. And many of them cannot support themselves and their miserable families unless they receive their wages every night'. When the Spanish market was dislocated in 1629 the 'workmasters' ceased to put out work to their employees and the result was the instant impoverishment of 'multitudes of those poor people'. Despite such crises, the numbers involved in rural industries grew throughout our period in response to both domestic and overseas demand. Dependent on the market for their food and upon uncertain employment for the means to buy it, their situation was rarely better than tolerable. As one anonymous observer said of industry in 1677, 'though it sets the poor on work where it finds them, yet it draws them still more to the place; and their masters allow wages so mean that they are only preserved from starving while they work; when age, sickness and death comes, themselves, their wives or their children are most commonly left on the parish'.[38]

Finally, our concentration on the rural majority must not preclude consideration of the towns. The fortunes of individual towns, as we have seen, varied a great deal and generalization is difficult. Nonetheless a few key points stand out. For the great merchants of the urban élite this was in general a period of prosperity, the more so if they were involved in the risky but highly profitable ventures of England's expanding overseas trade. Lower in the urban hierarchy the mounting prosperity of the gentry and yeomanry of the countryside rubbed off on the urban masters and professional men who supplied their needs for miscellaneous manufactures and services. In general this demand occasioned a growth in the range of occupations in the towns and a filtering down into quite small country towns of specialized services not formerly available at such a local level – those of doctors, lawyers and booksellers, for example. For the citizens of middling and upper rank, the period offered expanded opportunities and they in turn were able to offer employment to some of those who migrated to the towns. The most striking development in the economy and society of the towns, however, was the growth of that mass of unskilled urban poor who eked out an existence by irregular work as labourers, porters, servants, sweepers, boatmen and so forth. For them the period was one of deepening poverty. The labouring poor of London were described by a preacher to the Virginia Company in 1622 as people who rose early, worked all day and went late to bed, yet were 'scarce able to put bread in their mouths at the week's end and clothes on their backs at the year's end'. He recommended them as potential colonists. Their home country offered them little enough.[39]

The polarization of society

The socio-economic trends of the later sixteenth and seventeenth centuries clearly brought different consequences to different sections of the English population. As would be expected in such a highly stratified society the experience of the period was far from uniform. Some profited; some merely endured. Yet these variations of experience form a pattern which has been aptly summed up as a process of 'social polarization'. It is a term which subsumes a variety of specific points, but of these two stand out most clearly. First, there was a growing divergence in the living standards of rich and poor, and a redistribution of income towards the upper ranks of society. While the real incomes of the gentry, the yeomanry and the urban 'middling sort' expanded, those of the wage-earners who made up half the national population by the later seventeenth century generally declined. While the dietary standards of the prospering upper half of the population rose to new levels of variety and sophistication, those of the poor deteriorated. Whereas the period saw the erection of grander mansions by landowners and urban patricians and the rebuilding and refurnishing of the homes of the yeomanry and master craftsmen, it also saw a mushroom growth of bare cottages for the poor in country parishes and the emergence of squalid overcrowded pauper suburbs in the towns. In this sense the process of polarization is clear.

There is a further dimension to this process, however, for the pressures and opportunities of the period also produced a quickened pace of both upward and downward social mobility, leading over time to a significant modification of the profile of stratification in English society. This was achieved in several ways. On the one hand, the economic development of the period facilitated the expansion of certain occupations – notably in the professions, trade (both internal and overseas), service industries, manufactures and government service – opening new opportunities to place beside traditional avenues of upward social mobility for the children of the 'middling sort' of town and country. There was both an expansion of the 'pseudo-gentry' and a growing occupational complexity among the 'middling sort'. On the other hand, certain social groups, notably the husbandmen of the countryside and journeymen–craftsmen in the towns were depressed into the ranks of wage labour as a result of their inability to withstand economic pressures undermining their traditional place in society. Meanwhile, steady demographic pressure helped to swell the ranks of the labouring poor, either by encouraging the subdivision of formerly adequate agricultural holdings into the dwarf holdings of cottagers, or by simply multiplying the numbers of wage-dependent paupers at the bottom of society. In this sense too society was polarized.[40] Contemporaries noted both aspects of this phenomenon, but they were struck most forcibly by the very visible evidence of the increase of poverty.

Poverty, of course, was nothing new. English society had never been able to provide adequately for all its members. Yet the later sixteenth and early seventeenth centuries saw the growth of a poverty which was different in both its nature and extent from that which had been known earlier in the sixteenth century. In the villages and towns of the fifteenth and early sixteenth centuries, poverty had not been regarded as a major social problem. It was limited in extent and generally the result of particular misfortune – the death of a spouse or parent, sickness or injury – or else a phase in the life cycle, notably youth or old age. It was by no means the inevitable accompaniment of wage labour, which tended in any case to be a form of employment peculiar to a certain phase of the life cycle, early manhood, or else indulged in as a means of supplementing income. By the end of the sixteenth century and still more by the mid seventeenth century, the poor were no longer the destitute victims of misfortune or old age, but a substantial proportion of the population living in constant danger of destitution, many of them full-time wage labourers. In both town and country a permanent proletariat had emerged, collectively designated 'the poor'.[41]

The extent of the problem was frightening, though it varied, as might be expected, from area to area. Occasionally surviving local records permit an unusually detailed knowledge of the problem – as in one parish of Salisbury in 1635 where in addition to those paupers actually in receipt of poor relief a further one third of the inhabitants were regarded as poor. Again, at Heydon in Essex in 1625, some 43 per cent of householders were regarded as being on or below the poverty line, while a further 23 per cent (who held a house and four acres of land) were just above it and might easily be forced on to the relief system in a bad year.[42]

It is a dismal count. Yet these were the settled poor, relatively fortunate in that they had a recognized place in society and were eligible for parish relief under the Elizabethan Poor Laws. Beyond them and well outside the charitable consideration of the authorities, were the vagrant poor, the 'rogues and vagabonds' of picaresque literature. How many of them wandered the roads of the period, it is impossible to say, though their numbers were undoubtedly high. In 1695 Gregory King reckoned that there were 30,000 vagrants (one for every 182 of the settled population in his estimates), but this was just a guess, and in any case it is likely that by his time their numbers had diminished. Certainly they were a common enough sight. No fewer than 83 were punished in the two

Lancashire parishes of Rochdale and Middleton in the year ending August 1638, 153 in the parishes of Warrington and Winwicke in 1636. Sometimes accounts of them suggest that occasional individuals were indeed the colourful vagabonds of the contemporary literary stereotype; tricksters and ne'er-do-wells. More often, they were simply displaced people: usually young; mostly men (though a large minority were women); commonly unmarried (though there were some whole families on the road); generally drifting slowly from the north and west to the south and east, or between town and town. Often they claimed to have an occupation when they were examined by the authorities and frequently they were able to find seasonal work. Some even found permanent places and moved back into the settled population. More often they were hustled on their way by villagers who feared and suspected them, or whipped out of parishes by constables enforcing the vagrancy laws. Too many found a settlement only when their bodies were found in barns or under hedges on winter mornings, especially in years of food-shortage, their only memorials being brief anonymous entries in parish registers: buried 9 December 1592 'a poor woman which died in a barne at the parsonage whose name we could not learne'.[43]

Crisis and recovery

The chronology of change

So far our emphasis has been placed upon the identification of long-term socio-economic trends, many of which stand out best when viewed in long-term perspective. Nevertheless, it is equally important that attention be given to the periodization of the overall process of change. To some extent every region, even every town and village, had its own chronology of change, sometimes conforming to, sometimes out of step with the broader national trends. Overall, however, there is some justification for dividing the century into two periods of fifty years. The first, 1580–1630, was a period of gathering crisis, punctuated by a number of years of acute distress. The second, 1630–1680, saw the gradual stabilization of the forces underlying change in English society and the amelioration to some extent of the social problems so evident at the turn of the sixteenth and seventeenth centuries. Consideration of each of these subperiods in turn can do much to sharpen our appreciation of the course of change in the century as a whole.

The half-century after 1580 saw the peak of both the population expansion, renewed after the check of the mid sixteenth-century epidemics, and the long-term inflation of prices. These facts alone might have brought difficulties to the mass of the English people, yet they were exacerbated in their effects by the coincidence of a number of catastrophic harvest failures. In 1586, 1594–8, 1623–4 and 1630 harvest disasters brought dearths of national proportions, while in a number of other years, notably 1608 and 1614 deficient harvests caused more localized scarcities.[44]

These years of dearth severely affected all people dependent on the market for their food. They also, however, exacerbated the difficulties of many small farmers. The years after 1580 saw a quickening in the efforts of landlords to reorganize tenures and raise rents on their estates, as large numbers of tenancies granted in more favourable times began to fall in.[45] Many husbandmen, then, were feeling the pinch. They were also, in the years between 1585 and 1604, subjected to unusually high demands from the Elizabethan state in the form of war taxation and requisitioning of produce. Into this situation came the dreadful series of dearths of the 1590s, followed in the first decades of the seventeenth century by unusually good harvests. For many small farmers this alternation of scarcity and abundance seems to have proved the final straw, bringing indebtedness, inability to pay rents and eventual sale or abandonment of their lands. Margaret Spufford, in the closest study yet attempted of this phenomenon, has suggested that in Cambridgeshire it was the turn of the sixteenth and seventeenth centuries which proved the crisis point for the small farmers of corn-producing areas. In Chippenham, the middling fifteen to forty-five acre husbandmen survived well enough until 1598, but fell by the wayside in the succeeding decades while their lands were taken up by engrossing yeomen. In Orwell the same process of polarization came a little later, in the second and third decades of the seventeenth century.[46]

In industrial areas the chronology of crisis was rather different. England's cloth-producing districts had established a modest prosperity by the 1580s. The trade in the broadcloths produced in the south-west had revived and stabilized after the crisis of the mid sixteenth century, while the production of the New Draperies in East Anglia had expanded in response to the demand of new markets in southern Europe. The dearths of the 1590s brought terrible suffering to these industrial areas whose workers were almost wholly dependent on the market, since scarcity brought not only high food prices, but also a slump in demand for manufactures both at home and abroad. As the seventeenth century opened the situation improved once again until in 1614 the Cockayne project utterly dislocated the broadcloth industry, while in the 1620s war in Europe disrupted the markets for both broadcloth and the New Draperies. This crisis, which coincided with renewed dearth in 1622–3 and 1630 brought dreadful want to the weaving towns and villages and a degree of improverishment which was only slowly recovered from in succeeding decades.[47] For the weavers the decade of crisis *par excellence* was the 1620s, and this was equally true of the towns. They too suffered from the years of harvest failure, which brought not only distress to the urban poor, but new floods of subsistence migrants drawn from the countryside in hope of benefiting from the superior relief measures taken by urban authorities. They also, after 1580, suffered repeated blows from more frequent outbreaks of bubonic plague, each of which temporarily dislocated commercial life. Weakened by these crises and faced with the problem of an increasing burden of urban poverty, the towns were also to feel the effects of the commercial and industrial depression of the 1620s. Whether we view this decade as the lowest point in a long-term process of urban social crisis or simply as one more in a series of short-term crises, a matter on which urban historians disagree, there can be little doubt that it was a terrible period for the urban poor.[48]

In the years between 1594 and 1630, then, a series of crises, any one of which would have been bad enough in itself, served to exacerbate the effects of long-term changes in England's economy and society. The seriousness of this dreadful conjuncture stands well enough revealed in the impoverishment of small-farmers, artisans and the growing proletariat of town and country. Its starkest manifestation, however, is to be found in the recently discovered fact that within this period England became vulnerable in a way which had not been known for three centuries to actual 'crises of subsistence': famines.

This vulnerability stands best revealed in the evidence produced by the analysis of parish registers. When, in a year of high prices, burials of more than twice the annual average for the decade are recorded, together with a simultaneous drop in the number of marriages and conceptions (calculated on the basis of baptismal dates), famine is to be suspected. The gradual refinement and widespread application of this basic technique has resulted in an accumulation of evidence which tells a sombre story. Large areas of England suffered from famine in 1597–9 and again in 1623. In dealing with evidence of this kind, of course, we must be careful to avoid sensationalism. Regional vulnerability varied a great deal. The worst hit area was undoubtedly Cumbria, a region relatively remote from relief supplies, imperfectly incorporated into the national market and gradually subject to impoverishment as a result of the fact that prices for its chief product, livestock, lagged behind the prices demanded for the grain which the area was obliged to import. Again, Cumbria was a classic example of a pastoral area where demographic pressure had resulted in rural congestion and the fragmentation of holdings to support a substantially increased population. In 1586/7 dearth brought in its wake famine exacerbated by an epidemic of typhus, 'famine fever'. In yet more terrible disasters in 1597/8 and 1623 famine again decimated the population.[49]

Of these crises only that of 1597–8 came near to being national. It was precipitated by the last of a series of four catastrophic harvests, which had already drained the withstanding power of the rural population, and clear evidence of famine deaths has been found in Cumbria, Yorkshire, Northumberland and Durham, Staffordshire and upland Devon. Elsewhere, the crisis may have been more muted, though it was serious enough to show up in higher than average mortality in a national sample of 404 rural parishes analysed by the Cambridge Group for the History of Population and Social Structure. In the cities too (which were distinguished by their superior relief measures in years of dearth) it left its mark: Exeter, Bristol, Worcester and Newcastle all suffered unusually high mortality that year. The crisis of 1623, however, was more definitely restricted to the north of England – Cumbria, upland Lancashire, Northumberland and Yorkshire all being affected.[50]

With the exception of these crises, evidence of famine has not been found elsewhere, yet there is reason to believe that the aggregated statistics derived from parish registers, which make no distinction between the experience of different social groups, may in part conceal the extent to which an imbalance between population and resources had developed in this period. A recent study of the Forest of Arden, in which 'landed' parishioners have been distinguished from 'landless' cottagers and labourers, has revealed in the years 1613–19 a demographic crisis which affected only the landless poor. It passed through three stages. First in 1613–14 poor women bore children, but their children suffered a disproportionately high degree of infant mortality. Next in 1615–16 the fertility of poor women fell significantly. Finally in 1617–19 they recovered their ability to conceive, yet experienced many spontaneous abortions. All this suggests a situation of 'endemic food shortage leading to creeping malnutrition' among the poor of these five parishes.[51]

Finally, we may consider one more oblique indicator of the deteriorating position of the poor in this period. Demographic research has revealed that in the years between 1580 and 1620, and more particularly those between 1595 and 1610, the illegitimacy ratio reached an unprecedented peak. It is a phenomenon found almost everywhere, though the actual proportion of children born illegitimate varied from area to area. In the light of the usual circumstances surrounding illegitimate births, it seems likely that this remarkable phenomenon resulted from a period of unusual instability and insecurity in the courtships of the poor. In a deteriorating economic climate following the crisis of the 1590s it may well be that fewer and less stable opportunities existed for the poor to marry and set up independent families.[52]

Frequent disappointment in marital expectations is hardly something to be compared with the horror of widespread famine, yet both reveal, in different ways, the harsh realities of life in England at the turn of the sixteenth and seventeenth centuries. We still have much to learn of this period, but it seems possible that the years 1590–1630 may prove overall what, in writing of the earlier seventeenth century, Dr Bowden called 'among the most terrible years through which the country has ever passed'.[53] These years reveal much about both the nature of English society and the direction in which it was changing. Yet equally significant is the fact that the deepening socio-economic crisis of this period was gradually overcome. England's earlier experience of a serious imbalance between population and resources in the early decades of the fourteenth century had ended in a famine far more serious than those which afflicted the country in 1597 and 1623, and the situation had been reversed only after the catastrophic mortality of the Black Death. In the seventeenth century no such fortuitous disaster intervened. Indeed, after 1665 the plague actually vanished, for reasons which remain obscure. Yet the situation of crisis was alleviated nonetheless. By the mid seventeenth century England's economy proved capable of sustaining an increased population and the most significant fact about the famine of 1623 was that it was the last such trauma. Harvest failures in 1630 and 1646–9 brought suffering, but not widespread death. How was this momentous breakthrough achieved?

In the first place the years after 1620 saw a gradual stabilization of population growth. This was the result partly of fortuitous changes in the death rate – rising rates of infant, child and adult mortality brought about by the introduction of new infectious diseases – but it owed much also to human adaptation to a changed situation. A rising age of marriage, probably in response to the greater difficulties experienced in setting up independent households, led to reduced fertility. Again, within marriage, attempts appear to have been made to reduce fertility, possibly in an effort to limit numbers of dependent children so as to maintain threatened living standards.[54] Restrained fertility, even more than rising mortality, brought about a stabilization of population growth. At the same time reduced demographic pressure contributed to a falling-off of long-distance 'subsistence' migration.[55]

As population growth tapered off, the capacity to feed the enlarged population continued to grow. Agricultural innovations introduced earlier began to pay off in larger crops and this development, together with the continued improvement of internal distribution of produce through the market, helped to stabilize prices. Lower grain prices and improved distribution benefited the poor in general, but especially those of pastoral 'corn-poor' regions, who had been most vulnerable to the effects of harvest failure. They also encouraged continued cost-cutting innovations in arable farming. Techniques pioneered earlier were generalized to a greater degree, while a notable new trend was the planting of greater acreages of spring-sown crops which led to a better crop balance and reduced the risks of scarcity in a bad year. These trends were not uniformly beneficial. For some small farmers declining prices constituted a *coup de grâce* forcing them out of business. But in general the improved capacity of the agricultural economy to feed the population resulted in slowly improving real wages after a century of decline and brought relief, if not prosperity, to the poor of town and country. In turn, improved real wages released greater purchasing power in the home market, which, together with the stabilization and expansion of overseas markets, produced increased demand for manufactures and an expansion of industrial employment which assisted the absorption of the poor.[56]

This process of recovery and development is best illustrated at the level of particular localities. In Cumbria, for example, reduced population pressure as the seventeenth century advanced, together with better livestock prices, higher food output, closer integration into the national economy and an expansion of commercial and industrial employment, helped ensure that there was no repetition of the disaster of 1623. In the Forest of Arden, the early seventeenth century saw much wood clearance and reclamation of waste land, which was turned over to convertible husbandry. The larger farmers turned to more arable farming and dairying and were able not only to expand the food production of the area, but also to offer more employment in their dairies and in the more intensive arable husbandry. Work for perhaps 100 more agricultural labourers was created over a period of years, not to mention increased opportunities for casual employment among women and children. At the same time expanding hemp, flax, woollen, leather, metal working and building trades provided new opportunities for industrial employment. A new stability and modest well-being emerged in an area which had teetered on the brink of disaster.[57]

Such specific cases are revealing, providing us with only two of the many variants which together constituted a general amelioration of England's economic position. Most importantly, it was a recovery achieved by a complex process of development and not by the kind of straightforward reversal which might have resulted, for example, from simple demographic disaster. The vicious circle of Malthusian crisis had been overcome in England generations before this was to be accomplished in Scotland, France or Scandinavia. At the same time, however, it is vital that we appreciate that the dangers which had threatened English society in the first half of our period were overcome in a manner which preserved and rendered permanent most of the socio-economic changes of that period. England was a more complex, a more closely integrated and a wealthier society in 1680 than it had been a century earlier. But it was also, and remained, a more polarized society, bearing a heavier burden of permanent poverty than it had known. The poor were no longer vulnerable to mass starvation. Yet their presence in greatly enhanced numbers constituted the most visible evidence of the socio-economic changes of the period. It is a presence best evidenced in the assessments made for the Hearth Tax in the 1660s and 1670s, which listed householders exempted from the tax on the grounds of poverty. It must be remembered that by this time the economic situation of wage earners had improved and that those exempted in the tax lists represented only the destitute and near destitute. Many of those not exempted were only marginally better off. Nevertheless, the proportions exempt in different areas provide a revealing picture of the core of poverty. In rural Kent, 31 per cent of householders were exempt, in Leicestershire 30 per cent, in Shropshire 23 per cent and in Suffolk 37 per cent. In fielden Northamptonshire 35 per cent were exempt, while in the forest areas of the same county the figure was 44 per cent. Essex had an overall exemption rate of 38 per cent, ranging from 23 per cent in the parishes of the south of the county to 53 per cent in the industrial parishes of the north.[58]

Such figures serve to remind us that in the opinion of Gregory King, at least half his countrymen in 1688 were scarcely able simply to provide an adequate maintenance for their families. The poor had emerged as a massive and permanent element in English society. Coming to terms with the strains of that transition was to prove the most central theme in the social drama of the age.

6 *Order*

In the course of the later sixteenth and early seventeenth centuries, the gathering pace of economic change placed English society under considerable strain. To historians blessed with the benefit of hindsight the period may well appear one of gradual transition, albeit scarred by a cluster of serious short-term crises, a necessary prologue to the stabler and more prosperous situation of the later seventeenth century. To contemporaries, however, who lacked such knowledge of what was to come, the situation was far more worrying. If they were only dimly aware of the underlying causes of economic and social change, they were acutely conscious of the more pathological symptoms of the process of change. It was they who struggled with the problems of widespread poverty and vagrancy, they who tried to come to terms with changes which threatened their conceptions of a stable and enduring social order. Little wonder, then, that to some of them it appeared that the very bonds of society were endangered. Governments, all too often helpless to avert crises over which they had no control, watched anxiously for signs of unrest among the common people. Magistrates observed with disquiet the multiplication of thefts within their jurisdictions and the boldness and impunity of offenders. Ministers filled their sermons – especially those preached at assizes and quarter sessions – with vivid images of disorder, darkness, sickness and corruption. The times seemed out of joint.

Such fears may be exaggerated, but they were not entirely without justification. Historians of crime have discovered that the numbers of serious offences tried at county assizes did indeed rise rapidly in the course of the reign of Elizabeth – more rapidly than can be explained simply in terms of population increase – to reach a peak between 1590 and 1620.[1]

Even more worrying for the authorities was the incidence of riots in the English provinces. Every bad harvest year brought its crop of food riots, while most years witnessed minor agrarian disturbances, usually in resistance to enclosures. Such facts confirmed members of the governing class in their opinion that the common people, unless restrained with the bridle of good government, were singularly prone to disorder; 'as a Beast with many heads', as Christopher Hudson informed the justices of Lancashire; 'always apt to rebel and mutiny . . . on the least occasion', in the opinion of Sir John Oglander.[2] If further confirmation was required it could be found in occasional expressions of popular opinion which gave the authorities naught for their comfort. Anonymous libels and seditious utterances testify to the existence among at least some of the common people of a bitter hatred of the rich whom they regarded as exploiters: 'Yt wold never be merye till some of the gentlemen were knocked down' was the opinion of one prospective leader of an abortive Oxfordshire rising in 1596. Indeed, even in their supposedly humble petitions to the authorities in times of crisis, they could threaten as well as appeal for redress of their grievances. Unemployed Essex weavers in 1629, fearing that 'theire miseries are not Creditted', warned the king himself that but for the Earl of Warwick's intervention 'many wretched people would have gathered together in a Mutinie and have beene with your Ma:tye for they said words would not fill the belly nor Cloth[e] the backe'. The threat was scarcely veiled.[3]

In the face of threats of this kind, the government possessed only limited coercive power. The system of local administration and law enforcement built up over the centuries was an impressive monument to the institutional inventiveness of England's medieval kings, and through it the royal government was always potentially present in the localities. Yet the *effective* presence of the government could be far less impressive, for it depended above all upon the diligence and co-operation of essentially amateur, unpaid local officers, ranging from the Justices of the Peace of the counties to the petty constables of townships and villages. Such diligence and co-operation were not always forthcoming. Nor could the government fall back upon the services of a standing army, for its regular military resources prior to the civil wars were small. Even when local troops were raised and committed in the defence of public order, they could be far from reliable. In 1631 the Sheriff of Wiltshire was authorized to raise the train bands, supposedly the cream of the English militia, in order to eject one Thomas Carr from Clayhill Farm in Selwood Forest, following Carr's refusal to obey a decree of Chancery to surrender the farm to its proper owner. Fifty pikemen and fifty musketeers, accompanied by ordnance, duly advanced upon the farm which was held by 'a multitude of base and desparate persons' armed with muskets. When the defenders refused to surrender and instead presented themselves ready to fight, the men of the train bands suddenly discovered that only four of the musketeers were fully equipped with powder and shot and 'none could be gotten to light their matches', while the pikemen simply refused to put on their protective corselets. The Sheriff withdrew, explaining that he 'thought fitt to excuse my departure by reason of the foulness of the weather and the neereness of the night'.[4]

Central government and county justices

It was within the bounds of constraints of this kind that the governments of Elizabethan and early Stuart England had to operate. Like all governments, they were concerned with the maintenance of public order and they were well aware that they had more reason than most to fear for its stability. Faced with perplexing problems and acutely conscious of the deficiencies of the system of local administration, they responded by attempting to win the assent of the various social groups upon whose co-operation depended the maintenance of order.

This was achieved in several ways. On the one hand, they never tired of preaching the values of order and obedience. On the other hand, they dissociated themselves from the disorders and abuses of the times by insisting upon the punishment of offenders and the alleviation of distress. It was an age of proclamations and a period of great legislative activity. The desire of England's rulers for order and their sympathy with the victims of change were proclaimed from pulpits and at market crosses. They were also embodied in what Lambarde called 'stacks of statutes', many of them promoted by the government and ranging from the great Tudor Poor Laws, through the codification, modification and extension of the penal laws governing social and economic regulation, to acts aimed at the sterner punishment of particular offences. Such was the flow of legislation that handbooks of the law required frequent updating if they were to serve adequately as guides to the local officers charged with the duty of enforcement. Thomas Pulton's abstract of penal legislation, originally published in 1577, went through eight new editions by 1603. Michael Dalton's *Country Justice*, the favourite judicial textbook of the early seventeenth century, saw seven editions and revisions between 1618 and 1635.[5]

Some of this legislation was of largely symbolic value: it stated the good intentions of authority, re-emphasized traditional values and provided reassurance that something had been done to curb particular offences. Most of the new laws, however, were intended from the first to be enforced and it was in the sphere of the implementation of the law that Elizabethan and early Stuart governments most distinguished themselves.

That burden fell upon the broad backs of the Justices of the Peace, the ubiquitous local agents of the central government, and upon their counterparts among the ruling oligarchies of the towns. Although additional means were sometimes employed – the encouragement of private informers, the granting of patents to private persons to enforce particular statutes – the energies of the government were above all bent to the task of ensuring that local magistrates played their part effectively. They were watched over by the privy council; exhorted, encouraged, ordered and rebuked. They were inspected and reported upon by regional councils, lords lieutenant, bishops and above all by the assize judges who visited the counties twice every year and brought back their reports to Westminster. In accordance with such reports, county commissions of the peace were periodically reshuffled, putting out unsatisfactory magistrates, while deserving individuals were awarded the honour of inclusion.[6]

Nor were the justices simply prodded into a generalized activity, for they were provided with very specific instructions as to the particular laws deemed 'fittest to be put in execution'. In 1561 when such an 'abbreviate' of the penal laws was first sent down to the magistrates of the counties it had been greeted with dismay among those who received it. But magistrates gradually learned to expect and to accept such directives. By the 1590s the Lord Keeper regularly addressed the assize judges before their departure on circuit, giving them a 'charge' to be delivered to the justices who would greet them in the county towns. By the early decades of the seventeenth century such charges had come to assume a regular pattern: the poor were to be relieved, the markets supplied, the roads maintained, church attendance enforced, superfluous and disorderly alehouses suppressed, riots, robberies and vagrancy put down. In times of dearth they were supplemented by the Book of Orders, first issued in 1587, requiring the suppression of speculation in foodstuffs and detailing measures to be taken for the prevention of famine and the preservation of order.[7]

The result of this sustained pressure for effective local government was a gradual quickening of county administration which became most evident in the crisis years of the last decade of the reign of Elizabeth and was consolidated and extended under the early Stuarts. This development must not be exaggerated, of course, for the effective implementation of policy could still be inhibited in several ways. Some areas, such as the Yorkshire Dales or Cleveland, were inadequately staffed with resident justices. Some justices remained negligent – only three-fifths of Worcestershire justices were active in the reign of James I. Others were corrupt or partial in the use of their authority. Counties remote from central control might be slow to improve in administrative efficiency – like Northumberland where the governing magistracy remained negligent in the enforcement of famine relief, the poor laws and alehouse control as late as the 1620s. Even where magisterial activity intensified, it might be sporadic and pulsating rather than regular, distorted by local rivalries and factionalism, or highly selective in its application. In Norfolk the justices could enforce the whole panoply of penal legislation when they chose, but they did not often choose to do so, preferring to concentrate on matters related 'to their own concerns and not necessarily to dictates of central government'. Similarly in Sussex the increasingly active magistrates remained 'not susceptible to outside pressure unless it was in line with the purposes of government as they saw them'.[8]

Such selectivity was common, and it was of the first importance, for it serves to remind us that the enforcement of order was a process which depended upon multilateral assent to the policies of government. As pressure from above intensified, the institutions of county government became the framework for interaction between centre and locality, of a new kind. Whereas formerly, contact between central government and county justices had been to a large degree mediated through such leading provincial magnates as the Duke of Norfolk or the Earl of Westmorland, the intensification of administrative oversight, coupled with the Tudor policy of circumventing aristocratic influence in the provinces, brought about a much more direct relationship between the gentry rulers of the counties and the royal government. Justices meeting in quarter sessions became more aware not only of the duties required of them, but also of their own role as representatives and spokesmen of their counties. They debated policy, formulated opinion, corresponded and negotiated with the privy council, and in the process became more aware of their own need to influence national policy. It was a need reflected in their letters and petitions and in the activities of some of their number in Parliament. Indeed, as Dr Hassell Smith has argued, a close relationship existed between the developing responsibilities of local government, the pressure of central government for the enforcement of policy, and the grievances raised by the gentry representatives of the localities in Parliament. To this extent the administrative initiative of the later sixteenth and early seventeenth centuries played a major part in the development of the political consciousness of the provincial gentry. Nor indeed was this a process confined to the leaders of county society, for it involved also the minor gentry who served in the humbler offices of county administration and the yeoman freeholders who played their part in parish government and who had a voice in county elections. Although the latter groups might frequently follow the lead of their social superiors, they were by no means mere pawns. In the conduct of local affairs and in the quarrels and resentments to which the policies of the crown occasionally gave rise, they experienced a political education which was to have repercussions which reverberated far beyond the circumscribed spheres of their local communities.[9]

The tensions engendered by the demands of Elizabethan and early Stuart government were to reach their peak in the reign of Charles I, when a government determined to pursue unpopular policies and singularly deaf to local complaints, which were metamorphosed by parliamentary oratory into statements of constitutional principle, succeeded in sufficiently alienating the 'political nation' as to provoke the massive attack upon royal government which occupied the first session of the Long Parliament. Much as the magistracy might resent and resist government policy on particular issues, however, there was no disagreement on the basic question of the need to advance and preserve good order among its inferiors. Indeed, in this matter local justices could sometimes show zeal and initiative above and beyond what was officially required of them. Despite all qualifications, a great deal was achieved. It was an achievement which can be measured in the mounting bulk of the files of quarter sessions business handled by the justices. It is evidenced in the growing efficiency with which justices and their subordinates responded to the periodic crises of dearth years, drawing upon reserves of energy to regulate the market, organize relief and galvanize the whole system of social regulation into effective action. It is reflected in the manner in which the justices shouldered the increased burden imposed on them in the years after 1631 when the privy council, following the issue of the Book of Orders to meet the dearth of 1630–1, insisted upon the continuance in normal years of the special measures for poor relief and public order normally reserved for emergencies, and set the assize judges to supervise yet more closely the activities of the justices. Petty sessions, monthly meetings of justices for the divisions of their counties, which had been resented and generally unsuccessful when introduced earlier in the century, were now accepted and regularly kept. Above all, perhaps, the administrative achievement of the first half of our period is revealed in the gradual institutionalization of the poor laws. By 1642, despite the initial resentment of local ratepayers and the foot-dragging of parish officers, the poor rate, as Anthony Fletcher has observed, 'had become a fact of life'.[10]

Nor were these developments reversed by the revolt against royal policy which occasioned the constitutional revolution of 1640–1 and precipitated the slide of the nation into civil war. In the aftermath of the temporary disruption occasioned by the war, county justices met again and carried on as before. Petty sessions were retained. Poor relief (once erroneously thought to have been dislocated) was continued. The dearth crisis of 1646–9 was met and ameliorated in the usual way. Indeed, there is much evidence to suggest that, in many counties, the Interregnum witnessed a further intensification of the effective presence of government in the English localities. The institutions of county government were elaborated by the addition of committees responsible to Parliament. Participation in the principal offices of county administration was expanded by the inclusion of a broader spectrum of the minor gentry. County benches infused with religious zeal periodically attempted regulative initiatives against petty disorders and ungodliness, involving as their allies *ad hoc* committees of supporters drawn from the principal inhabitants of the parishes and townships.[11] In all these ways the authorities of the Interregnum further consolidated and extended the administrative achievement of Elizabethan and early Stuart government. Although their more radical innovations did not outlive the Restoration of 1660, much of what had been achieved by the three preceding generations was preserved. What had required initiative and determination on the part of successive governments now needed only administration by local magistrates who had learned to accept the burdens placed upon them and to share the attitudes and concerns of central authority. Innovations which had been greeted with dismay by their Elizabethan and Jacobean predecessors had become normalized.

The law and the local community

The heightened concern of central government with the problem of order thus led to both an elaboration of social and economic legislation, and a significant improvement in the enforcement of royal policy in the English provinces. It was a considerable achievement. Yet the extension of the effectiveness of local government was only part of the history of the problem of order in this period – if the best known part. Pressure from above for the creation of a more ordered and stable society could never have more than a very limited and temporary success if it was not accompanied by, and in broad conformity with, spontaneous local efforts to meet the needs and respond to the problems of the age. Government directives, as we have seen, had to pass through a filter of local interests before finding implementation in the counties. Similarly, at a more intimately local level, the attempts of the magistracy to put into execution the desires of the royal government could founder where they were not complemented by a ground swell of local support. This reality was enshrined in the very nature of the judicial and administrative system. Justices of the Peace could demand the implementation of policy and the prosecution of offenders in tones as peremptory as those of the privy council. In the absence of a professional police force, however, they were obliged to rely for the enforcement of the law upon the willingness of the governed to bring cases to their attention: upon such victims of crime as were prepared to initiate private prosecutions and upon the part-time, temporary officers of parishes and townships who were charged with the maintenance of the peace and the public presentment of offenders. Neither group could be relied upon to bring cases before the courts.

Private prosecution was an expensive and troublesome matter. If the loss or injury sustained by a victim of crime was small, then the bringing of a case, even where the offender had been apprehended, might not seem worth the loss of time and money involved. Accordingly, many crimes went unprosecuted. In the opinion of the stern Somerset justice Edward Hext, who complained to Lord Burghley of the laxity of law enforcement in 1596, 'the fyveth person that comytteth a felonye ys not browght to this tryall' either because of the negligence of constables in taking offenders, or because 'the symple man that hath lost hys goods, he ys many tymes content to take hys goods and lett them slypp, because he will not be bound to give evidens at the assises to hys troble and chardge'.[12]

Such reluctance was understandable. However there was also a more positive dimension to the frequently alleged unwillingness to prosecute. The law could be savage, for it was concerned with the exemplary punishment of that minority of offenders who were brought before the courts. Felonies, which included most serious crimes and extended down to the theft of goods valued at more than one shilling, were punishable by death, a situation which led Sir Henry Spelman to observe that, at a time when all other commodities had risen in price, only the life of man had grown cheaper. This harshness was to a considerable degree mitigated by the practice of allowing 'benefit of clergy'. Felons convicted for the first time who were capable of reading the 'neck verse' (Psalm 51, verse one) and thereby able to claim clerical status, were branded (to facilitate future identification) rather than hanged – an escape route taken by over 80 per cent of those convicted for stealing sheep or cows at Essex assizes between 1579 and 1603. Again the law might be softened by the willingness of a jury to reduce the valuation of the goods stolen so as to free an accused person from the threat of execution, or by the discretionary powers of judges to recommend pardons. Even so, such exercise of mercy could not be guaranteed. Perhaps 10–20 per cent of all convicted felons were condemned to death, and of these perhaps half were actually hanged. Devon saw some seventy-four death sentences a year between 1598 and 1639, London 140 a year in 1607–16. In the reign of Elizabeth probably seventeen people were executed every year in Essex, while the annual average for the mid seventeenth century was ten. In this situation, potential prosecutors could be more lenient than the law. Edward Hext believed that 'most commonly the simple Cuntryman and woman, lokynge no farther than ynto the losse of ther owne goods, are of opynyon that they wold not procure a man's death for all the goods yn the world', and that many of them 'uppon promyse to have their goods agayne wyll gyve faynt evidens yf they be not stryctly loked ynto by the Iustyce'.[13]

What was true of felonies, punishable by death, could also be true of misdemeanours punishable by whippings or fines; the more so when those who would be laid open to such punishment were neighbours with whom the private prosecutor would have to live long after the case was over. Accordingly, where disputes between neighbours threatened to deteriorate sufficiently to provoke a court case and even when actual offences were committed, a strong preference existed for informal mediation which might satisfactorily resolve the matter within the bounds of the neighbourhood. Local gentlemen, clergymen and prominent neighbours were commonly involved in mediation of this kind and local officers could also take a hand. When the tithingman and neighbours of one Wiltshire village discovered stolen corn in the house of one Thomas Morris, Morris entreated them 'to be good unto him and his children or else he should be utterly undone'. As a result, the tithingman Robert Toomer 'moved with pity, sought his neighbours that this business might be concealed'. Again, when John King, an Essex villager, stole eight hens in 1636, he was rapidly apprehended by the constable Thomas Burrowes, but 'did falle downe on his knees . . . and did desire him that he would not be the meanes to cast him away for a few hennes, for it was the first offence that ever he had donne'. Burrowes, taking upon himself the role of mediator, talked the matter over with the victim of the theft and having decided that it was the lesser of two evils, released the thief.[14] Such circumstances were not unusual. From the point of view of members of the village community the maintenance of order in the sense of restoring good relationships among neighbours might be better served by the avoidance of prosecution than by the stern enforcement of the law desired by such justices as Edward Hext.

If this was so in the case of felonies and disputes between parties, it was even more true of the enforcement of the regulative penal legislation so dear to the heart of the royal government. Constables elected for a single year and combining their duties with the normal pursuit of their livelihoods, or parish representatives serving on presentment juries at quarter sessions, commonly showed little enthusiasm for the task of nosing out and presenting offences of this kind. Nor was this simply a reflection of their inadequacy and inefficiency, as was commonly alleged by justices berating them for their lack of enthusiasm. Frequently they simply failed to share the law's definition of an offence, for the period witnessed the statutory proscription of many activities which were well established and sanctioned by local custom. In this situation, village officers were often willing to allow a considerably larger area of ambivalent, permitted behaviour than was compatible with the nice definitions of legislators. Again, they were unwilling to stir up trouble which might rebound against them by poisoning their relationships with their neighbours. The more conscientious among them generally preferred admonition to formal presentment of offenders, while those even less impressed with the demands of the law knew the value of a blind eye.[15]

Adam Martindale's experience in helping to enforce the strict sabbatarian legislation of 1656 in his Cheshire parish provides a revealing example of the dilemmas faced by officers charged with the implementation of such laws. He himself felt that the Act was too stringent, but as parish minister he was obliged to enforce it on pain of a £5 fine. Even so, he would have preferred to turn a blind eye when he could, but matters came to a head when he and the constable were obliged to act against a servant girl, since information on her offence of working on the sabbath was brought to them 'by such as we had reason to beleeve would complaine against us if we took not notice'. They then had the choice of either fining her five shillings if she was over 21 years old, or else requiring her master and dame to correct her. The constable was prepared to accept that she was under age, and although Martindale knew this to be untrue he succumbed to 'mine owne wife and severall others' who were 'importunate with me that I would not search it out'. Upon this he turned her over to the constable and her master who 'turned all into a jest; and her master plucking off a small branch of heath from a turfe, therewith gave her two or three such gentle touches on her cloathes as . . . would not have hurt an infant of two dayes old'. The matter might have ended there. Unfortunately the girl later died of fever and a malicious rumour arose that Martindale had caused her death by having her savagely whipped. He had to clear himself before a Justice of the Peace.[16]

Martindale was not the only local officer to experience the tension which could exist between the order demanded by the law and the problem of maintaining neighbourly relationships in the village. Many an officer who tried to execute the law was accused of spite and malice, or reproved for being 'too busie' or 'presyce'. Nor was he the only one to appreciate that in such small-scale communities it was exceedingly difficult to judge the behaviour of an individual without bringing into play a host of personal considerations which had no place in the statute book. What really mattered at this level was the maintenance of specific, local, personal relationships. In that task, the attempt to enforce conformity to an impersonal standard of legally defined order could be thoroughly counter-productive.

There were, then, strong elements of local discretion in the enforcement of the law, sufficient indeed to ensure that the cutting edge of the authorities' drive for greater order could be blunted when it threatened to come too sharply into conflict with the perceived needs of local society. But just as there were limits on the effectiveness of social regulation through the law, so also there were limits to local tolerance of offenders. For all their selective reluctance, people did use the courts a great deal. Indeed, they used them increasingly in the first sixty years of our period. If examination of their frequent unwillingness to go to law reveals something of the attitudes and values of the common people of the time, yet more can be learned by asking how and why they did use the courts. For if the village communities of the period were to some extent 'moral communities', in the sense that they placed a premium upon good neighbourliness and preferred local opinion to the impersonal values of the law, there were also boundaries to the moral community beyond which individuals could not stray with hope of impunity. The record of the local courts can help to reveal the nature of those boundaries and the extent to which they varied from place to place and from time to time.

Felonies and misdemeanours

Of the numerous felonies and misdemeanours listed in contemporary judicial handbooks, the great majority were comparatively rarely the object of prosecution. Public concern would appear to have been concentrated in the main upon four broad categories of offence: homicides; assaults and threats of violence; thefts (using this term to cover property offences ranging in seriousness from petty larceny to burglary and robbery); and finally a very broad category of offences relating to social regulation under the penal laws, but including above all prosecutions of unlicensed and disorderly alehouse-keepers, neglecters of church attendance, vagrancy, and offences under the laws governing cottaging and the taking in of 'inmates' or sub-tenants.

Of these offences homicide was undoubtedly regarded as the most serious. It was also the only offence of which we can be fairly confident that the record of prosecution comes close to being an accurate reflection of the incidence of the crime. Homicide was hard to conceal. Moreover, the laws governing homicide were already very sophisticated and procedures for dealing with violent or suspicious death were already well established. Where any person died by untimely means a coroner's inquest was rapidly convened (usually within days), and in accordance with its findings a prosecution might be made. Figures derived from surviving assize files suggest that, as William Harrison alleged, murder, with 'malice aforethought' was rare in England. Other forms of less culpable homicide, however, were not uncommon. Homicide accounted for 4.5 per cent of assize indictments in Hertfordshire and 10 per cent of assize indictments in Sussex in the reign of James I. In the estimate of Dr Sharpe, the leading student of this problem, the homicide rate in Essex between 1645 and 1679, expressed as homicides per 100,000 population, was approximately three times the homicide rate of mid twentieth-century England. Indeed, it may have been higher, given the ambivalent nature of some coroners' inquest returns which did not lead to prosecutions, although on the other hand it is important to remember that the inadequacies of medical care in this period meant that some victims of violence died who would almost certainly have been saved had better medical facilities and techniques been available. Richard Terry, a tailor, who died in 1617, no less than sixteen days after being struck on the head with a jug, for example, might very well have been saved under modern conditions. The homicide rate, then, was undoubtedly high by modern English standards, but it was not sufficiently high, all things being considered, to justify any suggestion that life could be casually taken.[17]

The circumstances of violent death do, however, suggest that this was a society in which violence might be resorted to comparatively readily. This should not be exaggerated. There were few deaths as a result of armed affrays or private wars; although these could still occur, as in 1589 when Sir Thomas Langton and eighty men attacked Thomas Houghton and thirty men at Lea Hall in Lancashire, killing Houghton, or in 1617 when Frances Robinson was besieged in Raydale House in Wensleydale by Sir Thomas Metcalfe and had to summon the help of her kin to raise the siege, one of the besiegers being slain.[18] But such events were uncommon and increasingly anachronistic, even in the supposedly lawless north of England. Most gentlemen settled their disputes at law, as indeed did many of their social inferiors. Nevertheless, the evidence of homicide cases carries the implication that many people were volatile and that quarrels could easily degenerate into violence, especially when assisted by drink.

There were few planned homicides and little calculated violence. The commonest circumstances were those of a disagreement leading to blows being struck and the commonest weapons used to kill were not swords or knives, though most men went armed, but either hands and feet or else commonplace implements seized and employed in a moment of passion. Moreover, such violence was relatively widely directed and less contained within the intense emotional setting of the family than is the case today. In Elizabethan and Jacobean Essex, Sussex and Hertfordshire some 18 per cent of killings were within the family (if we include resident servants), and in Essex between 1620 and 1680 some 21 per cent, as compared with approximately 50 per cent in modern England. Violence was more readily used – less circumscribed – in society at large; it was also used by people of all social levels.[19]

These conclusions receive further support when consideration is given to the less serious violence which resulted in prosecutions for assault and in the binding over of individuals to keep the peace. Assault was a misdemeanour, punishable by a fine, the size of the fine often being graduated according to the means of the offender. Unlike homicide, it was a very loosely defined offence and the actual circumstances involved could range from considerable violence against the person to merely threatening behaviour. But whatever the actual content of the offence, cases of assault were common. They were prominent in the business of assizes and even more so in the courts of quarter sessions, while the total number of cases of this kind is swelled still more when we include the many recognizances issued by justices requiring individuals to keep the peace towards specified persons with whom they had quarrelled. How many incidents went unprosecuted we have no way of knowing, though incidental references in local records to assaults which cannot be matched with any known court proceedings suggest that there were many.

The patterns of conflict revealed by assault cases and bindings to keep the peace are intriguing. A substantial minority of assaults were directed against local officers – constables, bailiffs or tax-collectors, a further reminder of the hazards of office for these individuals. Most, however, were between quarrelling neighbours, very often people of quite substantial standing in their villages, though it is likely that the incidence of assault among the poor is masked by the fact that they were those least likely to go to the expense and trouble of bringing cases. Where humbler people appear in assault proceedings it is very commonly as auxiliaries of their employers, patrons or relatives among the notables of a village, for not a few assaults involved small groups of people. The circumstances underlying these cases can only be reconstructed with difficulty, but where additional evidence is available it frequently appears that they were connected with other offences, such as trespass or disseisin (illegal ejection from property), and that these in turn were part and parcel of larger feuds and rivalries. In Terling in Essex, for example, two assault and two disseisin cases in the 1590s arose from a bitter dispute between Richard Rochester and his brother William, both yeomen, over rights of inheritance to the lands of their dead elder brother. Both men brought in auxiliaries from among their friends and employees, with the result that their quarrel reverberated throughout the community and periodically disturbed its peace during a period of several years.[20]

The fluctuating incidence of prosecutions for assault and bindings to keep the peace were doubtless related to the ebb and flow of conflict of this kind within local communities. As with homicides, no general trend can be discerned in court actions of this nature. Both categories of offence, however, reveal something of the nature of this society. Clearly it had a comparatively high tolerance level for minor violence and its members, at all social levels, were relatively ready to resort to threats and blows. Equally significant, however, is the evidence of the limits which existed on the readiness of individuals to take the law into their own hands. Recognizances of the peace were used frequently to contain disputes which threatened to escalate into violence. Actual assault gave rise to court proceedings rather than to the private pursuit of vendettas. Homicide was swiftly reported and punished. It was, by our standards, a relatively violent society, but it was also one in which violence was to a considerable degree contained by use of the law.

The relative violence of sixteenth- and seventeenth-century society impresses the modern student of the court records. It was not, however, so impressive to contemporaries for whom it was one of the normal realities of life. To William Harrison, as to most contemporary commentators on the subject of crime, the real problem of the age was not violence but theft, and such views derive much support from the evidence of the courts. Theft in its several forms (ranging from petty larceny through grand larceny to housebreaking, burglary and robbery) accounted for around three-quarters of all assize indictments and made a substantial contribution to quarter sessions business. Moreover, as contemporaries complained, it was almost certainly on the increase, prosecutions for theft accounting for the major part of the increase in indicted crime observable at the turn of the sixteenth and seventeenth centuries.[21]

Among those accused of theft there is little evidence of the existence of professional crime. Great cities, notably London, had an underworld of professional thieves, while cutpurses might make their appearance in country markets and highway robbers on lonely roads, but vocational crime of this kind was exceptional. In cases where details survive it is clear that most theft was opportunistic rather than planned, and though country villages had their persistent delinquents, these scarcely conformed to any of the picaresque types of professional thief colourfully portrayed in contemporary literature.[22]

The career of Jeremy Heckford of Marks Tey in Essex provides a less romantic example of petty crime in this period. In 1583 and again in 1584 he was in trouble for living out of service, as a result of which he absconded from his home village. Later in 1584 he was taken as a vagrant in Chelmsford and imprisoned on suspicion of felony. No indictment was entered against him, however, and he was released. By 1587 he was back in Marks Tey again, for in that year he was tried for stealing some grain and acquitted. In 1589 he was in trouble at the quarter sessions (together with his wife) for stirring up dissension in the neighbourhood by his evil tongue and was also indicted for the theft of two skins worth 2s. As a result of the jury's willingness to reduce the valuation of the goods, he was found guilty of petty larceny only and whipped. A year later he was indicted for petty larceny at the assizes, found guilty and whipped again. Finally, in December 1590 he was indicted for taking some hose and petticoats in Marks Tey, valued at two shillings and was again tried at the assizes. This time the valuation was not reduced. He was found guilty, pleaded benefit of clergy, failed to read the prescribed verse of scripture and was hanged.[23]

Men like Heckford were about as close as one might come to the existence of professional crime in the English countryside and clearly the term is quite inappropriate. At worst he was a nuisance and a persistent pilferer of his neighbours' goods, but he was hanged for it all the same when he pushed his luck too far. Most thieves were even less culpable and their crimes more occasional. Broadly speaking they fell into two categories. On the one hand, there were vagrants. On the other hand, there were individuals drawn from the lower strata of the settled population – labourers and servants in particular. What the records of theft make clear is that there existed whole strata at the bottom of society which were potentially criminal for the simple reason that occasional pilfering when the opportunity arose was part and parcel of their means of survival. This sombre reality is most graphically illustrated by the fact that within the general upward trend in prosecutions for theft, there were dramatic peaks in years of harvest failure and industrial depression – in Sussex, Hertfordshire and Essex in the dearths of 1586–7 and 1596–8, in Wiltshire during the depression years of the 1620s, in north Yorkshire during the famine of 1623. The implications are straightforward enough. Some of the rural poor stole when they got the chance, like the Hertfordshire woodcutter who came across a small pig feeding when he was working in Cheshunt Wood, killed it and took it to his mother's house 'to make merry with her'. Others, like Robert Whitehead, who took a sheep 'beinge a verie poore man and haveinge a wiefe and seaven smale children and being very hungery', stole when they had to.[24]

Most of the poor, however, did not steal at all, and of those who did, not all were prosecuted. While there seems little doubt that the upward trend in theft prosecutions resulted in part from deteriorating conditions for the mass of the population, increased destitution and vagrancy exacerbated by short-term economic crises, it would be unwise to make too simple an equation between impoverishment and crime. Local patterns of recorded crime could vary considerably. The Essex village of Heydon knew dreadful levels of poverty, yet it produced only one known felon in the whole reign of Elizabeth. The weaving townships of Halstead and Dedham experienced both depression and dearth in the years after 1590, yet while the former saw a sharp rise in indicted crime, the latter witnessed no change in levels of prosecution.[25] Such differences can only be explained in terms of the varying quality of the particular patterns of local social relations which could act either to inhibit or to encourage both the potential thief and the potential prosecutor. The rising tide of theft prosecutions at the turn of the sixteenth and seventeenth centuries must indeed reflect in part an actual increase in crime; but there is also evidence that it resulted in part from a greater willingness on the behalf of some victims of crime to prosecute; an erosion, under the pressures of the times, of the inhibitions of the more prosperous villagers who usually brought indictments.

Such a toughening of attitudes can be detected in the way in which certain ambivalent but customarily tolerated practices, such as the retention of a portion of grain by threshers, pulling wool off sheep's backs, gathering kindling or gleaning, were beginning, in some places, to be redefined and prosecuted as theft. The Berkshire yeoman Robert Loder knew that his labourers took some of his corn, but the fact did not worry him. 'Item that corne which my men doe steale (more than I allow of in a yeare),' he wrote in his accounts, 'although it be a thing uncertain, yet I thinke it may well be valued at xls.' Others were less complacent. One Hertfordshire farmer attacked local women for gleaning on his land 'as is usual for all the pore to do' in 1603, while six years later another accused his labourers of stealing his grain 'under colour of gleaning'.[26] Again, the prosecution – particularly in dearth years – of poor neighbours for milking a cow without permission or stealing a loaf or a piece of cheese, suggests the use of the courts to resolve conflict between expectations of neighbourly assistance and unwillingness on the part of some propertied individuals to meet such obligations. While theft was no more an automatic response to want than prosecution was an automatic reaction to theft, the rising incidence of theft cases suggests a deterioration of relationships within some village communities under the gradual pressure of the underlying socio-economic changes of the period. The man who was prepared to pay the costs of prosecuting a neighbour for the theft of a penny loaf or a kerchief was out to make an example and to draw more tightly the boundaries of permitted behaviour.

This aspect of the use of the courts can be explored more thoroughly by considering the last of our categories of prosecution – those cases brought under the regulative penal laws. As we have seen, there was a general unwillingness among village officers to seek out and prosecute those guilty of such 'crimes without victims': the widow who sold ale without a licence, the occasional drunkard or neglecter of church attendance or the craftsman who exercised a trade without having served an apprenticeship. This discretion, however, was qualified in three ways.

In the first place, persistent delinquents whose multiple disorders threatened the general peace and well-being of a community might find themselves hauled before the courts when they had exhausted the patience of their neighbours. John Voale of Portsmouth, for example, who was prosecuted at the borough sessions for drunkenness and swearing in 1661, had made himself odious to his neighbours by keeping a disorderly alehouse, making unwanted advances to married women, beating his wife and threatening to set his own house on fire, as well as by his generally rowdy behaviour when drunk.[27] Such a bad neighbour placed himself outside the moral community and, like the persistent thief, dissolved any sense of communal identity which might otherwise have restrained the parish officers.

Second, Justices of the Peace could sometimes force local officers into action. From time to time they might insist upon surveys of unlicensed alehouses or of recusants who absented themselves from church. More commonly they might question presentment jurymen closely on the prevalence of particular offences, or even issue specific 'articles' or sets of questions to petty constables, requiring them to produce written answers at the next sessions, and fining those of them who neglected to do so. Such regulative initiatives on the part of the authorities could be very effective indeed, bringing in literally hundreds of cases to a single meeting of quarter sessions, and they were often adopted at times of crisis, notably in dearth years. Initiatives of this kind, however, were exceedingly difficult to sustain for any length of time and such energetic action on the part of local officers was not usually required. In more normal times, constables could swiftly revert to their usual modest levels of activity. Similarly, members of presentment juries, even when obliged to listen to formal 'charges' reminding them of their duties, were commonly content to present 'all well', thereby assuring their superiors that order was satisfactorily maintained, while excusing themselves the unwelcome task of informing on their neighbours.[28]

However, not all local officers were so complacent. In the course of the early seventeenth century some showed a growing readiness to exert their brief authority and to attempt to establish a higher degree of social regulation within their communities. Activity of this kind is partly revealed in the records of presentment to the local courts and partly seen in other spheres of action. Whichever was the case, its primary characteristic was its selectiveness. It varied in intensity from place to place and it was concentrated upon a limited range of problems. Local officers, like the Justices of the Peace themselves, could choose to enforce what suited them and to ignore what did not, and the matters which commonly attracted their concern are of some interest. For the most part they confined themselves to offences against the cottaging laws, the harbouring of 'inmates', disputes over the settlement of paupers, bastardy, vagrancy, the prosecution of persons failing to attend church and above all the regulation of unlicensed and disorderly alehouses.

The reasons for this narrowness of focus were several, but they are not hard to discover. In repressing vagrancy, resisting the settlement of paupers, opposing the erection and maintenance of cottages which lacked the statutory four acres of land, preventing the taking in of 'inmates' and prosecuting the parents of bastard children, they were defending their parishes (and themselves as leading ratepayers) against actual or potential charges on the poor rates. Hence the readiness with which the parents of potentially chargeable bastards or paupers of uncertain settlement were taken before the justices; hence the growing numbers of prosecutions made under the cottaging laws; hence also the various forms of action taken by means other than prosecution before the Justices of the Peace. The church courts were also used to punish the mothers of bastards and to establish the paternity of children. Where manorial courts leet were still active they too could be employed to regulate cottaging and immigration – as at Stoneleigh and Solihull in Warwickshire where orders to this effect were made by the leets in 1613 and 1632. Similarly, the sanctions of the poor laws could be brought to bear informally, as at Braintree in Essex where the parish vestry frequently made such decisions as that 'The overseers shall give to old father Cleeves tenn shillings to releeve him in his necessity upon condicion he shall remove his son Dennis out of the Towne and not receive him any more into his house.' Informal action could even be taken, as we have seen, to inhibit the marriages of the poor.[29]

Action of this kind was crudely instrumental. It was intended to control the problem of poverty locally, but it also involved a greater sense of social distance between parish officers and the local poor. As the problem of poverty grew, ratepayers, charged with the administration of the poor laws and feeling in their own pockets the novel burden of its costs, could begin to regard the labourers and cottagers of their parishes less as neighbours and more as a potential threat, less as individuals and more as 'the poor'. It was part of what Robert Reyce, writing of early seventeenth-century Suffolk, called 'the corrupt and froward judgement of many in these days who esteem the multitude of our poor here to be a matter of heavy burden and a sore discommodity'.[30] Such attitudes were far from universal, but they were nonetheless widespread enough.

Attempts to contain and reduce the local problem of poverty can be seen as defensive initiatives on the part of parish notables. Where they sought to enforce church attendance and to extend closer control over both the numbers of alehouses and the myriad petty disorders associated with them, however, parish officers were taking a rather more positive step. They were attempting not simply to defend their parishes against potential expense, although that was part of it, but also to establish higher standards of social discipline among their neighbours. Of church attendance more will be said in Chapter 7. As for the alehouses, it can be asserted without exaggeration that at the level of the local community, the struggle over the alehouses was one of the most significant social dramas of the age.[31]

In the course of the later sixteenth and early seventeenth centuries, alehouses frequently drew the attention of legislators and administrators. An Act of 1552 laid down that all alehouses must be licensed by the Justices of the Peace, in the interests of preventing 'hurts and trobles . . . abuses and disorders'. The Book of Orders required the suppression of all superfluous alehouses in dearth years in the interests of preserving barley supplies. Other legislation fixed the price of ale and beer, forbade drunkenness and 'tippling' (sitting drinking in an alehouse for more than one hour in an individual's home township) and finally, in the Interregnum, the frequenting of alehouses on Sundays and fast days, while numerous local orders attempted to restrict the numbers of alehouses and to regulate the behaviour of alehouse-keepers and their customers.

All this was very well, but the problem remained that the populace at large was reluctant either to accept the law's definition of an offence in these matters or to enforce the law. Controlling the numbers of licensed houses was extremely difficult. Ale-sellers were generally drawn from among the village poor and the securing of an ale-selling licence could be a useful form of providing for them without bringing a charge upon the poor rates. Obtaining an alehouse licence for a distressed client was a common form of patronage and once a licence was given, the 'interest' of local gentlemen and village notables might be involved in its continuance. However many alehouses were licensed, numerous houses sprang up unlicensed, for ale-selling was a well-established by-employment of the poor which can be traced back in English village society to the thirteenth century. For all these reasons, involvement in the trade could proliferate to a quite astonishing degree, the more so in times of economic stringency. In surveys of forty Worcestershire townships conducted between 1634 and 1638 they were found to contain eighty-one licensed and fifty-two unlicensed houses. Twenty-five Essex townships surveyed in 1644 had fifty-five licensed and fifty-two unlicensed houses, while thirty Lancashire townships in 1647 had an astonishing eighty-three licensed and 143 unlicensed houses. This meant that these Essex villages had one alehouse for every twenty households, while in Lancashire there was one alehouse for every twelve. Clearly the laws were widely ignored.

As for the activities of alehouse-keepers and their customers, these did indeed include numerous minor disorders. Drunkenness, brawling, swearing, gaming, dancing and revelling were tolerated, especially on Sundays and holidays. Villagers haunted the alehouses when they should have been at church. Servants gathered in the alehouses, free from their masters' controlling supervision. Poor labourers sometimes drank their wages and left their families unprovided. Such disorders attracted the attention of magistrates and ministers, but they should not be exaggerated, and they must be placed in the context of a popular culture in which drink was the ubiquitous lubricant of popular sociability. The alehouses were the centres *par excellence* of the social lives of the common people, and to many the value of their services outweighed the problem of occasional disorders. On this issue Arthur Dent quoted the typical opinion of his parishioners: 'What I pray you, do you make it so great a matter if a man be a little overtaken with drink now and then? There is no man but he hath his faults: and the best of us may be amended.' Or again: 'If neighbours meete now and then at the alehouse . . . meaning no hurt: I take it to be good fellowship, and a good means to increase a love among neighbours; and not so hainous a thing as you make it.' Dent's reply to this 'objection' was characteristic of the authorities' perception of alehouse life: 'There is no true fellowship in it, it is meere impietie: if we may call it impietie for poore men to live Idlely, dissolutely, neglecting their calling, while their poore wives and children sit crying at home.' To moralists like Dent and to the many magistrates whom they influenced alehouses were conventionally dismissed as 'nests of satan', 'nurseries of all riot, excess and idleness', 'the fountains and well-heads from whence spring all our miseries', and rooting out these disorders was the very 'foundation of reformation'.[32]

Such alleged disorders could never be wholly eradicated. The moralists and magistrates, however, kept up their pressure, the former almost invariably building up their assize sermons to end with a ringing denunciation of alehouses and the latter instigating periodic purges of the ale trade. Urban authorities, anxious to extend greater discipline over the swelling, impoverished suburbs of the cities which sheltered numerous alehouses, often maintained sustained efforts to deal with the problem, though in the counties magisterial initiatives were more occasional. In the course of the early seventeenth century, however, a novel phenomenon appeared: parish and village officers also began to turn against the previously tolerated activities of their ale-sellers, and to act more regularly against disorders.

Action of this kind was not easy either to initiate or to sustain. Officers who tried it were courting unpopularity and they could be resisted in many ways: with informal sanctions of gossip and ridicule, with defensive petitions to the justices accusing them of acting only out of spite and malice against individuals, even sometimes with physical force. Not surprisingly, they sometimes failed in their attempts to extend control over their local alehouses. Whatever the outcome – and often they won – their activities are of some significance and their motivation worthy of consideration. In seeking to suppress alehouse disorders they were partly concerned to discipline the behaviour of servants and the poor (together with those who abetted and defended them) in the interests of preventing further impoverishment. But the most important aspect of their actions was perhaps less instrumental than symbolic; for in attacking the major centres of popular sociability they were dissociating themselves from the customary behaviour of their neighbourhoods and aligning themselves with a definition of good order and social discipline derived from their social superiors, from the sermons of their ministers and the 'charges' and orders which they heard at quarter sessions. That dissociation and realignment, that shift in perception, was expressed in the use of the machinery of social regulation to mark out new boundaries of permitted behaviour in their communities.

Implicit in developments of this kind was a new form of assent to the programmes of England's magistrates and moralists, and on occasion such a shift of attitudes was made explicit in petitions which expressed support for law, order and reformation and rejection of the behaviour of their disorderly neighbours. Such petitions generally came from small groups of parishioners who identified themselves in such terms as 'the inhabitants', 'the principall inhabitants', 'the best inhabitants', 'the honest neighbours' or 'the better sort'. They were often led by parish ministers and local officers and subscribed by yeoman farmers, substantial tradesmen and minor gentlemen. In their terms they echoed moralistic and magisterial statements on the problem of the alehouses, intermingling concern for godly and civil order with anxiety about impoverishment and resentment of the flouting of their own authority by their social inferiors. Petitioners from Manningtree in Essex in 1627 complained of alehouse-keepers who regarded 'neither Gods laws nor the kings' and were grown 'so Rusticall that for the better sort it is almost no living with them' and urged their suppression 'that so god may not be dishonored and that the officers may be encouraged'. The leading inhabitants of Flixton in Lancashire in 1646 complained of disorders which persisted in 'high contempt of ye ordenance of Parliament' and to 'the great grieffe of many godly people'. The inhabitants of Stock and Butsbury in Essex petitioned in 1629 denouncing the drunkenness and idleness of servants and poor men occasioned by the alehouses of the township and urging the justices to root out such 'styes for such swyne and cages of these uncleane birds', praising the 'most excellent lawes' passed by Parliament and condemning 'the slacknes of inferior officers and other inhabitants of parishes (where these evills abound) to informe the magistrates of the delinquents that such good lawes might be executed'.[33]

Petitions of this kind were by no means unusual, and they became increasingly common as the early seventeenth century advanced, reaching a peak during the Interregnum when many godly magistrates found themselves urged on in the task of reformation by petitioning groups of village notables. They represent the high water mark of success in the desire of the authorities of the day for greater order. The values of magistracy and ministry had found fertile soil among local notables who were prepared to endorse them and employ them to legitimize friction between themselves and their own social inferiors. In doing so, they cut through the tangle of loyalties and connections which might otherwise have inhibited action. They had learned to accept a stricter conception of order and having done so, they were ready to impose it.

The local institutions of justice and administration could thus be used not only to contain and resolve conflict between individuals within local communities, but also, increasingly, to express conflict between the interests and values of different social groups and to mark out and enforce new boundaries of permitted behaviour. The former phenomenon was general. People had much respect for the law and used it to settle their disputes. The latter trend was partial, but symptomatic of the tensions bred by some of the broader changes of the age. In the course of the earlier seventeenth century some localities did indeed develop tighter patterns of social discipline, signalled by a readiness to use the law and consolidated often by the subtler, less dramatic, sanctions of the poor laws. Elsewhere, however, such initiatives were temporary or even altogether absent. Where the problem of poverty (or rather the problem of the poor rate) did not assume serious proportions, where a large labour force of cottagers was to be welcomed by local employers, where the influence of reforming magistrates or ministers was not strong, then such innovations were less likely to be attempted at all. Yet elsewhere, innovations in social regulation might be tried, only to founder when they could not successfully be sustained. The larger the local population, the more scattered the pattern of settlement, the more even the distribution of wealth, the less developed the local structure of institutions, the less all aspects of local life from provision of employment to administration of the laws were in the hands of a tight local oligarchy, then the less likely it was that such innovations would succeed.

As a result of such variations of experience, local communities became to some extent differentiated between what later came to be termed 'closed' and 'open' parishes. The former were predominantly lowland, and fielden with highly concentrated landholding. They were small in area and population, nucleated in settlement and closely governed by parish oligarchs. The latter were either fielden villages with unusually dispersed landholding or else located in areas of extensive commons, in the forests, uplands and fens. In fielden regions they often served as reservoirs of labour for surrounding villages. Elsewhere, they were pastoral or industrial in economy, large, heavily populated, with dispersed settlement and looser local government. It is a crude typology, but one which contains much truth. As contemporaries well knew, it was in parishes of the former type that order was best maintained, both through the exercise of authority by magistrates, ministers and overseers, and through the existence of social conditions conducive to the establishment and maintenance of deferential relationships between superiors and inferiors. As for the inhabitants of the 'open' parishes, certainly they were often poor and they were not immune from government, but the different conditions of their existence and the more egalitarian structure of their communities helped preserve to them what their social superiors saw as a worrying degree of independence of spirit which they did not trouble to hide. In consequence they were much abused. Miners in the developing coalfields were seen as an almost savage race; dirty, ignorant, superstitious, improvident, drunken, immoral and unruly. They were described in the reign of James I as 'lewd persons, the scums and dreggs of many countries from whence they have bine driven', thieves, 'horrible swearers', 'daillie drunkerds' and 'notorious whoremongers', some allegedly having 'towe or three wyves a peece'. Clothworkers were considered 'of worse condition to be quietly governed than husbandmen'. The people of Pennine Lancashire were reported to be 'ignorant and careless', those of upland Northumberland to be 'as rude as the ground seems uncouth'. Woodlanders and forest dwellers in particular were singled out. To William Harrison they were 'ignorant . . . of any civil course of life'; to Norden they were 'naturally more stubborn and uncivill than in the champion countries'; while Aubrey saw them as 'mean people [who] live lawless, nobody to govern them, they care for nobody, having no dependence on anybody'.[34]

The existence of such variation and the persistence of such independence deserve emphasis, for they serve to remind us that the whole structure of order in the English provinces rested ultimately upon the basis of consent by the governed. Such consent (and the terms on which it was given or withheld) is most familiar to students of the period as a major theme of studies of the growth of resistance among the 'political nation' to the policies of Charles I, in the decades which preceded the constitutional crisis of 1640 and the outbreak of civil war. In the face of the threat posed by royal policies to their liberties, property and religion, the parliamentary gentry as a whole were ready enough to oppose the king by every legal means. In the final crisis some were willing to carry their opposition to the extreme of arms. Nor were these matters of significance only to the gentry, for the struggle of the 1640s also involved many of their social inferiors among the 'middling sort' who fought not simply as dutiful tenants but often as their own men defending their own cause. However, enough has been written of this in specialist political studies. What is of more concern to us here is the fact that the conditional nature of consent to authority extended also to the mass of the common people for whom the issues of the English revolution were of more limited significance. Whatever the achievements of Elizabethan and early Stuart local government (and they were sometimes considerable), the acceptance of authority by those who enjoyed 'neither voice nor authoritie in the common wealthe' depended not upon coercion, but upon assent. Such assent was not always fully or freely given, to be sure. It involved a frank enough recognition of the realities of power in society, and it more often took the form of passive acquiescence than that of positive affirmation. Nevertheless it was vital to the whole system; and just as justices or parish officers accepted, adapted or ignored the dictates of government according to their own lights when playing their part in the maintenance of order, so also the acceptance of their authority by the mass of the common people was partial and conditional. In the face of unpopular laws, they could ignore or evade them when they chose. But in a yet more fundamental sense, their acceptance of subordination fell short of a degeneration into submissiveness. It remained conditional upon the maintenance of certain reciprocal expectations between governors and governed. Deference was accorded in return for a reciprocal respect for particular rights and obligations. Where these conditions were undermined, the framework of authority could tumble with them. The result was riot.

Tumults and mutinies

Our period saw no major popular revolt on the scale of the Norfolk rising of 1549. It did, however, witness numerous riots. Indeed, it possessed an actual tradition of riot, a pattern of crowd action on the part of the common people, which is only now being fully recovered as a result of the research of such scholars as John Walter and Buchanan Sharp.[35] By 'riot', contemporaries meant the committing of an unlawful act by three or more persons assembled for the purpose, a legal definition which meant that many comparatively petty offences could be subsumed under the term. The more large-scale crowd actions with which we are concerned here, however, fell into two principal categories. First, there were food riots, involving the staying or seizure of foodstuffs by the crowd. Second, there were enclosure riots, involving the destruction of hedges and fences erected to restrict access to former common pasture land or to divide former common fields into compact, consolidated farms.

Food riots were particularly associated with years of harvest failure and resultant scarcity, though they could also occur as a result of the inability of unemployed industrial workers to buy foodstuffs in times of industrial depression. In years of particular difficulty they could be quite widespread – as in the dearth of 1630–1, when outbreaks of rioting were reported in Somerset, Wiltshire, Hampshire, Berkshire, Sussex, Kent, Hertfordshire and Suffolk. They were never, however, as widespread as is sometimes assumed. The records of the central government, which watched anxiously for outbreaks in times of particular difficulty, suggest that there were some forty outbreaks of rioting of this kind in the period 1585–1660. Essex, for example, witnessed ten known riots in the period, while in Kent such riots were very occasional, a flurry of disturbances in the 1590s being followed by a long period of quiet until renewed outbreaks in the 1620s and in 1630–1.[36]

Enclosure riots, in contrast, were less associated with particular years of distress. Their incidence related more to the local timing of agrarian reorganization, though on occasion riot actually occurred when a crisis such as a bad harvest year exacerbated long-standing resentment of earlier changes. Again, flurries of riots could occur when a particularly favourable opportunity seemed to present itself, or when rumours of action in one locality led to outbreaks of rioting in other places with similar grievances. Thus in the early 1640s as the structure of royal authority crumbled and during the early years of civil war, there were outbreaks of enclosure rioting in no less than twenty-six counties. In 1607 rioting spread across neighbouring areas of Warwickshire, Leicestershire and Northamptonshire in the 'Midland Rising', while in the years 1626–32 rumours of similar actions elsewhere contributed to the series of outbreaks in the royal forests of the west country known as the 'Western Rising'.[37]

We must be careful not to exaggerate the frequency of riots in England in this period. England was not a country seething with popular unrest. Nevertheless, rioting was sufficiently common in certain years to cause considerable unease to the governments of the period. Not surprisingly, the royal government tended to denounce all such actions as heinous examples of disobedience, threats to all order, authority and property and signal demonstrations of the anarchic propensities of the rude multitude. Its fears and protestations were given some colour by reported expressions of class hatred, worthy of Shakespeare's Jack Cade, on the part of rioters. The Somerset crowd which seized a load of cheese in 1596 was said to be animated by hatred of all gentlemen and by the belief that 'rich men had gotten all into their hands and will starve the poor', for example. It is doubtful how seriously such attitudes and reported utterances should be taken, however, for much of the drama of the government's statements and the crowds' menaces was indeed theatre. The government needed to present a stark portrait of the threat to order if it was to rally support among local magistrates and gentlemen, while the threatening postures of the poor were but a means to an end and very often no more sincere than their more accustomed postures of deference. Often it was no more than alehouse talk, but even when it was offered openly in defiance of authority it was belied by the actual actions of rioters.[38]

Riots in fact were very often more in the nature of controlled and remarkably disciplined demonstrations than abandonments of restraint on the part of the people. They defied authority, to be sure, but there was order in this disorder. In the first place, they presented no fundamental threat to the existing social order. Members of the crowd in the sixteenth and seventeenth centuries were animated by a coherent set of values and beliefs, but for the most part they possessed no vision of an alternative society to be built on the ruins of the old. Rioters were more limited in their objectives. They acted to defend what they regarded as their legitimate rights; rights which were threatened by the actions of unscrupulous individuals. These were not always legally enforceable rights, to be sure, but they were nonetheless valued for that. They were traditional rights, based on long usage, associated with particular patterns of established social relations and therefore possessed of a strong moral force.[39]

The most basic of these rights was the right to subsistence. This might be starkly presented in the actions of food rioters as the right to eat, to buy corn and cheese in the market place at reasonable prices, and not to be cheated by hoarders and speculators or deprived by the transportation of foodstuffs to other areas. It was less immediately visible, but no less present in the actions of other rioters who rose in defence of use-rights which were the bulwarks of their family economies against destitution. At Sydenham in Kent, for example, where over half the freeholders held less than five acres of land and two-fifths held only a cottage and garden, common rights were vital. When these were threatened, 500 householders protested that they were 'greatly relieved by the sayde common and would be utterly undone yf yt should be unjustly taken from them'. In the forests of Gillingham and Braydon in Wiltshire, cottagers who had no legal right to the use of the forests were willing to riot to defend their customary usage of the woodland commons, for they knew that both their livelihoods and their tenuous independence depended upon it. The fact that the disafforestation scheme provided for their compensation in the form of the setting aside of some of the newly enclosed land, the profits of which would be used for poor relief – and poor relief administered by those tenants who were better off and who accepted the enclosure of the commons – amply demonstrates what was at stake. Again, in the Forest of Dean in Gloucestershire, rioters tried to defend their traditional extra-legal mining rights which were threatened by the crown policy of leasing mineral rights to a single patentee.[40]

Rioters, then, acted always in defence of specific rights and customs which they wished to see respected and maintained. Both the timing and the geography of riots were shaped by the extent to which such rights were threatened at particular times and in particular places. Food riots in years of dearth or depression were commonest in the heavily populated industrial areas where large numbers of wage workers depended on the market for their supplies, in food-exporting areas where the local poor had to witness the transportation of food to which they believed they had a right, and in areas through which shipments of food passed on the way to the major urban markets. The counties surrounding London and Bristol and within the catchment areas of the food markets of those cities were peculiarly prone to outbreaks of rioting and, significantly, such outbreaks usually came on market days when local people found their markets ill-supplied or prices beyond their reach.[41] Enclosure riots were infrequent in counties such as Lancashire or Shropshire where plenty of common land remained and virtually absent in areas where there was little enclosure within this period. Trouble, however, came in parts of the midland counties where open fields were being enclosed either for pasture or for the introduction of convertible husbandry, in the fens and forests where drainage and disafforestation threatened to wipe out the commons, and in parts of the northern uplands where open hill-pasture was being enclosed by some landlords and common rights extinguished.[42]

By acting in defence of their perceived rights, rioters were defending a traditional order of their own. In doing so, they conducted themselves with remarkable restraint. Rioting was always a last resort. In the case of enclosure disputes, actual rioting was often preceded by appeals to the encloser, informal pressure to refrain from enclosing, anonymous threats and even litigation. Following the purchase of the manor of Willingham in Cambridgeshire by Sir Miles Sandys in 1601, for example, and his introduction of more rigorous estate-management policies, the tenants raised a joint fund to fight him at law over their common rights and to resist his enclosure of parcels of fen and common. In 1602, exasperated, they broke into an enclosed meadow and put in their cattle as a symbolic act of reclamation, an action which contributed to the temporary settlement of the conflict of interests between landlord and tenants by arbitration.[43] Again, in the case of food riots, actual outbreaks of rioting were usually preceded by urgent appeals and petitions to the local authorities whose duty it was to see the markets well-served and the poor relieved. Such appeals might include dark threats of what might come if popular grievances were not met – as when Wiltshire weavers pointed out in 1620 that 'to starve is woeful, to steale ungodly and to beg unlawfull, whereunto we may well add that to endure our present estate anywhile, is almost impossible'. Riot followed only if local justices proved either unwilling, unable, or too slow to take action. To this extent, rioting can be seen as a form of 'petitioning in strength and in deed'. As such it often worked in stimulating official action.[44]

If rioting was reluctant, it was also remarkably orderly. Violence against people was very rare and there were none of the atrocities associated with popular risings in France in this period. Indeed the crowds were frequently disciplined, assembling and marching in order, as in the Forest of Dean in 1631, when some 500 men 'did with two drummes, two coulers and one fife in a warlike and outragious manner assemble themselves together armed with gunnes, pykes, halberdes and other weapons' and set off to cast down enclosures. This looks like flat rebellion, but it is more likely that the rioters were simply employing the methods learned (and the equipment employed) at musters of the militia. Certainly they showed no desire to use their military strength, beyond firing off a few warning shots. Nor did rioters usually show much predisposition to fight, however well-equipped they were to do it. Their strongest weaponry was their sense of moral rectitude and this was clearly displayed in both the openness of their assembly and a strongly ritualistic element in their actions. The Dean rioters buried an effigy of their enemy, the patentee Sir Giles Mompesson, in one of his own ore pits. In other Forest of Dean actions and also in the Forest of Braydon, the riots took the form of 'rough music' or 'Skimmington rides', traditional forms of humiliation of moral delinquents. Elsewhere the overthrow of enclosures preceded ritual ploughing of land converted to pasture, or putting beasts into former common land, and the whole proceedings were sometimes rounded off with a bonfire. Indeed, some enclosure riots had an almost holiday atmosphere, which is the less surprising in that they frequently took place on traditional holidays.[45]

Not only were riots orderly for the most part, they were sometimes also legalistic. Loyalty to the king was sometimes stressed by rioters who did not wish to be misconstrued as rebels. Royal proclamations against enclosure or exploitation of scarcity conditions might also be cited as justification for action, and it seems significant that food rioters never attacked the rich in general, but confined their attention to the very middlemen in the victuals trade whom the government itself tended to blame for exacerbating distress in dearth years. Even then, the crowd did not always simply take food and make off with it. At Canterbury in 1596 rioters consulted an attorney's clerk as to the law before preventing grain from leaving the city, taking care 'not to meddle with the corn', and thus acting in accordance with proclamations restricting the movement of corn in time of dearth. Others in Somerset in 1629 stopped a grain shipment and returned it to its point of origin, then informed the nearest justice. Such actions displayed not so much a naive respect for the law as a canny ability to exploit its ambiguities. This could be shown in other ways too. Women were often prominent in enclosure riots in consequence of a popular belief that 'women were lawlesse, and not subject to the lawes of the realme as men are', while the destruction of fences and hedges was sometimes performed by two people at a time in hope of dodging the definition of riot as an unlawful act performed by three or more persons.[46]

For all this, rioters did defy authority. This did not mean, however, that they abandoned all respect for it. The conventional structure of authority might be retained in part, though obligations to recognize the authority of specific people had been repudiated. Sympathetic gentlemen might sometimes connive at, or even be involved in, popular action and the royal government appears to have preferred to believe that this was so in its investigation of particular disturbances, such as those in the western forests. It served to relieve its fear that the common people were capable of organizing resistance themselves. Such circumstances, however, were not common and enclosure riots were usually directed against the local landlord. On occasion clergymen or yeomen, the natural leaders of their communities, might take a leading part in enclosure disturbances, thereby preserving the conventional hierarchy of authority in truncated form. Nevertheless, if (as was increasingly the case) the yeomanry were not sympathetic, or were satisfied with the compensation they had received in enclosure agreements, then the poor could find leaders of their own. The history of riot provides not a few examples of such leaders: John Reynolds, alias 'Captain Pouch', who led the Midland Rising of 1607; 'Captain' Ann Carter who mobilized grain rioters at Maldon in 1629; Edward Powell, alias 'Anderson of the Fens', who led resistance to drainage and enclosure in Cambridgeshire; John Williams, alias 'Skimmington', one of the leaders of the Forest of Dean disturbances. The government liked to think of such leaders as agitators who seduced their followers from their due obedience to authority, but there is no reason to believe that this was so. Rather, they were carried forward on a wave of popular support. When asked who had incited her to riot, one of the women who supported Ann Carter replied simply, 'the Crie of the Country and hir owne want'.[47]

Riots, then, were not the desperate and bloody furies of a demoralized mob. Whatever their menacing postures, rioters were concerned with the rectification of specific grievances, and infused with a sense of justice and they conducted themselves with a quite remarkable degree of restraint. The authorities of the day, for all their rhetoric of 'tumults' and 'mutinies', appear to have recognized that this was so. Rioters were seldom severely punished – the fining or whipping of a few of those involved appears to have been the norm – and punishment was rapidly outweighed by authoritative action intended to satisfy the legitimate grievances of the crowd. Enclosure disputes commonly ended by being settled in the court of Star Chamber, often by arbitration, but usually in a form which preserved the interests of the enclosers and 'improvers'. Food riots generally resulted in the taking of swift action by the authorities to relieve want by putting into execution the relief measures customarily ordered in time of dearth. Such moderation in response complemented the moderation of the crowd and derived ultimately from the fact that the authorities, however inconsistent their actions at times, subscribed to the same set of values as those espoused by the common people. By such responses they regained a credibility which had been temporarily shaken and restored again the tacit understanding of reciprocal duties upon which the legitimacy of their authority rested. Such complacence, however, was within strict limits, for when the authorities were truly alarmed they could act with real severity. The Midland Rising of 1607 amounted to virtual insurrection and was put down savagely. The first Maldon food riot of 1629 was moderately punished, but a second outbreak was met with a commission of oyer and terminer which swiftly arrested and tried the leaders of the rioters and hanged four of them.[48]

When order seemed truly threatened, England's rulers were ready enough to maintain it by flat repression. What is most significant, however, is that they preferred not to, and that such exercise of naked power was rarely required. In the light of the frequently expressed fears of members of the governing class, it is indeed ironic that when a serious breakdown of authority in the state did occur in 1642, it was the result, not of the allegedly anarchic propensities of the 'beast with many heads', but of a struggle for power among England's rulers themselves. And despite the alarmist forecasts of nervous gentlemen, heightened by opportunistic enclosure riots, the descent into civil war was not accompanied by any major breakdown of the social order in the localities. Riot posed no lasting threat in a society in which few men imagined any alternative social order. It did however play its part in the establishment of the terms on which the common people gave their assent to the existing structure of authority. There was a strong element of negotiation in the tradition of riot which both rioters and the governing class understood. Riot was less a form of self-help than a way of demanding that certain legitimate rights of the common people be respected and that the authorities live up to the standards of their own paternalistic rhetoric. Surprisingly often, it worked.

Conclusion

Food riots were to continue to be a familiar phenomenon in England for more than a century after the close of our period, notably in the expanding areas of industrial production which had already been the principal sites of such action in the later sixteenth and seventeenth centuries. Enclosure riots, in contrast, gradually faded and died after the last major flurry of outbreaks associated with the civil war years.[49] The persistence and development of the former tradition of collective action bears witness to the continued vitality of popular attitudes towards the right ordering of the market in time of scarcity. Such concepts retained their relevance in communities in which a steadily growing proportion of the population was wholly dependent on wages and their purchasing power for its subsistence, and in which a widespread consciousness of common interest in the face of market fluctuations was reinforced by a continuing common experience. The dying away of resistance to agrarian innovation, however, suggests a fading consciousness of traditional popular rights and a declining capacity for collective action in their defence. Resistance, as might be expected, lasted longest in the loosely controlled and populous forest and fen areas where large populations of commoners had most to lose. Even there, however, the issue had been largely settled by the 1660s in favour of the 'improvers', though in some fenland and forest areas resistance spluttered on into the eighteenth century. In fielden areas, the gradual decline of the small tenantry left rural society increasingly polarized between two principal groups. On the one hand, there were the large yeoman farmers who now held the vast majority of commonable land. Whereas formerly such leaders of village society had often identified themselves with the cause of their neighbours, they had come to appreciate that their own best interests lay with enclosure and improvement. They realigned themselves accordingly. On the other hand stood the growing mass of agricultural labourers who had lost both their claim on the land and their capacity for effective common action. They rarely retained common rights, for they rarely possessed agricultural holdings. Nor were they in any position, dependent as they were on the good offices of the farmers for employment, housing and poor relief, to oppose piecemeal enclosure by agreement among their betters.

The history of riot thus provides evidence of a readjustment of attitudes, interests and social relations in English rural society which closely parallels the developments which we have already seen reflected in the changing use by English villagers of the local institutions of law and administration. In both cases the issue turned essentially upon the realignment of the vitally important middling group in rural communities, the yeomanry and minor gentry, the cocks of the parish. As the beneficiaries of economic change they had become increasingly distanced in their interests from their poorer neighbours. As the officers and representatives of their communities they had learned to identify themselves, albeit selectively, with the programme of order and social discipline with which the Elizabethan and Stuart state had attempted to contain, dampen and defuse the pressing problems of socio-economic change. Accordingly, the penetration of central government demands into the localities and the institutional development which accompanied that process became more than a defence of the existing social order; it became also a vehicle of change, a mode of expressing and furthering, within the forum provided by the law and local administration, the shifts in social alignments and relations which accompanied changing social realities. Of those realities, the most significant was the emergence of the labouring poor as a massive and permanent social problem; and it was in the modification of relations between the mass of the poor and those who employed them and who were charged with their government and their relief that the administrative innovations of the period left their most permanent legacy.

By the later seventeenth century, after the working through of the processes of adjustment and conflict in English local society which we have traced, two forms of equilibrium had been arrived at. On the one hand, there was that mixture of relief and control represented by the poor laws, providing in its balance of communal identification and social differentiation a powerful reinforcement of habits of deference and subordination. The deserving poor were to be relieved, the undeserving were to be disciplined, and the criteria of merit were defined for each locality by tight oligarchies of leading ratepayers, vestrymen and overseers. In London, as Dr Pearl has shown, relief was customarily granted 'on terms which explicitly enjoined behaviour in strict conformity to the *mores* of the ratepayers', a code which could be 'brutally indifferent to the wayward or their offspring'. It was much the same in many a country parish. At Tynemouth in Northumberland, the charity established by Gilbert Spence was 'carefully and warylie distributed . . . alwaies regarding that no part thereof be given to needles lewde and idel persons, nor to drunkards, swearers or any infamous persons notoriouslie detected of any vile or wicked crime'. At Terling in Essex relief given to the able-bodied poor under the terms of Henry Smith's charity excluded all persons already on parish relief and all poor who had not been settled residents for five years. In addition, it was stipulated that no part of the charity be given to poor people who were 'guilty of excessive drinkinge, profane swearing, pilfering and other scandalous crimes or are Vagrants or are Idle Persons or have been incorrigible when servants or do entertain inmates'. All those who received relief in clothing were to be given 'upper garments on the right arm of which shall be a badge with the letters H. S.'.[50]

In such communities, the coupling of generosity in relief with the demand for social conformity to new canons of respectability and the badging of the poor (which became national policy following an Act of 1697) enshrined and symbolized the social transition of the age. Elsewhere, however, a different situation prevailed. The fabric of order woven by Tudor and Stuart local government, as we have seen, frayed at the edges. There were whole communities where the drive for tighter social discipline had achieved only limited success, in which the rulers of the parish enjoyed only severely qualified authority, and in which social relations were characterized not by control and deference but by dissociation and mutual wariness. It was a stand-off, best expressed in the theatre of menace which was a central element in the continuing tradition of riot. This was an alternative outcome to the social processes of the day which could deeply affect the texture of local life. But it was no less a product of those processes than the outward order and theatrical deference of the closed parish. In 1667 the cottagers of Kingswood Forest, near Bristol, were described as a people existing 'without government or conformity in idleness and dissoluteness'. They were not 'responsible to any Civil officer or Minister for their behaviour or Religion' and lived 'in a lawless manner, almost every cottage selling Ale without lycence and keeping what rule they please and never going to Church and in pilfering and stealing'.[51] What is most striking in this description is the sense of shocked dissociation. The inhabitants of Kingswood had kept their independence, but at the price of being regarded by their betters as an almost alien culture. It is a reminder that the process of social differentiation of the later sixteenth and seventeenth centuries, whatever its outcome, was one not simply of economic interests or administrative efficiency, but of attitudes, of values and of social perception.

7 *Learning and godliness*

On Sundays in the later 1620s, the village of Eaton Constantine in Shropshire echoed to the sounds of music and dancing. In the mornings the aged parson would say common prayer briefly in the church – often employing a lay reader to read it for him, for his eyesight was failing – and 'the rest of the day even till dark night almost, except eating-time, was spent in dancing under a maypole and a great tree . . . where all the town did meet together'. Not quite every inhabitant gathered for this communal merriment, however, for near to the dancing place stood the house of Richard Baxter the elder, a yeoman freeholder of modest prosperity – 'free from the temptations of poverty and riches', as his son later put it. Baxter did not participate, for he was one of those who suffered 'the derision of the vulgar rabble under the odious name of a Puritan'. In his youth he had shared some of the ungodly pastimes of the day, being particularly given to gaming, but in later life he had undergone a religious conversion. In this experience he had owed little to the aid of the established church of England, most of the local clergy being 'poor ignorant readers and most of them of scandalous lives'. He was, however, a literate man and 'by the bare reading of the Scriptures in private, without either preaching or godly company, or any other books but the Bible', he had weaned himself from the customary behaviour of the neighbourhood and learned to adopt a stricter course of life. In his house Sundays were spent in reading the Scriptures, a godly exercise rendered difficult by 'the great disturbance of the tabor and pipe and noise in the street'. His son Richard junior, hearing the sounds of the revellers, often felt his mind 'inclined to be among them' and sometimes indeed 'broke loose from conscience and joined with them'. 'But when I heard them call my father Puritan,' he later recalled, 'it did much to cure me and alienate me from them; for I considered that my father's exercise of reading the Scripture was better than theirs, and would surely be better thought on by all men at the last; and I considered what it was for that he and others were thus derided.'[1]

Those Sundays were among the most formative experiences of the young Richard's life, remembered long afterwards when he had established himself as one of England's foremost and most respected nonconformist divines. As yet he had little inkling of the mysteries of salvation. His father's 'serious speeches of God and the life to come' had indeed possessed him with 'a fear of sinning', but though he was already acquainted with the historical books of the Bible, he 'neither understood nor relished much the doctrinal part and mystery of redemption'. That was to come later when, at 15, his soul was awakened by reading 'an old torn book' called ***Bunny's Resolution*** lent to his father by a day labourer who sometimes read the service for the parson, and his faith was advanced by reading Richard Sibbes' ***Bruised Reed***, bought by his father when 'a poor pedlar came to the door that had ballads and some good books'.[2] What he *was* conscious of was the profound alienation of his father's household from the customary culture of their neighbours, their withdrawal from that culture, that world of shared values, meanings and practices, and their seeking of an alternative guide to living in the word of scripture. It was an experience which was so to haunt Baxter as to make him in later life one of the most sensitive analysts of the growing cultural differentiation within English society which was one of the most significant developments of the age. For the course of social change in late sixteenth- and seventeenth-century England involved not simply the polarization of wealth and poverty, shifts in the profile of social stratification and changes in the quality of social relations within local communities; it involved also a novel cleavage in beliefs, attitudes and values and the development of bitter conflict over the symbolic forms in which they were expressed and embodied. In short, it involved cultural change. Change of this kind had its origins well before our century of main interest, and was to exert its influence long afterwards, but it was both accelerated and consolidated in the course of the late sixteenth and seventeenth centuries. Both its nature and its significance can best be appreciated by exploring the interconnected developments of our period in the fields of education and religion.

Educational opportunity and popular literacy

Few periods of English history can boast such a conspicuous enthusiasm for the benefits of education. It was a period of marked advance in the provision of educational facilities and a time of growing demand for education at all levels. To the founders of new schools and colleges it appeared that education would provide both an answer to society's ills and a guarantee of social well-being. It would train up good men, virtuous rulers and useful citizens in accordance with the ideals of the humanists. It would advance the Protestant Reformation by banishing ignorance and implanting knowledge of the truth. It would provide opportunities for the advancement of talented children from humble origins in an orderly process of social mobility. It would promote the prosperity of the commonwealth and strengthen the bonds of the social order.[3]

The educational imperative of the day was thus a powerful mixture of idealism and practicality and it proved to have an extensive appeal. At the pinnacle of the educational hierarchy the numbers of students attending the universities of Oxford and Cambridge and the Inns of Court in London rose dramatically in the course of the reigns of Elizabeth and the early Stuarts, so much so in fact that, despite the foundation of new colleges and the erection of new buildings, these institutions experienced severe problems of overcrowding. In the market towns and parishes of the countryside, endowed grammar schools multiplied. Some owed their foundation to single benefactors like Sir William Paston, who established his school at North Walsham in Norfolk in 1604, to the intent that young boys 'might become good and profitable members of the church and commonwealth', through being 'restrained of their overmuch liberty and . . . instructed as well in the principles of religion . . . as in the dutifull obedience and subjection to their naturall Prince and other Magistrates'. Others represented a more widespread popular initiative, as when 102 of the inhabitants of Willingham in Cambridgeshire raised the sum of £102 7s. 8d. between them in 1593 to endow their school, or when the inhabitants of Solihull in Warwickshire erected a schoolhouse for their schoolmaster in 1615, requiring him to instruct his pupils in 'the Church Catechism & in good manners, & to read write & understand English, Latin & Greek, & to cast Accompt the best he can', 'and that so farr as to fitt them for the University'. Where ambitions did not extend so high, there was a proliferation of petty schools, kept by a single master who imparted the skills of literacy to local children. Such schools were often held in the church and taught by the vicar, or curate, or by schoolmasters who passed on as soon as ecclesiastical preferment came their way. Accordingly they were commonly temporary or intermittent in existence. They were also, however, extremely numerous and their contribution was of the first importance, both in preparing children for the grammar schools and in providing a basic education for those who progressed no further up the ladder of educational attainment.[4]

This expansion of educational facilities was not a linear trend and it was not uniform across the kingdom. The growth of the universities suffered a temporary setback between the 1590s and the 1610s, for example, while student numbers suffered a severe decline from the 1670s onwards. Again, the provision of schooling in the provinces varied much from time to time and from place to place, and its expansion halted in the years after the civil wars. The overall achievement, however, was very considerable. By the 1630s, a more substantial proportion of the population than ever before was in receipt of higher education, while schooling of all kinds was available to an extent which had never before been experienced. Most market towns had a grammar school capable of preparing boys for the universities. In Kent half the parishes and townships of the diocese of Canterbury had a school at one time or another in the period 1600–40. In Leicestershire there were schools in twelve market towns and licensed schoolmasters in at least seventy villages in the same period. Some 52 per cent of the parishes of the midland diocese of Lichfield had a schoolmaster at some time between 1584 and 1642, while some 24 per cent had schoolmasters continually and probably had well-established schools. In Cambridgeshire in the years 1574–1628, twenty-three villages had schools, while a further nine had schoolmasters continuously and fifty-five more had schoolmasters from time to time. Only twenty-two villages are not known to have employed a schoolmaster at any time.[5]

Despite the setbacks suffered in the later seventeenth century, as both enthusiasm for education and activity in school-founding waned, the evidence of school foundation makes it clear that the period between the accession of Elizabeth and the outbreak of the civil wars had witnessed something of a revolution in the provision of educational facilities. Yet if there was an 'educational revolution', as Lawrence Stone has argued, it was one which was highly selective in its impact upon society. Educational provision expanded certainly; access to education, however, remained limited. Above all it diminished sharply as the social scale was descended.

This was for several reasons. In the first place education was costly. Even village schoolmasters had to be paid, and not all parents were either willing or able to meet the costs of even a basic education for their children. Nor were tuition fees the only problem, for even where these were waived, as was sometimes the case in endowed 'free' schools, parents had to face the expense of books, candles and writing equipment, while if a child was placed in a grammar school at some distance from his home there was board and lodging to be paid for too. (William Stout's father paid the considerable sum of £4 a year for his board when he attended the school at Heversham in Westmorland.) The higher the degree of education sought, the greater the cost. At the universities, boys from humble backgrounds might benefit from closed scholarships, or work their way through their training as 'servitors' or 'sizars', waiting upon their wealthier fellow students. But in order to have attained university entrance they would already have had to be maintained at school until their late teens – a formidable burden for any parent. As for the Inns of Court, they offered no such avenues of advancement for the poor student. Maintaining a youth at an Inn meant expenditure of at least £40 a year, a very sizeable slice from the annual income of even the more wealthy of English families.[6]

Such financial considerations were in themselves sufficient to place severe constraints upon the educational opportunities of children from all but the most prosperous of families. But fees and maintenance costs were not the only factors to be considered. Many families could not easily afford to forgo the benefits of their children's labour once they had reached an age at which they could contribute to their own livelihood, and this was a factor which could seriously affect both the question of access to education and that of the level of educational achievement. Many children sent to school spent only a very brief time there, while others had their education severely disrupted. Thomas Tryon, a tiler's son, was sent to school in his Oxfordshire village at the age of 5, but later recalled, 'I scarcely learnt to distinguish my letters before I was taken away to work for my living.' He was subsequently employed at spinning and carding and then as a shepherd until, at the age of 13, 'thinking of the vast usefulness of Reading', he bought himself a primer and persuaded his fellow shepherds 'to teach me to Spell, and so learn'd to Read imperfectly, my Teachers themselves not being ready Readers'. None of them could write at all, presumably because they had left school early, before they were taught this skill, which was customarily embarked upon only after the attainment of a reasonable reading standard. Accordingly Thomas, a determined youth, learned to write from a local schoolmaster at the cost of one sheep.[7]

Thomas Tryon's case was probably typical of many, though all too few possessed his strong motivation to seek a basic education. Even among more fortunate children similar factors could come into play somewhat later in their educational experience. William Stout's parents were fairly prosperous and 'very careful to get us learning to read as we came of age and capacity, first at a dame schoole and after at the free schoole at Boulton'. Nevertheless the labour needs of the family farm disrupted their subsequent education, for as William recalled, 'As we attained to the age of ten or twelve years we were very much taken off the schoole espetialy in the spring and summer season, plow time, turfe time, hay time and harvest . . . so that we made smal progress in Latin, for what we got in winter we forgot in summer, and the writing master coming to Boulton mostly in winter, wee got what writing we had in winter.'[8]

Circumstances such as these could clearly have very adverse effects upon the educational achievement of even those children lucky enough to be kept at school for part of the year and to attend schools kept by competent masters. Josiah Langdale, son of a Yorkshire yeoman, was another boy who 'made a little progress in Latin, but soon forgot it'. 'I had not time for much Schooling,' he explained, 'being closely kept to what I could do in our way of Husbandry.'[9] This was not simply a question of parental poverty or parsimony, however, it was also a matter of the perceived need for education on the part of parents. To the gentlemen who swarmed into the universities in the later sixteenth and early seventeenth centuries, education had become a social necessity and higher education a desirable means of shaping themselves to the fashionable pattern of the gentleman scholar. To the aspirant clergyman or lawyer, education was an essential professional qualification. To the would-be apprentice, a tolerably sound grounding in reading, writing and accounting was essential for future success in trade. To the average countryman, however, reading and writing were certainly desirable but not absolutely necessary, while additional skills might seem something of a luxury. 'We can learn to plow and harrow, sow and reape, and prune, thrash and fanne, winnow and grinde, brue and bake, and all without booke and these are our chiefe businesse in the country', opined Nicholas Breton's 'countryman'. To Thomas Carleton's father, a Cumbrian husbandman, reading was only part of his son's education, and perhaps not the greater part. Thomas described himself as 'educated sometimes at school, sometimes with Herding, and tending of Sheep, or Cattel, Sometime with the Plow, Cart, or threshing Instrument, or other lawful labor'. William Stout's father 'minded to get [him] *constantly* to schoole', only when it had been decided that William should be 'placed to some trade or other imployment'. Adam Martindale's relatives advised his father 'to take me off learning and set me to somewhat that might be me a subsistence; alledging too many instances of such as made no advantage of their learning, though they had been brought up so long to it as to be fit for nothing else'. Whatever the aspirations of contemporary educationalists, most parents who made stipulations for their children's education in their wills required only such education as was 'proper to their degree and calling' or else necessary for a specific purpose, such as apprenticeship. While basic literacy was clearly valued in itself, additional education was sought primarily as a means to some 'advantage'. Where no advantage was perceptible, it was the less likely to be either sought or sustained.[10]

As a result of these constraints, many of the children of poor families whose means were small and whose incentive to seek education was weak, received little or no formal education, even in villages where schooling was available. If they learned to read and write it was either at a very young age, with the risk of subsequently losing the skills, or informally. Children from more prosperous families were commonly grounded in basic literacy, but they were unlikely to proceed to the grammar schools unless they were destined for trade or for clerical careers. It is a situation well-attested by surviving lists of admissions to the endowed schools of the period. Of the eighty-six pupils at Bury St Edmunds grammar school in 1656, over half were of gentle birth, while the greater part of the remainder were the sons of clergymen, professional men or the wealthiest urban tradesmen. The rural 'middling sort' were little represented and there was not one pupil of truly humble origins, despite the fact that the statutes of the school required preference to be given to poor boys, provided they could read and write. Similarly at Colchester Free Grammar School, of 165 boys admitted in the period 1637–42, 31 per cent were sons of the gentry, 20 per cent of the clergy and professions, 37 per cent of wealthy tradesmen and only 12 per cent sons of yeomen. Husbandmen and labourers were not represented at all. Places in the endowed schools, then, were largely and increasingly monopolized by the rural and urban élite, a tiny proportion of the national population. What was true of these schools was even more true of the institutions of higher education. The student body of Oxford was fairly evenly divided between youths of gentle birth, most of whom did not actually take degrees, and youths of 'plebeian' origin who sought degrees as qualifications for clerical or professional careers. Few of the latter were of humble origins. Similarly at Cambridge, examination of the admission registers of four colleges reveals that some 33 per cent of students admitted were gentry children, 22 per cent sons of the clergy, 16 per cent sons of substantial tradesmen and only 15 per cent sons of yeomen. Moreover, as the seventeenth century advanced the social exclusiveness of the universities grew. Student numbers were to fall, but of those students who continued to enter the universities even fewer were of plebeian origin. As for the Inns of Court, their social exclusiveness was even greater throughout our period. Of the entrants in the period 1610–39, some 90 per cent were sons of the aristocracy and gentry, most of the rest being drawn from the highest ranks of trade and the professions.[11] Educational opportunity for boys was thus grossly biased by wealth. For girls it was doubly discriminatory. Access to the grammar schools and universities was closed to them whatever their rank, and though gentlewomen might be well taught by domestic tutors, few other girls were able to proceed beyond the attainment of literacy in a petty school, if that.

Inequality in access to educational institutions, however, is only one way of discerning the limitations which remained in educational opportunity and achievement within our period. Even more revealing is the evidence of adult illiteracy provided by the analysis of the ability of individuals to sign their names. This measure is now generally accepted as a good indication of the ability to read fluently, since writing, as we have seen, was taught only after the achievement of a satisfactory reading standard. The evidence of subscriptions to the Protestation Oath, taken in 1642, suggests that by this date adult men were still 70 per cent illiterate overall. While a decisive advance had been made in the education of the upper strata of society, the great majority of the English people were unable to read fluently. Moreover, those who had achieved literacy were drawn for the most part from the upper and middling ranks of the social scale. Analysis of ability to sign wills, marriage licence bonds and allegations, court depositions and other documents providing evidence of the social status of signatories, makes it abundantly clear that, while illiteracy had been annihilated among the gentry and very substantially reduced among yeomen and tradesmen, comparatively little progress had been made either lower in the social scale or among women. Gentlemen deponents in the ecclesiastical courts of Durham were still 30.5 per cent illiterate in the years 1565–73, but these illiterate gentlemen were for the most part older men. By 1626–31 the Durham gentry were completely literate. Leicestershire yeomen who had been 77 per cent illiterate in the 1590s were only 55 per cent illiterate by the 1640s. The husbandmen and labourers of Leicestershire who had been 87 per cent and 100 per cent illiterate respectively in the 1590s, however, were still 81 per cent and 96 per cent illiterate respectively in the 1640s. Educational expansion had produced not a literate society, but a hierarchy of illiteracy which faithfully mirrored the hierarchy of status and wealth. Ecclesiastical court depositions taken in East Anglia over the whole period 1580–1700 reveal that gentlemen deponents were 2 per cent illiterate, professional men entirely literate. Yeomen were 35 per cent illiterate and tradesmen and craftsmen 44 per cent illiterate overall (though within the latter category, achievement ranged between 6–12 per cent illiteracy for merchants and shopkeepers to 88 per cent illiteracy for poor artisans). Husbandmen, however, were 79 per cent illiterate, labourers and servants 85 per cent and women 89 per cent. While absolute levels of achievement varied from area to area and over time, the hierarchy of illiteracy is found everywhere. The conclusion is inescapable. The first great onslaught on popular illiteracy in English society had been so channelled and diverted by the varying ability of different social groups to afford schooling for their children and by differences in their perception of the value of literacy, as to produce a society markedly differentiated in terms of education. It is a telling commentary on the realities of the age that although more than 100 of the villagers of Willingham (many of them illiterate) had subscribed to found a school in 1593, analysis of their wills, and of the subscriptions to a common agreement made almost a century later in 1677–8, indicates that though overall levels of illiteracy had been greatly reduced, the improvement had been largely confined to the upper reaches of village society. In Willingham, as elsewhere, 'literacy and prosperity were very strongly related'. So, too, were illiteracy and poverty.[12]

Education and social change

The educational expansion of the later sixteenth and seventeenth centuries was thus severely limited in its social impact and no amount of enthusiasm over the progress of school foundation can disguise the fact. Its effects, both direct and indirect, were nonetheless of the first significance and it is these that we must now consider. Three aspects of the role of education in promoting social change stand out above all. First, the contribution of education to the development of a greater degree of cultural cohesion among the English ruling class. Second, the gradual incorporation of literacy into the popular culture of England. Finally, the notable expansion of the cultural horizons of at least one section of the common people.

Among the gentry and aristocracy, the sixteenth-century transition from elementary education by domestic tutors to formal education in the grammar schools and from education by service in aristocratic households to attendance at such central educational institutions as the universities and Inns of Court, contributed markedly to the growth of a homogeneous national culture among the English ruling class. For them the educational initiative of the age was less a question of access to basic education, for they had that already by the mid sixteenth century, than a matter of the nature and degree of education which they now received. In the grammar schools they received a largely standardized education in humanist rhetoric and religious knowledge of a kind formerly reserved, for the most part, to the clergy and a narrow cultural élite. In the universities and Inns of Court they rarely pursued the established curricula of studies with any assiduity, and still more rarely obtained degrees or legal qualifications. But they did acquire, in common with their peers, the general education in mind and manners considered appropriate to men of their station. At Oxford and Cambridge, the tutorial system evolved alongside the formal lectures of the universities as a means of meeting their special needs, and from their tutors they received a broad-based education in the classics, logic and rhetoric, history, theology and modern languages. Meanwhile, outside the walls of the colleges, additional facilities developed to cater for them. In Cambridge in the 1650s, for example, Bassingbourn Gawdy not only studied under his tutor's direction, but also learned French and mathematics from private teachers in the town, in addition to which he attended classes in fencing, dancing and riding. Facilities of this kind also grew up around the Inns of Court, to add further accomplishments to the smattering of legal knowledge picked up by gentlemen benchers, while the location of the Inns provided the further advantage of facilitating the introduction of young gentlemen to the delights and dangers of the capital. Finally, for those with a taste for them, both London and the university cities offered sermons aplenty in their numerous churches, the pulpits of which were occupied by some of the leading preachers of the day.[13]

The common experiences provided by the transformation of gentry education thus contributed much to the development of a degree of cultural cohesiveness which went over and beyond common consciousness of rank. Those of the lesser gentry whose education did not carry them outside the borders of their counties nonetheless experienced a common intellectual training. Those scions of more substantial landed families who resided, however briefly, in the central institutions of education, were enabled to consolidate and extend that training, while at the same time doing so in a context and among companions which promoted their self-awareness as members of a national ruling class. The cohesiveness and sense of identity, which the meetings of quarter sessions had helped to develop at the level of the county, were complemented and expanded at the level of the nation by the experience of higher education. As our period advanced, more people sought that experience. Whereas in 1584 only 48 per cent of the Members of Parliament had experienced education at the universities or Inns, by 1640–2 some 70 per cent of members had undergone higher education. In 1584, some 54 per cent of the active justices of Somerset and 50 per cent of those of Northamptonshire had attended a university or Inn or both, but by 1636 the respective proportions were 86 per cent and 82 per cent. Of the 247 heads of Yorkshire gentry families in 1642, 172 had been university educated and 164 had attended an Inn. Only after the 1660s, as the humanist ideal of the gentleman scholar gave way to that of the worldly superficiality of the 'man of quality', and as the universities became stigmatized by association with an outmoded learning, an unfashionable gravity and, by implication, the origins of the civil wars, did gentry involvement with formal higher education begin to wane.[14]

By then, however, the cultural transformation of the ruling class was essentially complete. The English intelligentsia had ceased to be a branch of the clergy and aristocracy, and had come to incorporate a significant proportion of the propertied laity. Some of them, indeed, became scholars of considerable distinction. Early seventeenth-century Kent could boast among its gentry such scholars as the astronomer Thomas Digges, the political theorist Sir Robert Filmer, the antiquarian Sir Edward Dering, with his library of over 200 volumes, and the classicist and Hebraist Sir Norton Knatchbull. East Anglia too had its share of such luminaries, while distant Yorkshire produced at least forty gentlemen who composed works for circulation among their families and friends. Among such men, county society could take on the aspect of a 'dispersed university', in Peter Laslett's phrase. Even among those whose intellects were less highly attuned and who lacked the polish of the cultured 'virtuoso', many had shared what Mervyn James has described as 'the experience first of assimilating and then of manipulating and using a generalized system of cultural standards and values'. That experience is evidenced in the libraries of the gentry, some modest, some remarkably extensive. It is discernible in the growing ease of expression demonstrated in their letters and in the common attitudes and values displayed in them. It is attested in the vigour with which they came to express their convictions and their grievances in 'generalized constitutional, religious or philosophical terms'.[15] The educational transformation of the ruling class cannot be held, as some contemporaries believed, to have caused the Great Rebellion of the 1640s. But it had a great deal to do with the manner in which the political and religious conflicts of the period were perceived, articulated and debated.

Lower in the social scale, the 'educational revolution' had equally significant effects, though of a somewhat different nature. However circumscribed the advance of popular literacy, there had nonetheless been a marked improvement in the educational levels of at least a section of the population at large. Moreover, this improvement, once set in motion, was one which contained the seeds of further development. England, as David Cressy has written, had become 'a partially literate society . . . undergoing transition to widespread literacy'.[16] It is the nature of that transitional process which must concern us. For crucial to the future development of popular literacy was the fact that within our period literacy had become incorporated into the very structure of the popular culture.

Overall levels of illiteracy were still exceedingly high, as we have seen, yet there were variations in the degree of popular literacy from place to place as well as between social groups. If we consider only the illiteracy levels of particular counties, as revealed in the Protestation returns, such variations may appear of little significance. The 117 Cornish parishes making returns had an overall male illiteracy rate of 72 per cent. For twenty-seven Huntingdonshire parishes the rate was 68 per cent, for forty-nine Nottinghamshire parishes 76 per cent and for thirty-one Sussex parishes 68 per cent. No distinctive regional pattern emerges. But there are two further observations to be made. First, the towns, as might be expected, were considerably less illiterate than the countryside. Five parishes in Chester had a male illiteracy rate of only 41 per cent, while the two London parishes for which usable returns survive had the remarkably low rate of 28 per cent. Clearly the conditions of urban life provided both the opportunity and the incentive to produce a wider spread of literacy even among the mass of the urban poor. Second, while county rates of illiteracy were generally within a fairly narrow range, the illiteracy rates of individual parishes *within* counties could vary enormously. In Cornwall, the worst parish for which we have evidence had an illiteracy rate of 92 per cent, but the best had a rate of only 54 per cent. In Essex, the worst parish had a rate of 82 per cent, yet the best had one of only 36 per cent. Comparable rates for Surrey were 91 per cent and 29 per cent, for Lincolnshire 94 per cent and 50 per cent, for Nottinghamshire 93 per cent and 27 per cent.[17] Doubtless such variations owed their existence to a host of local factors – the availability of schooling, the local distribution of wealth, the local occupational structure, the influence of individual clergymen and schoolmasters, for example. The important point to grasp, however, is that despite the gross overall social bias in the attainment of literacy, there were places, whether great cities or tiny hamlets, in which a much more widespread literacy had been achieved. Some husbandmen, artisans, labourers, servants and women *could* read and write.

The spread of literacy had not yet transformed the educational levels of the mass of the common people – that process was to take a further two centuries and to be achieved finally only with the advent of compulsory primary education. It had, however, made an initial penetration which went beyond the 'middling sort' of town and country who were its principal beneficiaries. In a very real sense, reading and writing had become established as part of the popular culture of England, skills everywhere apparent among some people and in some degree. Once put to use in a wide variety of social contexts, they became an increasingly familiar part of everyday experience. As this development proceeded, further advances in popular literacy were rendered not only possible, but probable, by virtue of the facts that people's lives were increasingly touched by literacy and that informal communication of the skill was rendered more possible. Nicholas Breton was certainly too patronizing when he put into the mouth of his 'countryman' the opinion that 'with us, this is all we go to school for: to read Common Prayers at church, and set down common prices at Markets; write a letter and make a Bond; set down the day of our Births, our Marriage day and make our Wills when we are sicke for the disposing of our goods when we are dead'. Even if it were so, these were matters of sufficient usefulness to impress upon people the value of literacy once they saw its skills regularly employed in such ways. The villagers of Ashton, who came to Roger Lowe to get him to write a letter to a sweetheart or relative, or to have him draft a bond or a presentment for the assizes, witnessed the value of literacy. The Durham husbandman John Taylor who suspected his half brother of trying to lay hands on his land by 'bringinge certain writeings to me which I could not certainly tell what they were . . . all which I did refuse to seale' knew the disadvantages of illiteracy. So did the Worcestershire constable who was so impressed and baffled by 'a leaf of paper written folded up', handed to him by a servant girl who had 'a purpose to be merry' at his expense, that he thought the hue and cry had been raised.[18]

By the early seventeenth century the unlettered majority of the English population were everywhere faced in one degree or another with the applications of literacy and the products of a literate culture. It was a situation admirably symbolized by the fact that some of the traditional products of the oral culture had come to be disseminated primarily by means of the printed word. The 'romances, fables and old tales' with which the young Richard Baxter was 'extremely bewitched', the 'old fables' like '*George* on horseback or *Bevis of Southampton*' which the young John Bunyan loved (and drew upon when he later came to write his *Pilgrim's Progress*), were introduced to them through the medium of the printed word. Again, over 3000 separate ballad titles were entered with the stationers' company between 1557 and 1709, most of them before 1675. They were sold by singers in the streets, by chapmen like the pedlar who called at Richard Baxter's home and at fairs and markets, and they sold in thousands. Nicholas Bownde, the Norfolk Puritan, complained that even the illiterate poor bought them and set them up in their cottages 'that so they might learne them as they have occasion'. In his opinion the advent of the printed ballad had actually revived and reinvigorated a dying aspect of the popular culture.[19]

In the hearing of tales and ballads, as in the making of wills and the writing of letters, the illiterate villager might well be content to rely upon neighbours and workmates or upon the services of the minister and schoolmaster. But how much better it was to have the skills oneself. Thomas Tryon, it will be remembered, was encouraged to learn to read when he considered 'the vast usefulness of reading'. He was able to learn informally because of the availability of help and advice from a group of semi-literate shepherds. Nor was he motivated by a single use of literacy. The motivation to learn was the stronger, as Thomas Laqueur has rightly pointed out, because reading and writing had become sufficiently deeply implanted in daily life to encourage people to seek literacy as a means of enabling them 'to function more effectively in a variety of social contexts'.[20] The advent of widespread popular literacy was to be a slow process, achieved against the odds by the mass of the population. The incorporation of literacy and its products into the popular culture of England, however, had set that process under way.

The educational achievement of the later sixteenth and seventeenth centuries, limited as it was, thus laid the foundations for further advance. But this was not its only significance. Literacy not only complemented and enriched the popular culture, it also assisted in the expansion and transformation of the cultural horizons of a significant minority amongst the common people.

Literacy was not simply a set of skills with numerous practical applications. For those who chose to use it to that end, it could be a means of breaking down the boundaries imposed upon the mental horizons of the illiterate by the limitations of their own experience and memories. Literacy could liberate the mind. There were those among the 'middling sort' of town and country who shared the educational experience of the gentry, generally with a view to advancement in clerical or professional careers. But even among those less fortunate, there is evidence enough of the development among some of a passion for print, an intoxication with the world of information and ideas opened to them by literacy. Adam Martindale who had been given an ABC by his godmother at the age of 6 and learned to read 'by the help of my brethren and sisters that could read and a young man that came to court my sister' became an assiduous reader and 'fell to reading the bible and any other English book'. His later determination to pursue formal education and eventually a clerical career grew directly from an altogether exceptional, and in the view of his relatives, inappropriate, intellectual curiosity. Thomas Tryon, having learned to read and write, became so intoxicated with the delight of reading that he sat up at night during his apprenticeship and carried his studies so far as to become deeply involved with contemporary medical and astrological writings. Roger Lowe was another apprentice who sat up reading at night. Arise Evans so loved books that while working his way to London at the age of 22, he stopped off for three months at Coventry 'by reason of an old Chronicle that was in my master's house that showed all the passage in Britain and Ireland from Noah's Flood to William the Conquerour'. 'It was a great volume,' he recalled with relish, 'and by day I bestowed what time I could spare to read and bought candles for the night, *so that I got by heart the most material part* of it.' During the particularly hard winter of 1683, William Stout was 'earnestly invited to sit by a good fire with the family', but preferred to busy himself in his master's shop, 'where, when out of necessary business, I passed my time in reading; or improving my selfe in arethmatick, survighing or other mathamatikall sciences. . . . And made some progress in *more than my present station required*'.[21]

Such assiduous readers were doubtless a minority, but they were a significant minority, and they must be placed in the context of a broader reading public which also had an appetite for information, albeit of a less rarefied nature. That this was so is amply evidenced in the growth during the earlier seventeenth century of the trade in almanacs, a kind of publication which formed a bridge between the popular and high cultures of the day and between the affairs of the localities and those of the nation. By the 1660s some 400,000 almanacs were being sold every year, enough to provide a copy each to two-fifths of the households in the kingdom. They generally cost between 2d. and 6d. and they were aimed at a market among the 'middling sort' of people. In them could be found a varied fare, including a calendar, information on fairs, roads and posts (often adapted to the needs of particular localities), farming hints, popularized scientific knowledge, historical information, sensational news, astrological predictions and, at the height of the genre in mid century, a good deal of social, political and religious comment. The almanacs alone could do much to extend the mental horizons of those who bought and read them. Some readers even used the blank sheets provided to keep diaries of their own, the content ranging from simple memoranda to entries evidencing a degree of introspection and reflection rendered the more possible by virtue of the skill of writing.[22]

Literacy could thus provide access to knowledge of many kinds, to the distant events of the day, to historical facts and interpretations, to the secrets of nature. It could also provide independent access to a body of literature which to many people was of even greater importance – to the Scriptures and to the proliferating vernacular literature of the English Reformation. One of the most striking features of the expansion of popular literacy is the extent to which the *initial* achievement of literacy among the common people was in excess of the functional necessity for the skills. Literacy had many applications, yet it was only as they became commonplace that these everyday uses of literacy acquired a significance sufficient to encourage parents to put their children to school and unlettered adults to learn to read and write. In the initial impulse towards literacy there was a further, quite specific motivation, and there is every reason to believe that this incentive was primarily religious. The growing vernacular literature of the age was above all a religious literature and the books possessed by the growing minority of testators whose inventories listed books were above all bibles, prayer books, psalm books and devotional works. The sale of primers and grammars, of chapbooks and almanacs may well have provided much of the bread and butter turnover of the increasing numbers of specialist booksellers to be found in English provincial towns, but the backbone of the trade was the demand for stronger stuff. The Warrington bookseller whose inventory, taken in 1648, listed over 1200 volumes had plenty of 'Home books', 'Plaine Primers' and 'Accidences' to guide the budding reader, and a fair selection of classical literature for the grammar school boy and cultured gentleman. He stocked Shakespeare and Cervantes too; but the heart of his stock lay in the 110 bibles, several dozen psalters and devotional works by Erasmus, Andrewes, Sibbes, Stubbes, Perkins, Robert Bolton, Thomas Shepherd, John Saltmarsh and a host of others.[23]

The possession and availability of such books does not, of course, prove that they were widely read, but it would be unduly cynical to assume that the 'Book of Martyrs, Eusebius and Josephus, with one great bible' possessed by a Westmorland Quaker family in 1679, or the old Bible and two small books listed in the inventory of a Petworth shearman in 1615 were merely status-enhancing accoutrements. On the contrary, we know that these books were commonly prized and read assiduously. Richard Baxter's father read his Bible and put his son to read 'the historical part of the Scripture' which 'greatly delighted' the boy. Josiah Langdale lost his Latin, but 'endeavoured however, to keep my English, and could read the Bible, and delighted therein'. In Henry Newcome's Cheshire parish in the later 1640s, 'the people came with Bibles, and expected quotations of Scripture'. Roger Lowe seized the opportunity when visiting a friend to spend a morning reading the 'Booke of Martirs'. Adam Eyre spent 1s. on a copy of John Saltmarsh's *Divine Right of Presbyterie Asserted*, published only a few months earlier, while on a visit to Halifax in

January 1647 and within a month had taken advantage of the enforced leisure of the winter season to spend three days considering its 'Arguments for Independency'. In March that year, he lent his neighbour Mary Greaves his copies of Saltmarsh's *Smoke in the Temple*, published in 1646, and William Dell's collected sermons, while borrowing a copy of Tobias Crisp's sermons from her and a copy of John Archer's *Personall Reigne of Christ upon Earth* from another neighbour.[24]

The newly literate 'middling sort' of England, together with the minority of their social inferiors who had learned to read and write thus constituted a reading public from the first. More specifically, they constituted a series of overlapping reading publics, which taken together provided the mass market for the enormous and variegated outpouring of printed matter which followed the collapse of effective government control of the press in 1640. Some might content themselves with ballads, fables and almanacs. Some, like Bunyan or Vavasour Powell, might graduate from romances, newsbooks and the like, to stronger meat. Adam Eyre's little library covered the range from almanacs and Dalton's *Country Justice* through Raleigh's *History*, a work on *The State of Europe* and Foxe's 'Book of Martyrs' to the puritan tracts and sermons which he exchanged with his neighbours.[25] Whatever the case, reading had come to involve people of middling rank throughout the nation more closely and directly with the currents of contemporary social, political and religious ideas. As that involvement grew, notably in the heady days of the civil wars and Interregnum, the appetite for print grew with it. It was a development which might make some of them merely more informed followers of the lead of their social superiors and religious teachers, but it could also have further effects. Where new ideas, new alternatives of thought and new models of behaviour came into conflict with local custom, they could promote a degree of cultural differentiation within local communities of an altogether novel type. Again, where readers became sufficiently informed and confident in their judgements and were drawn to consider alone matters formerly communicated to them only through intermediaries among their social superiors and religious mentors, they could strike out for themselves. All of these possibilities were to be most clearly demonstrated in the field of religion.

Religion and magic

In 1580, England had been a Protestant kingdom for almost a generation. It was not yet, however, a reformed nation. While initial conformity to the Protestant settlement of 1559 had been fairly rapidly established, the greater and more fundamental task of bringing home the teachings of the Reformation to the mass of the population remained unfulfilled. 'Three parts at least of the people', complained a puritan document in 1584, were 'wedded to their old superstition still'. This was not to suggest that they remained practising Catholics, though a tiny minority did. It was to assert rather, that the Anglican Church had not yet succeeded in its primary duty of transforming the devotional habits of the common people. The Church of England, like the reformed churches of Europe and the post-Tridentine Catholic Church itself, still faced the task of transforming what John Bossy has termed the 'collective Christians', inherited from the medieval church, into the individual Christian believers of the post-Reformation ideal. Protestantism was a religion of the word. Accordingly, religion as a system of ingrained observances, as a 'ritual method of living', in Keith Thomas's phrase, must give way to a religion based upon the internalization of a specific set of theological beliefs and expressed in the conforming of the individual life to the scriptural laws of God.[26]

It was no easy task. For if the reformed church had adopted a single image of the road to salvation and a purified model of devotion, rejecting the syncretic accretions and the 'blind formality' of medieval religion, its pastors faced a people far more eclectic in its beliefs and more inclined to respect than to reject its customary beliefs and practices. In part it was a problem of the persistence of Catholic and sub-Catholic rituals and devotions among a people for whom the efficacy of those religious rituals, which it valued, depended upon a continued adherence to traditional forms. In Lancashire in 1590, a county where the hold of the Anglican Church was at best tenuous, even apparent Anglicans had their 'beades closely handeled' in church and insisted upon traditional rituals at baptisms, weddings and funerals: holding wakes, transposing the wedding ring from finger to finger at the naming of the persons of the Trinity, and asking for the triple submersion of the child. They were also in the habit of crossing themselves 'in all their actions'. In Cleveland it was reported in the 1580s that 'when any dieth, certaine women sing a song to the dead body, recyting the journey that the parte must go' – doubtless the Lyke Wake Dirge, a song riddled with pagan imagery. Elsewhere in the north there was continued reverence for ancient crosses, or even their sites, and burial parties on their way to the church might circle them sunwise before passing on their way. Such survivals might perhaps be expected in what Sir Benjamin Rudyerd later called 'the utmost skirts of the North where the prayers of the common people were more like spells and charms than devotion'. However, similar practices were not uncommon elsewhere. Holy wells were still venerated, saints were still respected and appealed to, and numerous calendrical rituals survived which were not only occasions of festivity and merriment, but also credited with preventive or prophylactic power.[27]

Mere persistence of habit, however, was not the only problem. For in their continued adherence to traditional rituals and observances, the people were demonstrating an understandable reluctance to part with any agency which afforded them reassurance, protection, support and comfort in the face of a hostile environment and the unpredictable whim of supernatural powers. While they might respectfully accept the explanations of the nature of the spiritual world offered to them by their formal religion, few saw this as incompatible with supplementary beliefs. They were primarily concerned less with the path to salvation in the next world than with coping with the dangers and misfortunes which beset them on earth. This attitude opened the door to the coexistence of overlapping systems of belief and to the continued vitality of numerous practices which, in their preoccupation with the mechanical manipulation of unidentified supernatural 'power', can best be described as magical.[28]

It is in the nature of their approach to the explanation and relief of human misfortune that the beliefs and attitudes of the mass of the common people can be most sharply distinguished from those of their religious teachers. To the Reformation theologians, the daily events of life were not random. All happenings, all blessings and misfortunes, reflected the workings of the providential purposes of an omnipotent God. Accordingly, they instructed their flocks to see in misfortune the judgement of a just God upon their sins or the testing by God of the faith of the godly. Alternative explanations of misfortune, in terms of the operation of good or evil spirits, the neglect of omens and observances, the caprice of fortune or the malice of those with power to curse and ban, were played down if not actually denied.

Providence provided the godly with a coherent explanation of the ups and downs of daily life. In their diaries they noted the everyday course of God's providences to them. Adam Eyre was providentially preserved from a falling chimney stack. Ralph Josselin's daughter was saved by God's providence from serious hurt when she was struck by a horse. It was a flexible doctrine; but it could be a hard one. Often enough the purposes of God could seem strange, and his judgements out of all proportion to the sin of the persons on whom he visited them. The death of Adam Martindale's second son John, named after an earlier child who had also died young, troubled the Martindales, 'fearing lest we had offended God by striving with his Providence to have a John'.[29] It was a doctrine which provided no sure means of relief save by prayer and repentance. Moreover, it was an explanation of misfortune which posed a fundamental threat to the self-esteem of the sufferer, the more so to those of the poor whose constant insecurity and deprivation could be interpreted at best as a testing of their faith and at worst as a judgement on their unworthiness.

Accordingly, the appeal of the providential theodicy was limited. Many preferred other, older explanations, less coherent, to be sure, 'made up out of the debris of many different systems of thought', as Keith Thomas has put it, but powerful in their attraction. Misfortune was attributed not so much to the judgements of God as to ill-luck at best, or at worst the malign practice of witchcraft. Comfort in adversity was found less in prayer and earnest reformation of life than in simple stoicism or in the mechanical rituals of counter-magic. The ministry of the word held no monopoly of guidance and consolation, but was flanked by the shadowy ranks of diviners, astrologers, 'wise women' and 'cunning men'. Such ritual manipulation of supernatural power was wholly incompatible with orthodox divinity. God was to be supplicated, not commanded, and to tamper with magic could only be to sup with the devil. Nevertheless, villagers would travel miles to consult a respected cunning man at a time when distances of two or three miles over bad roads were considered a sufficient excuse to neglect the unfamiliar ideal of weekly attendance at divine service. The reason was simple enough. Magic catered for needs which were still felt, but which were no longer met by a 'purified' church.

The strength and ubiquity of magical beliefs is best evidenced in the numerous records of witchcraft trials.[30] Witchcraft in England was not primarily associated with the worship and service of the devil, though some educated contemporaries saw it as such, and the witchcraft statute of 1604 makes reference to the diabolical compact. Both the law and popular attitudes were far more concerned with simple 'maleficium', the power to do harm by use of unidentified supernatural powers. Witchcraft was not employed as an explanation of all misfortunes; general or national disasters were accounted for by the judgement of God, or the machinations of such bogeymen as the papists. Where an individual was conscious of having sinned, a providential explanation might be adopted. Witchcraft was reserved above all as an explanation of individual misfortunes in which the particular event could be linked to the known malice of a neighbour, yet for which there was no obvious natural explanation. The classical circumstances of a witchcraft accusation were those in which a quarrel between neighbours, often accompanied by threats or curses, was succeeded by the occurrence of an inexplicable misfortune. Thus, in 1616, Mary Smith of King's Lynn was accused mistakenly by Elizabeth Hancocke of stealing a hen. Mary, who already enjoyed a bad reputation in the neighbourhood, retaliated by calling her accuser 'proud Jinny' and 'wished a pox to light upon her'. Within hours Elizabeth was mysteriously taken ill and continued bedridden for three weeks. Her father then visited a cunning man, who confirmed that his daughter was bewitched, purported to show him the face of the witch in a glass, and provided him with a recipe for 'witch cake' which successfully counteracted the spell. Elizabeth recovered and later married, but within the year, following a further quarrel between her husband and Mary Smith, she had a recurrence of her malady. This time a court case was brought. Other accusers appeared with similar accusations and Mary Smith, who confessed herself to have been brought to witchcraft by the envy of her neighbours and the temptation of the devil, was hanged in January 1617.[31]

In the first half of our period there were many such accusations heard in English courts. The peak of prosecutions was reached in the last two decades of the sixteenth century and cases continued to be brought regularly in the first decades of the seventeenth century. Thereafter, their incidence fell off rapidly. Those accused of witchcraft were usually women. They were commonly old and often widows. They were almost invariably neighbours of their accusers, and they were usually of lower social status than those persons who they were alleged to have harmed. The quarrels which triggered suspicions of 'maleficium' were commonly the result of breaches of charity or neighbourliness – the turning away of an old woman who had come to beg or borrow from a neighbour being a common pattern. In the light of these facts, it seems probable that the rising tide of witchcraft accusations in the latter part of Elizabeth's reign provides yet further evidence of the tensions and conflicts generated within local communities by the broader socio-economic pressures of the day. Such tensions were not in themselves new; nor were witchcraft beliefs. But the convergence of socio-economic trends, which accentuated conflict between neighbours, with changes in the willingness of the church to provide protective or counter-magic, made possible the peculiar concern with the offence demonstrated at the turn of the sixteenth and seventeenth centuries. Witchcraft trials thus offer both an oblique indicator of the process of social change in the English localities, comparable to that provided by other forms of criminal prosecution, and striking confirmation of the existence of complexes of popular beliefs which carry the historian deep into an alien mental world. As Alan Macfarlane has written, the confessions taken in the course of witchcraft cases reveal that 'overlapping with the ordinary physical world was a sphere inhabited by strange, evil creatures, half-animal, half-demon. A world full of "power" both good and evil'.[32] Nor can it be dismissed as the fantasy world of a deluded minority for it was fully credible not only to the accused witches themselves, but to the neighbours who denounced them, the magistrates who examined them, and the judges who sentenced them.

The existence of this alternative world of belief and practice did not escape the reforming ministers of the day. For the most part they shared the popular belief in the possibility of witchcraft. Their opposition was to the continuance of magical practices and this, together with the persistence of traditional forms of devotion, they attributed above all to the gross ignorance of the common people in matters of faith. Such ignorance could be formidable indeed. In 1598 one Essex minister complained that the formal religious knowledge of half the population would disgrace a 10-year-old child and alleged that 'the poor people do not understand as much as the Lord's Prayer'. A little later, Nicholas Bownde, a Norfolk preacher, claimed that the people knew far more of the adventures of Robin Hood than they did of the Scriptures. 'They are utterlie ignorant in and never so much as have hard before of many textes that are alleaged in the sermons', he declared elsewhere, '. . . Nay the common stories of the bible they are unacquainted with: feare them with this or that judgement executed . . . comfort them with such a mercie shewed . . . it moves them not; they are altogether strangers in these matters.' In 1602 another minister argued that in parishes lacking preachers the people were as ignorant as heathens, citing his experience that in one parish of 400 souls, not one in ten had any knowledge of basic Christian dogmas.[33]

Such allegations are perhaps to be taken with a pinch of salt, for the standards of these ministers were high. What primarily concerned them was less ignorance of the words of the Lord's Prayer, or the details of Bible stories, but the general lack of 'saving knowledge', of the precise content of doctrine and of the straight and narrow path to salvation. It was not so much that the people stood outside the world of orthodox religion. Some of them may have done so, especially in areas of heath, forest and fell, lamentably badly served by the church. But most did not. They thought of themselves as Christians and valued some of the services of the church greatly, notably the sacraments of baptism and burial. The problem lay rather in the quality of their religious lives.

William Perkins maintained that they held too many 'erronious and foolish opinions' which were 'flat against the true meaning of the law of God', such as, 'I. That they can love God with all their hearts, and their neighbours as themselves; that they feare God above all, and trust in him alone; and that they ever did so. II. That to rehearse the Lord's praier, the beleefe, the tenne commandements (without understanding of the words and without affection) is the true and whole worship of God.' Feeling themselves secure 'because their mindes are forestalled with this absurd conceit that they are not in danger of the wrath of God', they were content to take their standards of behaviour not from the law of God contained in scripture, but from the more familiar canons of good neighbourliness. They thought 'that if they have a good meaning, and doe no man any hurt, God will have them excused both in this life and in the day of judgement'. It was a general analysis endorsed by Arthur Dent, who agreed that 'the common sort of people thinke indeed that all religion consisteth in the outward service of God'. He vividly illustrated his case in his remarkable book *The Plaine Mans Pathway to Heaven*, published in 1601 and later recommended by Robert Bolton as showing the common people 'excellently laid out in their colours'. The book takes the form of a dialogue between a minister, an 'honest man' and two villagers who meet them while on their way to buy a cow for £4, 'a great price'. In the course of the conversation, the improbably named villagers, Asunetus and Antilogon, duly equate devotion with repetition of the Creed, the Lord's Prayer and the Commandments and the saying of their prayers at night in bed. Godly living is to 'say no body no harme, nor doe noe body noe harme and do as he would be done to'. When Asunetus, broken down by the minister's searching questions, realizes at last that he is in danger of damnation, Antilogon exclaims: 'Damned man, what speak you of damning? I am ashamed to heare you say so, For it is well knowne that you are an honest man, a quiet liver, a good neighbour and as good a townsman as any in the parish. . . . If you should be damned I knowe not who shall be saved.'[34]

Our sympathies may lie with the hapless villagers, but those of contemporary divines, and especially the puritan preachers who formed the vanguard of militant Protestantism, did not. 'So long as they live in ignorance', wrote Perkins, the people lived 'either of custome, or example, or necessitie, as beasts doe, and not of faith: because they know not God's will touching things to be done or left undone'. Ignorance bred profaneness of life. It allowed people to continue to believe 'that a man may seek to wizzards and soothsayers without offence, because God hath provided a salve for every sore'; that blasphemous swearing was no sin; that fornication was 'but the tricke of youth'; that pride was 'but a care of honestie and cleanlines'; that covetousness was 'but good husbandry'; that 'a man may doe with his owne what he will and make as much of it as he can'; that working, sporting or revelling on Sundays was not offensive to God; that drunkenness and alehouse haunting were 'good fellowship'; that the upholding of popular festivities of manifestly pagan origin was a thing indifferent; that sober godliness was 'affected preciseness'. A people ignorant was a people unreformed.[35]

The godly and the multitude

The task of reformation was daunting, but it was not one which could be shirked. Indeed, it was rendered the more urgent by the common belief of England's Protestant divines that they were living in the last days of the world. The latter days were a time of iniquity. Antichrist was loose in the world, and the godly were enlisted in a cosmic war between light and darkness, Christ and the devil. In this momentous struggle, England was deemed to have a special place, for the historical justifications which had been produced to legitimize the very existence of the Church of England had succeeded in grafting on to the already fierce nationalism of Tudor Englishmen the notion that the English were the chosen people of God. John Foxe, in his *Acts and Monuments*, the famous 'Book of Martyrs', had demonstrated that God's Englishmen had ever stood in the forefront of the Lord's battles. (A grateful government ordered a copy to be placed in every parish church.) If the English, under their godly prince, were God's elect nation, then they should be active, standing forth like Joshua for the Lord. To fail in this duty was plain apostasy. The Elizabethan preacher Christopher Fetherston wept to consider 'with what blessings the Lord hath endowed us above all nations, and howe wee by our lewed and wicked lives doe more dishonor him almost then any other nation'. To continue to do so was to court disaster, for England's God was a jealous God, ever ready to pour forth his wrath on an unreformed and sinful people by visiting them with his judgements of dearth, pestilence and the sword.[36]

Reformation was a divinely imposed duty which the English could shirk only at their peril. Accordingly, the appeal for reformation was to echo from the pulpits for the better part of a century, reaching a crescendo in the time of the civil wars and Interregnum. It was an aspiration, however, which the Elizabethan church was initially ill equipped to realize. In the immediate aftermath of the Protestant settlement, it suffered from a severe shortage of manpower which took time to overcome. In 1576, some 14 per cent of the church livings in Lincolnshire were still vacant, while as late as 1610, thirty out of the eighty-five chapelries which served the needs of Lancashire were unmanned. Nor were the clergy always adequate to the task of implanting the saving knowledge of the gospel. Of 396 clergymen, tested for their knowledge of the Scriptures in the Archdeaconries of Lincoln and Stow in 1576, only 123 were found to be adequately qualified for their duties, while in the Archdeaconry of Leicester in the same year, only twelve out of ninety-three clergymen were 'sufficient' in scriptural knowledge, many of the remainder being regarded as 'mere ignorant' and some as 'utterlie ignorant'. In the Archdeaconry of Chichester in 1585 only thirty-five of the 120 clergy were able or willing to preach to their flocks. By the standards of the day this was not too bad. Lancashire south of the Lune had only twenty-three preachers to serve its 102,500 communicants, and of these only seven were 'able and painfull' men, while Northumberland never had more than three or four preachers throughout the 1580s and 1590s. If this were not sufficiently disturbing, too many of the clergy lived lives too closely akin to those of their flocks to make them suitable instruments of reformation of life. George Dobson, vicar of Whalley in Lancashire, can serve as an example. He was twice in trouble with the bishop for drunkenness in the later 1570s and was described as being too much given to participation in dancing competitions 'with a full cup on his head, far passing all the rest – a comely sight for his profession'.[37]

The inadequacy of the clergy should not be exaggerated. Few clergymen were truly scandalous in their lives. Again, deficiencies in the standard of clerical education are partly attributable to the fact that many of them had been trained for the performance of an essentially sacerdotal role rather than for the educational and pastoral role now demanded of the Protestant clergy. Nevertheless the state of the clergy undoubtedly inhibited the progress of reformation. Nor was the task of improving clerical standards made any easier by the fact that many clerical livings were so poor. In 1585 Archbishop Whitgift reckoned that only some 600 of England's 9000 livings were adequate for the proper support of an educated minister. The problem was that the tithes of many parishes had been impropriated by laymen (62.6 per cent of those in the province of York and 40 per cent of those in the province of Canterbury) who enjoyed considerable revenues from these tithes but left only a pittance for the vicar. Thomas Mychell of Ridgwick drew £100 a year from the tithes of Goring in Sussex, but left only £7 for the vicar's maintenance. It was perhaps an extreme case, but many vicars lived on pittances or gave up their time to other employments in order to live. William Harrison refuted the charge that the 'thred-bare' gowns of the clergy were the price of their having taken so enthusiastically to clerical marriage. They were, he argued, the fault of greedy patrons 'for such patrons doo scrape the wooll from our clokes'. The sufferings of the beneficed clergy were even more acute for their curates. In the Archdeaconry of Chichester in 1585 many curates were forced to support themselves as husbandmen, fishermen, tailors, weavers and the like.[38]

Poverty encouraged pluralism and pluralism led to non-residence, two further charges frequently levelled against the clergy. But even where the churches were staffed, in some areas the parochial structure of the church was wholly inadequate. Cheshire had 500 townships but only seventy parishes. Weardale and Teesdale had only one parish church and one chapel each. In Lancashire, only eleven parishes corresponded to single townships, and some parishes were vast: Whalley covered 180 square miles, Lancaster 100 square miles, Blackburn, Eccles and Rochdale 70–80 square miles each. Nor was it only in the 'dark corners' of the north that such conditions existed. The parochial structure of much of Kent was dense, yet Cranbrook parish in the Weald, with some 2000 communicants in 1597, contained five distinct hamlets, not to mention many isolated farms and cottages. Some of the parishioners were five miles from their church, along lanes which were regarded as virtually impassable in winter.[39] Clearly in parishes of this kind, the exercise of close pastoral care over the local population was virtually out of the question for even the best intentioned of ministers.

In the face of the conspicuously unreformed nature of the people and the manifest deficiencies of the church, two complementary though distinguishable strategies for improvement had emerged by the beginning of our period. On the one hand, the ecclesiastical hierarchy sought to improve the quality of the clergy and to lay greater stress upon their pastoral duties, while at the same time using the machinery of the church courts to enforce ritual conformity, to regulate the more dubious of popular ritual observances and to punish moral lapses among the population at large. On the other hand, the sterner puritan divines, who were the most enthusiastic proponents of godly reformation, proposed a strategy which was much more forthright in its recommendation of a blend of punishment and preaching, of 'sword' and 'word'. While they did not ignore the ecclesiastical courts, they called also for the passage of severe laws against sin and for their enforcement with the aid of the secular magistrate. The more ungodly features of popular culture were to be eradicated rather than contained, while at the same time every effort must be bent to the creation of a powerful preaching ministry.

Throughout the first half of our period these two initiatives proceeded side by side. Although none of the problems of the church were fully solved, a good deal was achieved, notably in the improvement of the quality of the clergy. Much ecclesiastical patronage remained firmly in the hands of the laity, but bishops were able to insist upon a higher standard among candidates for the ministry, while lay patrons themselves often took pains to procure good men for their livings. In Lincolnshire, Warwickshire, Wiltshire and Sussex, the years between 1580 and 1630 saw marked, though gradual improvements in the numbers of clergy, their educational qualifications and their willingness and ability to preach. In the diocese of Worcester, where in 1580 only 23 per cent of the clergy had degrees, 52 per cent were graduates by 1620 and 84 per cent by 1640. Efforts were made to improve clerical stipends, commonly through the piecemeal activity of pious laymen and patrons, though there was a more systematic attempt on the part of the puritan 'feoffees for impropriations' to buy up tithes and use them to augment the livings of godly preachers. Pluralism and non-residence were reduced, while attempts were made to supply preaching ministers and places of worship in areas inadequately served by the church. In the north the early seventeenth century saw the building or rebuilding of chapels of ease in vast upland parishes and their endowment by pious benefactors. Meanwhile, numerous 'lectureships' were established to increase the availability of preaching, commonly in market towns where market-day lectures might reach a broad audience of visiting countryfolk.[40]

By the 1630s the English church had witnessed the emergence of a resident, graduate clergy. It was a development of considerable importance. Many parishes now contained a resident intellectual for perhaps the first time in their history. The quality of the new clergy, of course, varied, but many were highly learned men, to judge by their libraries, and most were at least in touch with contemporary religious debates. Moreover, they were men trained to see their role primarily as one of pastoral care. Whether puritans or not, many were concerned to improve the standards of religious knowledge and moral conduct of their flocks; and they were the better placed to exercise this role in that many of them were now both socially and culturally distanced from their charges in an altogether novel way. The new clergy were commonly drawn from the upper and middling ranks of society: sons of the upper yeomanry, urban tradesmen, the gentry, and increasingly, members of clerical dynasties. They were less likely to be drawn from the ranks of the local peasantry and more likely to be outsiders. Even if they did return to serve in their counties of birth, they had generally undergone higher education in the universities. For all these reasons, they were less attuned to the local customary standards of devotion and behaviour which they were charged with transforming.[41]

The pastoral capability of the church had thus been greatly enhanced and the penetration of the Reformation deepened. At the same time the efforts of the clergy were backed by a reinvigorated apparatus of ecclesiastical discipline. The church courts, which had undergone something of an eclipse in the decades immediately following the Reformation, were to a large degree revived in the last decades of the sixteenth and the early decades of the seventeenth century. Ecclesiastical judges laboured to maintain clerical standards, and to admonish those of the laity who failed to take communion annually or to attend church or catechizing. They acted to restrain what the church saw as the grosser remnants of popish superstition, prosecuting cunning folk, reproving those who clung still to Catholic practices, and seeking to dissociate the church from popular festivities and ritual observances of dubious origin. In 1582, for example, the Archdeacon of Middlesex forbade interludes, dancing, games and the performances of minstrels in either the churches or graveyards within his jurisdiction. In 1584 the Archdeacon of Oxford reproved the churchwardens of Woolton for permitting 'evell rule done in the church by the Lord and the Ladie on Misomer day', those of Dunstowe for 'kepinge enterludes and playes in the churche . . . upon their wake-daye' and those of Sowthstooke and Boarton for permitting dancing in their churchyards at Whitsun. Villagers from Goldhanger in Essex found themselves in trouble in 1601 for dancing in service time on Whitsun Tuesday, while in May 1622 several inhabitants of Shottery in Warwickshire were admonished for 'dauncing the morris in evening prayer time'. At Eccleston in Lancashire, a parish long neglected by the church, the appointment of a sternly Protestant vicar in 1626 led to prosecutions in the church courts for bowling in service time, burning candles in a superstitious manner and kneeling by a corpse set down beside an ancient cross, blessing sick cattle and using invocations on the bodies of men and beasts, dipping a child in the font after it had been baptized and even refusing communion bread at the minister's hands. And meanwhile church courts throughout the kingdom continued to deal with the moral failings of the populace, with sexual lapses, drunkenness, and the rest, admonishing offenders and enjoining them to perform penance before their neighbours.[42]

By such activity, the church certainly hoped to eradicate the grosser superstitions of its flock. More broadly, however, it aimed less at the suppression of either sin in general or the various manifestations of popular culture than at their containment and regulation. The church courts dealt with many 'cunning men' and diviners, but they did not instigate a witchhunt. Prosecutions for 'maleficium', or black magic, went to the secular courts and even here they were spontaneously brought by the victims of alleged witchcraft rather than sought out by the authorities. Popular festivities were driven from the church and churchyard, but they were not the object of an official campaign of suppression. Their disappearance in some areas may have owed more to their expense in a period of inflation and to the withdrawal of support by leading villagers than to formal ecclesiastical hostility. Indeed, the church scarcely possessed the capacity to conduct campaigns of repression against any of the offences falling within its jurisdiction. While ministers or apparitors could initiate prosecutions in the church courts, and often did, they still relied for the most part upon the presentments of church wardens who, like village constables, knew when to turn a blind eye. Moreover, the sanctions available to ecclesiastical judges were weak. They could enjoin penance or excommunicate, but they had little coercive power and both citations to appear before the courts and sentences of excommunication were often enough ignored by offenders.[43] The administration of ecclesiastical discipline, nevertheless, provided a constant reminder of the standards which were enjoined upon parishioners by their ministers and a steady pressure for the adoption of higher standards of both life and devotion.

Both the 'toyish censures' of the church courts and the policy of containing rather than suppressing the more profane aspects of popular culture were the object of criticism from the puritan preachers, who constituted the most aggressively Protestant wing of the Anglican Church. They were ready enough to use the church courts, however, for the regulation of the behaviour of their parishioners, despite their resentment of the way in which the courts were sometimes employed to restrain the excesses of ministers who failed to conform to the Anglican ritual. In addition they exhorted and encouraged the godly laymen who, coupling appeals for greater order with appeals for reformation, sought sterner action against sin. In Parliament, laws were pushed through for the punishment of drunkenness, swearing, alehouse disorders and profanation of the sabbath, while unsuccessful efforts were made to legislate against sexual misdemeanours. Nor were the godly laity loath to use their authority in the task of reformation. Urban magistrates instituted policies of social regulation in which their concern for godliness and order were inseparably intermingled. Parish squires and village oligarchs, urged on by their ministers, sought the suppression of alehouses, as we have seen, or the uprooting of customary festivals. At Bruen Stapleford in Cheshire, the puritan squire John Bruen employed his servants to throw down maypoles and crosses. At Keevil in Wiltshire in 1611 the minister persuaded the jurors of the manor court to order the removal of a 'Kynge howse' set up as a bower for dancing and revels. In Norfolk and Suffolk, puritan justices used their courts of quarter sessions and petty sessions to attempt to impose moral discipline. They even went so far in 1578 as to draw up a Code of Discipline which was exhibited in the churches of the Bury St Edmunds area and which laid down punishments for popery, failure to attend church, disturbing church services, witchcraft, blasphemy, railing at ministers and magistrates, gaming, usury and other moral offences. Elsewhere justices fought an intermittent war against the common sins of the time and the disorders allegedly attending traditional festivities. In Devon, for example, suppression orders were issued against church ales in 1607, 1622 and 1627, while in Somerset such orders were made in 1594, 1596, 1608, 1624, 1628 and finally in 1632[44]. The godly were active across the nation.

By the 1630s England had a better ministry than ever before, and had witnessed a good deal of activity directed at the reformation of popular manners and the inculcation of Protestant devotion. The English could be regarded as fairly thoroughly Protestantized. The devotional clauses of their wills were generally unimpeachably Protestant (though admittedly many of these were actually written by ministers or schoolmasters). Virulent anti-popery had become part of the national psychology (though it was more fiercely directed against Catholic enemies abroad than towards the recusant minority at home). Catholicism survived largely as 'a nonconformism of the gentry', while even in those areas of the north where Catholicism retained a hold on some of the common people, they were generally an introverted minority clustered near the manor houses of their recusant landlords.[45] Popular religion had been to a large degree purified from the dubious accretions of medieval syncretism. Standards of church attendance were probably better. Godly preachers had winnowed out their converts and the sober lay piety of the puritan ideal had many adherents throughout the kingdom. Yet England was not reformed in the sense advocated and indeed expected by the preachers.

The trouble was that the reforming achievement was patchy, both geographically and socially. Whereas some parishes appeared models of godly discipline, notably the 'puritan' parishes of East Anglia, others remained uneasily contested between the innovating ideals of reformation and the persistence of the traditional popular culture. At Terling in Essex, preaching and pastoral care had produced a strong base of godliness among the parishioners, among whom 'the best', according to their minister, were 'a fasting and a praying people'. Sunday dancings and alehouse disorders had been put down, church attendance was good, swearing was 'well reformed'. The parish officers were increasingly respectable in their own behaviour and kept their neighbours on a tight rein. At Keevil in Wiltshire, however, an uneasy compromise existed. Early in the seventeenth century the minister had done his best to establish more than the minimum standard of religious observance, both by preaching and by the exercise of discipline. However, he failed to find strong support. His attempt to suppress summer revels in 1611 resulted in some of his parishioners getting up and singing an obscene libel against him; thereafter both he and his son and successor appear to have settled for a reasonable standard of ritual conformity. Dancing in the Bower on Sundays after prayers was still the norm in Keevil in 1624. Yet elsewhere the impulse of reformation had still scarcely been felt. In the New Forest, it was alleged in 1634, people went 'ten times to an Alehouse before they goe once to a church'. At Admarsh in Bleasdale in Lancashire, as late as 1650 there was a chapel but 'neither minister nor maintenance and . . . the people thereabout are an ignorant and careles people knowing nothing of the worship of God, but live in ignorance and superstition and six miles from any church or chapell'.[46]

The limits of reformation were not confined merely to the unevenness of geographical penetration. Even in apparently well-reformed parishes with high levels of church attendance, the truly godly commonly found themselves in a minority. For many of their neighbours church attendance remained a gathering of neighbours rather than an intensely spiritual experience. George Widley described them in 1604 'gazing about the Church as if they should be asked that question when they come home, What went you to the Church to see? and not what to heare: their eyes are on everyone, save on the teacher on whom they should be fastened'. John Angier, who in 1638 preached a series of sermons on the subject, dwelt on the spiritual unpreparedness of the people, their arriving at church late and leaving early, their failure to join in the psalm singing, whispering and joking and standing up to gaze around. At best, they were given to kneeling down in ostentatious private prayer at inopportune moments, while at worst they stretched out to sleep, a 'very generall' practice. It was scenes such as these, which are well documented in the records of the church courts, which led Nicholas Bownde to describe popular church attendance as 'unprofitable wandringe to the church and home again'. 'Did not authority command and generall example forcibly perswade and desire to avoid shame constrain', concluded Angier, 'they would not afford their company at all; and when they do come, they bring the same affections wherewith they go about their other occasions: And why so? They see no good in preaching, prayer, sacraments. What profit is in them? What good comes by them? They have too low thoughts of Gods Worship, as if it were only outward and did onely deserve the worst part, the presence of the body.'[47]

Such criticisms could be directed against inattentive church attenders of every rank, but they were most commonly directed at the mass of the poor. It was they who were most lax in their church attendance and they who were least orderly when they did attend. The sober piety of the Reformation ideal could appeal to people of all ranks, and demonstrably did so, but it found its most receptive audience among a minority of the gentry, the yeomen and craftsmen of the villages, and the merchants, tradesmen and artisans of the towns. It was they who formed the reading public for devotional works, they who practised sermon repetition and family prayers in their households, they who signed petitions against disorders which dishonoured God and they who promoted or supported local campaigns against ungodliness. Where they possessed the social power, they could call the tune in parish life; where they did not, they might form, like Richard Baxter's father, beleaguered islands of godliness. Whichever was the case they were a minority in an unregenerate world. At worst they might be the object of the mockery of an ignorant multitude described by Robert Bolton as 'a kind of people who yet lie in the darknesse of their naturall ignorance and dung of their own corruption'. At best they might sit like Symonds D'Ewes, struggling to be an attentive, critical, 'rational hearer' of the sermon, while surrounded by 'the brute creatures that were in the church with me, never regarding or observing any part of divine service'.[48]

The significance of the 1630s in the religious history of the period is that the decade saw the final parting of the ways between the hierarchical and the puritan approaches to the problem of reformation. Under Archbishop Laud and the Arminians, the church was prepared to settle for decency and formality in public worship. Sermons were played down and the ritual element in worship was enhanced. Theology was liberalized, moving away from the daunting Calvinism of the Elizabethan and Jacobean church and towards a gentler, more comprehensive road to salvation. Attacks on the popular culture were abandoned in favour of attacks on nonconformist ministers. It was a policy symbolized in the King's Declaration of Sports of 1633 which sanctioned traditional Sunday recreations and seasonal feasts, subject to their being preceded by divine service and conducted in an orderly manner. Given the state of religion in England it was a perfectly reasonable policy. But to many Englishmen it looked too much like popery and to the most zealous of the puritan preachers it appeared to be an abandonment of the struggle to win the people to godliness before it was half won.[49]

With the meeting of the Long Parliament, the overthrow of the Arminian ascendancy and the outbreak of the civil wars, the puritan demand for reformation, muzzled for a decade, was revived amidst a frenzy of excitement. Whatever the constitutional origins of the struggle, religious enthusiasm was the principal motivating force of many of the gentry and 'middling sort' who rallied to defend the parliamentary cause, and in the mouths of army chaplains and parliamentary preachers, the cause of constitutional reform was rapidly eclipsed by demands for cultural revolution. In 1642 Thomas Case preached to Parliament that God was saying to England 'Thy people shall be all righteous' and urged the bringing in of 'the mixt multitude' by 'the Conversion of Some' and 'the punishment of others'. Three years later Nicholas Proffet urged that to bring the nation to God, 'instructions and corrections must be used; Magistrate and Minister, the Word and the Sword must be joined'. As regards 'the stupidity and profannesse of the multitude', he advised in a frenzy of Christian charity, 'that in as much as no instructions noe admonitions will worke on such men, the blueness of the wound might be applied'.[50]

Such advice did not fall on deaf ears. In the aftermath of the wars and subsequently during the Interregnum, sterner laws were passed for the suppression of ungodly behaviour. Justices of the Peace made fitful attempts to discountenance profaneness by suppressing sports and revels, surveying and purging alehouses and ordering sterner punishments for the parents of bastards. More importantly, the church was purged of 'scandalous' ministers – albeit some of them were more scandalous for their political opinions than their morals. Vetted preachers, many of them young men fresh from the universities, were put in to replace them. Sequestered tithes formerly owned by Catholics or royalists, together with the confiscated incomes of bishops, deans and chapters were employed to augment poor livings and to fund preachers in the remaining 'dark corners of the land'. The church was surveyed and plans were set on foot to reorganize parish boundaries so as to facilitate church attendance and closer pastoral care. It was a remarkable programme, and by the later 1650s, England had probably never had a better manned and financed church or a more active preaching ministry.[51] Yet this also failed.

The activity of the Interregnum certainly completed the penetration of the English provinces by the Reformation. The ministers won many new converts: 'there was much work now on foot with souls', observed Henry Newcome. Yet the greater task of winning over the people to godliness remained unfulfilled. Nor was this something which could be attributed simply to the inability of the secular magistracy to sustain a campaign of repression against ungodliness, or to the political impossibility of erecting an effective system of Presbyterian church discipline to replace the machinery of the Anglican Church. The failure lay primarily in an inability to communicate meaningfully with the common people. The enthusiastic preachers of the Commonwealth Church discovered what some of their predecessors had found long before: that most of the people were 'sermon-proof'. Richard Younge dismissed them as 'those blocks that go to Church as dogs do, only for company and can hear a powerful Minister for twenty or thirty years together, and minde no more what they hear then the seats they sit on'. It was a judgement shared by one of the king's preachers in Lancashire thirty years before, though he put it more gently. 'People heare much, learne little and practise lesse,' he advised the Bishop of Chester, 'which cannot be imputed to the want of good preaching, but rather to the want of good hearing.' Arthur Dent agreed that much preaching was 'but a breath from us and a sound to them'.[52]

It was a disillusioning experience for men who had placed so much emphasis on the creation of a preaching ministry. Yet to their credit some of them analysed the problem with some sympathy and sophistication. To Richard Baxter, who agreed that sermons often failed, it was not simply a question of the common people's stupidity or inattention, but a problem of their educational levels. Sermons failed to move people because they tended to 'over-run their understandings and memories'. The people were not stupid, but they were unlettered. They lacked not only personal knowledge of the Scriptures, but also experience in the handling of abstract concepts and the vocabulary with which to apprehend the significance of intricate questions of doctrine. 'Many men have that in their minds,' he argued, 'which is not ripe for utterance; and through ill education and disuse, they are strangers to the expressions of those things which they have some Conceptions of.' Failing to understand the mysteries of the path to salvation, they tended to fall back on 'an ungrounded affiance in Christ that he will pardon, justifie and save them'. Failing to appreciate the requirements of godliness, they lived according to custom.

To Baxter the remedy lay in patient catechizing and private discourse which would impart to the people not simply the words of the catechism, but an appreciation of their significance couched in 'homely expressions'. 'I have found by experience', he claimed, 'that an ignorant sot that hath been an unprofitable hearer so long, hath got more knowledge and remorse of conscience in half an hours close discourse, then . . . from 10 years publike preaching.' 'Poore ignorant people' should be dealt with 'very tenderly . . . for matter of knowledge and defect of expression if they are teachable and tractable'. It was no answer 'to reject them so hastily as some hot and too high professors would have us do'.[53]

Partly as a result of his influence and of the example of his Worcestershire association of ministers, major catechizing exercises were begun in several areas in the later 1650s. But it was a forlorn hope. Adam Martindale, who took part in a major catechizing plan in Cheshire in 1656 found it impossible to deal adequately with all the people under his charge. Even among those he dealt with, he had to surmount such obstacles as 'the unwillingness of people (especially the old ignoramuses) to have their extreme defects of knowledge searched out, the backwardnesse of the prophane to have the smart plaister of admonition applied . . . and the businesse (reall or pretended) left as an excuse why the persons concerned were gone abroad at the time appointed for their instruction'. The proselytizing effort of the Interregnum failed. Those ministers who tried to serve all the people under their charge had to learn to live with the type of experience recorded by Henry Newcome when he visited the sickbed of a 'poor ale man' in 1655: 'I dealt as well as I could with him; but saw with him (as I had done many times before, and have done since. . .) how hard it is to get within poor persons . . . to fasten anything upon them of their danger and concernment.'[54]

'Getting within' was the whole point of the puritan effort. Yet what the Interregnum saw was not the transformation of England into 'a land of saints and a pattern of holiness to all the world' as Richard Baxter had hoped,[55] but the disintegration of English puritanism into a multiplicity of denominations and sects. Side by side with that process went the alienation from what remained of the national church of those common people who found themselves both the object of the cultural aggression of the godly and at the same time excluded from the communion of the faithful.

In the proliferation of the sects and in the vitality of debate over religious belief we have incontrovertible evidence of the extent to which one part of the common people – notably the literate 'middling sort' – had become closely involved with the central issues of the day. Steeped as some of them now were in scriptural knowledge, they were prepared to take up positions of their own on matters of faith, to the very evident discomfiture of the clergymen who regarded themselves as the guardians of Protestant orthodoxy. For them the relative religious toleration of the 1650s provided unprecedented opportunities for self-expression and spiritual exploration of an entirely new kind. Soldiers of the New Model Army took to preaching and expounding the Scriptures to their fellows. 'Seekers' of various kinds wandered the countryside. Adam Eyre pondered the arguments for Independency in his Yorkshire farmhouse. Villagers at Terling in Essex broke away from the tutelage of their theologically orthodox pastor under the influence of Baptist evangelists and Quaker pamphlets.[56] A century of educational improvement and religious change had bred up individuals who had sufficient self-confidence to find their own paths of the spirit and to judge for themselves the requirements of salvation.

In the vitality of their thought and the frequent theological and social radicalism of their ideas, the Interregnum sects provided much of what was truly revolutionary in the English revolution, as Christopher Hill has shown. They horrified their social superiors with the prospect of a 'world turned upside down'. Nevertheless the experience of some, significant as it was, must not blind us to the experience of the majority. Ralph Josselin, vicar of Earles Colne in Essex, referred to three groups among his parishioners in the course of the 1650s. First, there was 'our society', a group of deeply religious individuals drawn largely, though not exclusively, from the most substantial members of the village, which met to 'discourse of the principles of religion'. Second came 'my sleepy hearers', the majority of simple church attenders. Finally, there were 'the families that seldom heare'. When a decision was taken by the godly to hold a communion service in 1651 'divers . . . that wee could not comfortably joyne with' were turned away. Eventually only thirty-four persons were admitted.[57]

Here as in many other parishes the effective ministry of the pastor had become confined to a minority and the central ritual of the faith had become an exclusive rite. Similarly, at Altham Chapel in Lancashire, the group which covenanted together to form an Independent congregation in 1651 consisted of only twenty-nine persons (fourteen of them women), representing, it would seem, only twenty of the 150 families which the Church Survey of 1650 reported as inhabiting the chapelry. Between 1651 and 1662 only thirty-two persons had been added to this group and in 1656 the comment 'no conversion work in Altham' was entered in the church book. In the same year the minister, Mr Jolly, complained to Major-General Worsley that 'not one in twenty . . . go to any place of worship on the Lord's Day, but sit in their houses'. It was scarcely surprising, for though he invited others to join the covenant and offered instruction to the 'ignorant and scandalous', Jolly was withholding baptism from the children of non-members.[58]

What was spiritual liberty to some could amount to deprivation and exclusion for others from valued services of the church, and the extent of the alienation of the mass of the unregenerate population from the Commonwealth Church is perhaps best evidenced in the clear under-registration of the parish registers of the Interregnum. That alienation and exclusion may also provide a further form of explanation of the limited success of the enthusiastic preachers sent out to win the people to godliness. Among the common people there had always been a truculent resistance to the demands of the radical reformers among the clergy, born not simply of ignorance but of resentment of their cultural aggression, and reinforced by a long tradition of anti-clericalism. One Wiltshire girl resentful of her minister's action against sports and games and his enthusiasm for catechizing, described his sermons in 1624 as 'such a deale of bibble babble that I am weary to heare yt and I can then sitt downe in my seat and take a good napp'. Her opinion was echoed by James Nicholson of Aysgarth in Yorkshire who expressed the view in 1633 that 'the preaching of the gospel is but bibble babble and I care not a fart of my tail for any black coat in Wensleydale and I had rather hear a cuckoo sing'. The situation created by the demands of another eager cleric at Womersley near Pontefract was vividly summed up by a servant who remarked to a friend, 'Its sharp shiting in a frosty morning.'[59]

Such attitudes were not submerged in the religious enthusiasm of the Interregnum. If anything they were reinforced. Little wonder then that what had begun with such high hopes of godly reformation ended in the spontaneous wave of conspicuous ungodliness which greeted the Restoration of the King in 1660. Adam Martindale was not the only godly minister to wake up one May morning to find that 'the rabble of prophane youths and some doting fooles' had put a maypole on the green again. Henry Newcome, travelling through Leicestershire and Rutland, 'found May-poles in abundance as we came, and at Oakham I saw a morris-dance, which I had not seen of twenty years before'. 'It is a sad sign the hearts of the people are poorly employed', he reflected, 'when they can make a business of playing the fool as they do. This I found, that in most places they either have had bad ministers to rejoice in, or else good ones whom they hate.'[60]

The dual legacy of the Interregnum was on the one hand the various branches of dissent and on the other hand a restored Church of England purged of nonconformist ministers which made few demands on its members other than their official conformity. The former were disproportionately, though never of course exclusively, drawn from among the 'middling sort of people': minor gentry, yeomen, husbandmen, tradesmen and their families.[61] Their very presence served as a reminder of the revolutionary years and of the fact that English Protestantism could never again be contained within the walls of a single church. But their withdrawal into nonconformity represented also a retreat from the ideal of national reformation. The emotional exhaustion of the Interregnum experiment and its failure had left their mark. Sober respectability had triumphed over radical enthusiasm. As for the church, until 1689 it still formally embraced the whole of society. In some areas its authority was effectively re-established, together with the exercise of ecclesiastical discipline, and strenuous efforts were made to combat dissent and to restore ritual conformity to the standards of the 1630s. There were parishes enough where the absence of nonconformists and the combined influence of squire, parson and leading parishioners permitted a reassertion of the spiritual hegemony of Anglicanism. At Clayworth in Nottinghamshire there were no known dissenters. The church remained the centre of the community, and at Easter in 1676, 200 of the 236 inhabitants eligible to take communion did so. Elsewhere, however, such efforts were fitful or fruitless and a very different situation prevailed. The poor married in church, brought their children for baptism and their dead for burial, but for many that was the limit of their dealings with formal religion. In the rural deanery of Sutton in Kent it was reported in 1680 that 'there is great reason to complain of many of ye meaner sort of people besides dissenters from ye church who absent themselves from ye publicke worship, and this is ye generall complaint of all parishes amongst us'. Ralph Josselin's sermons were attracting audiences of only seventy to 100 in 1663 and 1664, and he recorded his surprise when, on one occasion, he found 'divers of the ruder sort of people hearing'. The population of Earles Colne was approximately 1000. Only once did Josselin enter in his diary 'the church where I preacht full, multitudes standing without at windows'. He was recording one of his dreams.[62]

Cultural differentiation

In 1580 illiteracy was a characteristic of the vast majority of the common people of England. By 1680 it was a special characteristic of the poor. At the time of the Armada, rural England possessed a vigorous popular culture of communal recreations and rituals. By the time of the Exclusion Crisis this traditional culture had been greatly impoverished, while its surviving manifestations were discountenanced by respectable society and participation in them was largely confined to the vulgar. In the middle of the reign of Elizabeth, English villagers had largely shared a common fund of traditional beliefs, values and standards of behaviour. By the last years of Charles II's reign that common heritage had become the property of those 'rusticall', 'rude', 'silly ignorants' who remained wedded to their superstitions and their disorders. The spread of popular literacy and the progress of the Reformation had opened up new cultural horizons to a section of the common people. Yet they had also brought about a widening fissure between polite and plebeian culture, the informed and the ignorant, respectability and the profane multitude. It was a process revealingly paralleled in what Keith Thomas has described as 'the decline of magic'. As the seventeenth century advanced witchcraft prosecutions declined while the tensions which had given rise to them eased. Yet the decline of magical beliefs was a far more selective process. It occurred among theologians no longer willing to concede the devil any other than spiritual power. It was evident among judges whose reluctance to convict for a crime so difficult to prove as witchcraft ripened into flat scepticism, and among the magistrates and jurymen whom they influenced. Among intellectuals influenced by the rationalist thinkers of antiquity, the new mechanical philosophy and the canons of experimental proof, the whole basis of magical beliefs withered and died. Yet there is abundant evidence that they retained their vitality and their currency among the lower strata of the rural population.[63]

The distancing of mind and manners which added a cultural dimension to the polarization of English society should not be crudely exaggerated. But it was a reality nonetheless. It is nicely illustrated by the fact that in the mid and late seventeenth century popular beliefs and practices began to arouse the curiosity of antiquarian gentlemen. To Sir Thomas Browne in his *Vulgar Errors* and John Aubrey in his *Remaines of Gentilisme and Judaisme* the beliefs of the common people were an alien world and an interesting object of study. The poor had become not simply poor, but to a significant degree culturally different. Richard Baxter had been right when he judged as a child that his sober, Bible-reading father would be 'better thought on . . . at the last'. The dancing villagers of the 1620s had become by 1691 a sort of people whom Baxter himself, now one of England's most respected divines, could sum up when searching for a suitable collective description, as 'the rabble that cannot read'.[64]

Conclusion: nation and locality

The impact of social change in late sixteenth- and seventeenth-century England presents itself to the historian as a series of localized social dramas. In the levelling of an enclosure or the staying of a load of grain, the prosecution of a witch, the conflict attending the putting down of a popular festival or the suppression of alehouses, we find revealed the tensions generated by the economic, administrative and cultural developments of the day. Such incidents, redolent of underlying processes of change, provide our surest indication of the gradual process of social transformation. They are scattered in time, for the process of change was slow. They are dispersed in place, for it was uneven. Taken together, however, they constitute a sure guide to both its course and its nature. In the preceding chapters I have sought to present characteristic examples of such events and to explain the changing social realities from which they sprang. What remains is to make sense of the process as a whole.

Social change in our period was fuelled by the convergence in time of forces of demographic, economic, cultural and administrative change, active in the nation at large. Its course was determined by the way in which their impact was registered, absorbed or deflected by different social groups within the intimate contexts of thousands of provincial communities. In this interpenetration of the national and the local, the general and the particular, lies the key to both the local diversity of the social experience of the period and its essential regularities of pattern. For if English society was varied, its diversity was contained within a discernible range. If it was highly localized, its localism was qualified by its openness to a set of common influences. What the later sixteenth and seventeenth centuries witnessed was an intensified interaction between the locality and the larger society, which both drew together provincial communities into a more closely integrated national society and at the same time introduced a new depth and complexity to their local patterns of social stratification. The outcome was a series of adjustments in local social relations which gave rise to the characteristic conflicts of the age.

In the interconnected demographic and economic developments of the period both dimensions of the process of change are made abundantly clear. The growth and redistribution of the national population and the quickening of economic activity to which it gave rise, furthered the development of a national market which bound together, in a mesh of interdependence, the diverse regional economies of provincial England. Yet demographic expansion and economic change served not only to unite, but also to divide. To those well-placed to take advantage of the market opportunities of the day, notably the gentry, the merchants and tradesmen of the towns and the yeomanry of the countryside, it brought an unprecedented level of prosperity. To those smallholders for whom the demands of rising rents cancelled out the profits to be made from marketing their surplus produce, however, or whose withholding power in the face of harvest failure was weak, it was a time of chronic insecurity. Some were driven from the land. Others eked out a more marginal living on subdivided holdings. As for the labouring poor, the period saw both an absolute and relative expansion in their numbers and a deepening of their poverty which was alleviated only late in the seventeenth century.

Demographic expansion and economic development thus had the effect of advancing the economic integration of English society while, at the same time, modifying its structure and exacerbating its inequalities of wealth. It was a process of fundamental importance in the overall course of social development and it was made possible only because of certain pre-existing characteristics of local society. English society was already deeply permeated by the ethos of agrarian and commercial capitalism. Inequality of wealth and opportunity was nothing new. Beneath the rhetoric of contemporary ideals of commonwealth was concealed the cold reality of a harsh, competitive, contract society. Within the flexible structure of the neighbourhood there already flourished a cultural emphasis on the interests of the individual nuclear family which was a powerful enough incentive to override traditional social obligations where there was gain to be made. Such attitudes needed only the opportunity to express themselves more fully, and in the fiercely competitive climate of the late sixteenth and seventeenth centuries they found it. As a result there was a gradual pushing apart of the clusters of social groups which constituted the established social hierarchy. The 'middling sort' moved closer to their immediate superiors among the gentry and urban élite in both interests and life-style. They were steadily distanced from those of their neighbours for whom the pressures of the age outweighed its opportunities. It was a polarization which took different forms in different localities, in accordance with the particular structure of the local economy. But it was everywhere an inescapable fact.

The broader implications of these developments are best seen in the differentials which they entailed in the life experiences and opportunities of families of different rank. To some the period brought dramatic rises in living standards, better housing and more elaborate furnishing, cash in hand for the purchase of land, the setting-up of sons and the marriage portions of daughters. It offered new chances of upward social mobility both for themselves and their children, on whose education and advancement they laid out much of their new wealth. Many, however, found themselves sunk ever deeper in the age-old struggle for existence. They were harder put to it to marry and set up their own independent families. They could do little more for their children than feed and protect them when they were young and place them with a good employer when they were of age to fend for themselves. The tensions engendered by the process of polarization are clearly evidenced in the strain placed upon the established patterns of social relations within local communities. Conflict and suspicion between neighbours show themselves in the upward trend of theft prosecutions, the hostilities laid bare by witchcraft accusations and the harrying of inmates, cottagers and pregnant servant girls. The difficulties experienced in reconciling the contradiction between the realities of an advancing agrarian and commercial capitalism and the demands of traditional social obligations are thrown into bold relief by the explosion of frustration and despair in riot. Throughout English society it was becoming ever harder to preserve the balance between communal identification and social differentiation upon which the stability of the social order rested.

Such problems would have proved sufficiently difficult had they occurred in isolation. What made them the more traumatic was the convergence in time and the superimposition in place of other processes of social change. Educational advancement, religious reformation and the thrusting out into the provinces of the demands of a more aggressive state all served in their turn to intensify the interaction of centre and locality. The development of grammar school and higher education enhanced the cultural homogeneity of the English ruling class by providing for them a standardized mental training in common institutions of learning. The spread of literacy among the 'middling sort' made possible a broadening of the mental horizons of this section of the population and their closer assimilation to the attitudes and values of their social superiors. The advancing tide of the Protestant Reformation brought home to the localities new ideals of religious devotion, stricter standards of personal conduct and a new providential theodicy. It swept up an expanded proportion of the population into the currents of religious debate. The enhanced presence and activity of government in the localities brought to those involved in local administration a more acute awareness of the purposes and responsibilities of government and a more direct concern with its policies.

As a result of these interconnected processes of change, our period witnessed the increasingly close involvement of provincial Englishmen of upper and middling rank in national affairs. Indeed, one of its most striking features, taken as a whole, is the emergence of 'the people'. Their entry on to the stage of national history can be witnessed in their participation in religious movements and controversies and in their demonstrable awareness of and concern with national political events. It is shown above all in the fact that the English revolution of the 1640s was not an affair confined to the aristocracy, the greater gentry and their retainers, but involved the aspirations and willing participation of thousands of their immediate social inferiors among the minor 'parochial' gentry and the 'middling sort' of town and country. Of course, these changes did not cause the English revolution; but they most emphatically helped to make it what it was.

It is a familiar story, well told in a whole literature of specialist studies. Less generally appreciated, however, is the extent to which these changes also wrought their effects upon the patterns of social relations within England's local communities, and it is upon this issue that I have deliberately concentrated my attention. For at the level of the local community the most striking feature of these changes is the extent to which their benefits were socially circumscribed. Education, for the most part, was for those who could afford it. The mass of the poor were excluded. Literacy had indeed been incorporated into the popular culture and the seeds of further advance had been sown. But as yet the transition to mass literacy had scarcely begun. The reformers of popular beliefs and manners were successful above all among the middling and upper ranks of urban and rural society. Their efforts brought not national renewal, but a polarization of godliness and ungodliness which had social as well as spiritual dimensions. Participation in government involved for the most part those whose inherited or achieved social position entitled them to rule: the gentry and urban oligarchs who filled the offices of their counties and cities, the parish notables who represented their communities as presentment jurymen and governed them as vestrymen and overseers. To those over whom they exercised their powers, the governmental achievement of the period and the elaboration of local institutions to which it gave rise were experienced primarily as the threat or actuality of a greater degree of social regulation. They were less participants in than objects of a regenerated and extended system of social control.

Through the superimposition of educational, religious and administrative innovation within the intimate context of individual local communities, the existing trend towards social polarization, enhanced social conflict and the realignment of social groups became charged with an element of normative conflict. Differentiation of values and a shattering of shared attitudes and understandings added a new dimension to the existing polarization of wealth. Local norms of behaviour came into sharp conflict with attitudes and values introduced from outside the local community. A novel respectability emerged which was defined in opposition to and was singularly hostile towards, a popular culture which was slowly transformed into a culture of poverty.

In this process a crucial role was played by the 'middling sort', the local notables who were both the principal beneficiaries of change and the brokers who mediated between forces active in the larger society and their polarizing local communities. To them, by virtue of their strategic position in the structure of local society and the social power which they controlled, fell the task of defining the terms upon which external influences were incorporated into the fabric of the local social system. It was a responsibility of unenviable difficulty, which could involve acute conflicts of loyalties and roles. Yet, for the most part they settled that conflict by aligning themselves with the forces of change. The pressure of their economic interests, in a period fraught with risk and pregnant with opportunity had already led many to enter a closer alliance with the 'improving' gentry. They were readier to agree to schemes of enclosure and improvement, less likely to head resistance to innovation, save where their personal interests were directly at risk. Where they were also caught up in other changes which sapped their sense of identification with their poorer neighbours and promoted a closer assimilation to the attitudes and values of their social superiors and religious mentors, this realignment could become more complex and above all more consistent. Leading ratepayers who administered the poor laws found a new institutional expression of their identity as a group which at the same time differentiated them sharply from those whom they relieved. Parish officers who had adopted new standards of order became more conscious of the necessity of regulating the 'disorders' of the poor. Literate churchwardens influenced by the sober piety of the Reformation ideal found themselves allied with their godly ministers in restraining the profaneness of the multitude.

This complex process of realignment is clearly revealed in the enhanced activity of censorious churchwardens, in local attacks upon traditional recreations, in the manipulation of the poor laws as instruments of social regulation, and above all in the numerous local campaigns over the suppression of alehouses. At the level of the individual town and village, the 'middling sort' of England were withdrawing themselves from the popular culture of their neighbours and allying themselves as willing auxiliaries of the magistrates and ministers whose values they had come to share just as surely as they shared the economic interests of the gentry. That achieved, they were exerting themselves in a redefinition of local social relations, attempting to mould their communities into conformity with standards of behaviour which accorded with their interests and reflected their prejudices as ratepayers, masters, employers and pillars of the church.

The very frequency of such localized social dramas provides a clear indication of the extent to which this process was a national phenomenon. It was, nonetheless, one which varied in its chronology, its complexity and its outcome. The timing of change could vary from county to county and from parish to parish in accordance with differences in the particular point at which the forces of innovation gained precedence over the tenacity of custom. The complexity of the process of differentiation could also vary. In some parishes conflict between the 'best inhabitants' and the poor was fought out in a rough rustic vernacular which owed little to the legitimizing rhetoric of statutes or sermons and much to the level of the poor rate. Elsewhere it involved a comprehensive effort to establish order and promote reformation. Nor were such efforts everywhere successful in the redefinition of the boundaries of permitted behaviour and the establishment of tighter patterns of social disipline. Variations in the social, economic and institutional structures of local communities could deeply influence the relative ability of the innovators in local life to call the tune. Here, they successfully imposed their *mores*; there, they stood aloof, dissociated but powerless in the face of the truculent resistance and effective independence of their inferiors. Elsewhere, there were communities so remote from the influence of church and magistrate that the effort was never made. But whatever the practical outcome in particular localities, it reflects only variation of response to a common process of change. It remains the case that a deep social cleavage of a new kind had opened up in English society. It was one not simply between wealth and poverty, but between respectable and plebeian cultures, and it followed the line which divided not the gentry and the common people, but the 'better sort' and the mass of the labouring poor.

This process of transition was essentially completed by 1660, following the marked furtherance of its national penetration which resulted from the social and religious policies of the Interregnum. Thereafter it was simply consolidated. Demographic stabilization and economic growth eased the tensions generated by the process of economic polarization, though without reversing its outcome. The swollen mass of the poor remained. Emotional exhaustion with the drive for reformation after the failures of the Interregnum dampened the cultural aggression of the godly. Yet their social values were preserved in the dominant conception of respectability. A novel reluctance of central government to interfere in the running of local administration blunted the edge of the drive for order. However, the poor laws and petty sessions remained.

In the last two decades of our period the heat had gone out of the situation. Yet the relative social tranquillity of the later seventeenth century must not be mistaken for a reversal of the social forces active in the preceding three generations. It was an equilibrium established on new terms. Those terms had been proposed in the clash of interests and ideals which attended the changes of the later sixteenth and seventeenth centuries, and hammered out in conflicts which had involved every group in local society. The outcome was embodied in the social relations of thousands of local communities. The rulers of English local society had learned to live with their poor by winning the deference of some, enforcing the compliance of others and keeping their distance from those whom they could neither control nor coerce. It was not their preferred solution to the problem of how to reconcile a socio-economic order which implied the existence of mutually antagonistic classes with their cherished ideal of a stable, hierarchical society. It was, however, the best they were able to achieve.

Notes and references

Introduction

1 A. S. P. Woodhouse (ed.), *Puritanism and Liberty: Being the Army Debates (1647–9) from the Clarke Manuscripts with Supplementary Documents*, 2nd edn (London 1950), pp. 17–18.
2 E. P. Thompson, 'Patrician society plebeian culture', *Journal of Social History*, vol. 7 (1974).

Chapter 1: Degrees of people

1 F. J. Furnivall (ed.), *Harrison's Description of England*, New Shakspere Society, 6th series, no. 1 (London 1877), pt 1, p. 105; P. Laslett, *The World we have Lost*, 2nd edn (London 1971), p. 66.
2 Furnivall (ed.), *Harrison's Description of England*, pt I, ch. 5, 'Of degrees of people in the commonwealth of England'.
3 F. J. Fisher (ed.), *The State of England Anno Dom. 1600 by Thomas Wilson*, in *Camden Miscellany*, vol. 16, Camden Third Series, vol. 52 (1936), p. 17 ff. The relevant section of Wilson's account is also reprinted in J. Thirsk and J. P. Cooper (eds.), *Seventeenth-Century Economic Documents* (Oxford 1972), pp. 751–7.
4 King's table has been frequently reprinted; see Thirsk and Cooper (eds.), *Seventeenth-Century Economic Documents*, pp. 780–1, or Laslett, *The World we have Lost*, pp. 36–7.
5 For a useful discussion of such social descriptions, see D. Cressy, 'Describing the social order of Elizabethan and Stuart England', *Literature and History*, no. 3 (1976), pp. 29–44.
6 L. Stone, *The Crisis of the Aristocracy 1558–1641* (Oxford 1965), pp. 49–97; G. E. Aylmer, *The King's Servants: The Civil Service of Charles I 1625–42* (London 1961), pp. 261–2.
7 Fisher (ed.), *The State of England*, p. 22; Thirsk and Cooper (eds.), *Seventeenth-Century Economic Documents*, pp. 780–1; Stone, *Crisis of the Aristocracy*, ch. 3; B. G. Blackwood, *The Lancashire Gentry and the Great*

Rebellion, 1640–60, Chetham Society, 3rd series, vol. 25 (1978), p. 10; J. T. Cliffe, *The Yorkshire Gentry from the Reformation to the Civil War* (London 1969), p. 6.

8 Blackwood, *The Lancashire Gentry*, p. 5; Stone, *Crisis of the Aristocracy*, p. 51.

9 G. E. Mingay, *The Gentry: The Rise and Fall of a Ruling Class* (London 1976), pp. 58–9.

10 Stone, *Crisis of the Aristocracy*, ch. 4; Mingay, *The Gentry*, p. 13; Cliffe, *The Yorkshire Gentry*, p. 29 ff.; C. W. Chalklin, *Seventeenth-Century Kent: A Social and Economic History* (London 1965), p. 191; Blackwood, *The Lancashire Gentry*, pp. 12, 14–15, 30 n.29.

11 Blackwood, *The Lancashire Gentry*, p. 11; B. W. Quintrell, 'The government of the county of Essex, 1603–1642' (unpubl. PhD. thesis, University of London, 1965); W. B. Willcox, *Gloucestershire 1590–1640* (New Haven 1940), ch. 4; G. P. Higgins, 'The government of early Stuart Cheshire', *Northern History*, vol. 12 (1976), pp. 33–4, 40; T. G. Barnes, *Somerset 1625–40: A County Government During 'The Personal Rule'* (Oxford 1961), pp. 11–13.

12 Cliffe, *The Yorkshire Gentry*, p. 16; Blackwood, *The Lancashire Gentry*, p. 18 ff. and Appendix 1.

13 R. Grassby, 'Social mobility and business enterprise in seventeenth-century England', in D. Pennington and K. Thomas (eds.), *Puritans and Revolutionaries: Essays in Seventeenth-Century History Presented to Christopher Hill* (Oxford 1978), pp. 355–81; V. Brodsky Elliott, 'Mobility and marriage in pre-industrial England' (unpubl. PhD. thesis, University of Cambridge, 1978), p. 64 ff.

14 P. Clark and P. Slack, *English Towns in Transition, 1500–1700* (Oxford, 1976), pp. 117–120.

15 Aylmer, *The King's Servants*, p. 263; W. R. Prest, *The Inns of Court under Elizabeth I and the Early Stuarts: 1590–1640* (London 1972), pp. 26–31; P. Clark, *English Provincial Society from the Reformation to the Revolution: Religion, Politics and Society in Kent, 1500–1640* (Hassocks 1977), p. 276; B. P. Levack, *The Civil Lawyers in England, 1603–1641* (Oxford 1973), pp. 10–11; L. Stone, 'The size and composition of the Oxford student body, 1580–1910', in *idem* (ed.), *The University in Society: Vol. 1, Oxford and Cambridge from the Fourteenth to the Early-Nineteenth Century* (Oxford and Princeton 1975), pp. 18–19.

16 Thirsk and Cooper (eds.), *Seventeenth-Century Economic Documents*, p. 756.

17 A. Everitt, *Change in the Provinces: The Seventeenth Century*, Occasional Papers of the Department of Local History, 2nd series, no. 1 (Leicester 1970), p. 43 ff.

18 Clark and Slack, *English Towns in Transition*, pp. 117–20; Grassby, 'Social mobility and business enterprise', p. 358.

19 M. Campbell, *The English Yeoman Under Elizabeth and the Early Stuarts* (New Haven 1942), p. 7 ff.; Laslett, *The World we have Lost*, p. 45. This

generalization does not apply to parts of north-east England in which the term 'yeoman' was used more generally to describe small farmers.

20 C. S. Orwin and C. S. Orwin, *The Open Fields*, 3rd edn (Oxford 1967), ch. 9; M. Spufford, *Contrasting Communities: English Villagers in the Sixteenth and Seventeenth Centuries* (Cambridge 1974), pp. 138–9.

21 J. C. Hodgson (ed.), *Wills and Inventories from the Registry at Durham*, vol. 3, Surtees Society, vol. 112 (1906), pp. 100, 122, 126.

22 P. J. Bowden, 'Agricultural prices, farm profits, and rents', in J. Thirsk (ed.), *The Agrarian History of England and Wales, Vol. IV, 1500–1640* (Cambridge 1967), pp. 657–9; Furnivall (ed.), *Harrison's Description of England*, pt 1, pp. 151–2.

23 Campbell, *The English Yeoman*, p. 217; G. E. Fussell (ed.), *Robert Loder's Farm Accounts*, Camden Third Series, vol. 53 (1936), pp. 47–74.

24 M. Brigg, 'The Forest of Pendle in the seventeenth-century', pt. 1, *Transactions of the Historic Society of Lancashire and Cheshire*, vol. 115 (1962), pp. 74–5; P. Tyler, 'The status of the Elizabethan parochial clergy', in G. J. Cuming (ed.), *Studies in Church History IV: The Province of York* (Leiden 1967), pp. 96–7; cf. for a recent analysis of 3281 inventories from fourteen counties, D. Cressy, *Literacy and the Social Order: Reading and Writing in Tudor and Stuart England* (Cambridge 1980), pp. 137–9.

25 A. M. Everitt, 'Farm labourers', in Thirsk (ed.), *Agrarian History*, pp. 398, 400–3, 420.

26 ibid., p. 437; F. Hull, 'Agriculture and rural society in Essex, 1560–1640' (unpubl. PhD. thesis, University of London, 1950), pp. 498–500; Essex RO Transcript no. 448, new series; Chalklin, *Seventeenth-Century Kent*, p. 249.

27 Bowden, 'Agricultural prices', p. 657; A. Clark, *The Working Life of Women in the Seventeenth Century* (London 1919), pp. 65–80; K. Wrightson and D. Levine, *Poverty and Piety in an English Village: Terling, 1525–1700* (New York, San Francisco, London 1979), pp. 39–42.

28 Everitt, 'Farm labourers', pp. 438, 442, 446–7, 450–3.

29 W. G. Hoskins, *The Midland Peasant: The Economic and Social History of a Leicestershire Village* (London 1957), pp. 166–7; Wrightson and Levine, *Poverty and Piety*, pp. 22–3; Brigg, 'The Forest of Pendle', p. 88; J. Thirsk, 'Industries in the countryside', in F. J. Fisher (ed.), *Essays in the Economic and Social History of Tudor and Stuart England* (Cambridge 1961); D. Hey, *The Rural Metalworkers of the Sheffield Region: A Study of Rural Industry before the Industrial Revolution*, Occasional Papers of the Department of Local History, 2nd series, no. 5 (Leicester 1972), pp. 19–31, 34; G. D. Ramsay, *The Wiltshire Woollen Industry in the Sixteenth and Seventeenth Centuries*, 2nd edn (London 1965), pp. 16–17.

30 Wrightson and Levine, *Poverty and Piety*, pp. 103–6; J. A. Sharpe, 'Crime and delinquency in an Essex parish 1600–1640' in J. S. Cockburn (ed.), *Crime in England 1550–1800* (London 1977), pp. 93–4; J. D. Marshall, 'Social structure and wealth in pre-industrial England' (unpubl. paper to the

139th Annual Meeting of the British Association for the Advancement of Science, 1977), p. 20; V. Skipp, *Crisis and Development: An Ecological Case Study of the Forest of Arden 1570–1674* (Cambridge 1978), pp. 80, 82; Furnivall (ed.), *Harrison's Description of England*, pt I, p. 134.

31 J. Patten, *English Towns, 1500–1700* (Folkestone and Hamden, Conn. 1978), ch. 4; Clark and Slack, *English Towns in Transition*, chs. 8 and 9.

32 G. A. J. Hodgett, *Tudor Lincolnshire* (Lincoln 1975), pp. 4–5; Blackwood, *The Lancashire Gentry*, p. 6.

33 M. J. Ingram, 'Ecclesiastical justice in Wiltshire, 1600–1640, with special reference to cases concerning sex and marriage' (unpubl. D.Phil. thesis, University of Oxford, 1977), pp. 63–6; Chalklin, *Seventeenth-Century Kent*, pp. 246–7; J. Thirsk, 'The farming regions of England', in Thirsk (ed.), *Agrarian History, passim.*

Chapter 2: Social relations in the local community

1 W. G. Hoskins (ed.), *The History of Myddle by Richard Gough* (Fontwell 1968). Gough's *History of Myddle*, first published in its entirety in 1874, is available in several modern editions. It also served as the basis of an illuminating recent study of the parish: D. G. Hey, *An English Rural Community: Myddle under the Tudors and Stuarts* (Leicester 1974).

2 Hey, *English Rural Community*, p. 190 ff.; W. L. Sachse (ed.), *The Diary of Roger Lowe 1663–74* (London 1938); Wrightson and Levine, *Poverty and Piety*, pp. 74–9.

3 P. Spufford, 'Population movement in seventeenth-century England', *Local Population Studies*, no. 4 (1970), pp. 46–7; P. Laslett and J. Harrison, 'Clayworth and Cogenhoe', in H. E. Bell and R. L. Ollard (eds.), *Historical Essays 1600–1750, Presented to David Ogg* (London 1963), pp. 174, 177.

4 A. Sturm Kussmaul, 'Servants in husbandry in early-modern England' (unpubl. PhD. thesis, University of Toronto, 1978), ch. 4 (Dr Kussmaul's thesis is shortly to be published by Cambridge University Press under the same title); Elliott, 'Mobility and marriage', pt 2; J. Patten, *Rural-Urban Migration in Pre-Industrial England*, Oxford University School of Geography Research Papers, no. 6 (1973).

5 Everitt, 'Farm labourers', p. 434; Laslett and Harrison, 'Clayworth and Cogenhoe', pp. 177–80; Wrightson and Levine, *Poverty and Piety*, pp. 79–81; D. Souden, 'Movers and stayers in family reconstitution populations, 1600–1780', forthcoming in M. Kitch (ed.), *Migration in Pre-Industrial England.*

6 J. A. Johnston, 'The probate inventories and wills of a Worcestershire parish, 1676–1775', *Midland History*, vol. 1 (1971), p. 29; Sharpe, 'Crime and delinquency', p. 94; Hey, *English Rural Community*, pp. 117, 141–2, 170, 173–6; Wrightson and Levine, *Poverty and Piety*, pp. 81–2; P. Clark 'Migration in England during the late seventeenth and early eighteenth centuries', *Past and Present*, no. 83 (1979); cf. M. Chaytor, 'Household and

kinship: Ryton in the late sixteenth and early seventeenth centuries', *History Workshop*, no. 10 (1980), pp. 31, 58 n. 12.

7 P. Clark 'The migrant in Kentish towns 1580–1640', in P. Clark and P. Slack, *Crisis and Order in English Towns 1500–1700: Essays in Urban History* (London 1972), pp. 134–8.

8 For a lucid statement of this viewpoint, see J. Bossy, 'Blood and baptism: kinship, community and Christianity in Western Europe from the fourteenth to the seventeenth centuries', in D. Baker (ed.), *Sanctity and Secularity: The Church and the World* (Oxford 1973).

9 P. Laslett, 'Mean household size in England since the sixteenth century', in P. Laslett and R. Wall (eds.), *Household and Family in Past Time* (Cambridge 1972); N. Goose, 'Household size and structure in early Stuart Cambridge', *Social History*, vol. 5 (1980). For a valuable discussion of some of the circumstances which could modify this norm, see Chaytor, 'Household and kinship', pp. 36–47, 54–7.

10 Wrightson and Levine, *Poverty and Piety*, pp. 84–7; A. Macfarlane, *The Origins of English Individualism: The Family, Property and Social Transition* (Oxford 1978), pp. 75–6; Hey, *English Rural Community*, pp. 203–4. Clusters of kin-linked households in Ryton, County Durham, are examined in Chaytor, 'Household and kinship', pp. 45–9. How typical they were in this large and economically complex northern parish remains uncertain.

11 L. Lancaster, 'Kinship in Anglo-Saxon society', *British Journal of Sociology*, vol. 9 (1958), pt. 1, p. 232, pt. 2, p. 272, and *passim*; Macfarlane, *Origins of English Individualism*, pp. 144–7; S. J. Watts, *From Border to Middle Shire: Northumberland 1586–1625* (Leicester 1975), p. 25 ff.

12 Everitt, *Change in the Provinces*, p. 27; Cliffe, *The Yorkshire Gentry*, p. 10; A. Fletcher, *A County Community in Peace and War: Sussex 1600–1660* (London 1975), p. 25.

13 A. Macfarlane, *The Family Life of Ralph Josselin, a Seventeenth-Century Clergyman: An Essay in Historical Anthroplogy* (Cambridge 1970), p. 157 ff.; Wrightson and Levine, *Poverty and Piety*, pp. 91–4; Johnston, 'Inventories and wills of a Worcestershire parish', p. 32.

14 R. J. Spence, 'The pacification of the Cumberland borders, 1593–1628', *Northern History*, vol. 13 (1977), pp. 61–2; Watts, *Border to Middle Shire*, p. 27.

15 Fletcher, *County Community in Peace and War*, pp. 44–8, 52; Everitt, *Change in the Provinces*, pp. 26–7; M. James, *Family, Lineage and Civil Society: A Study of Society, Politics and Mentality in the Durham Region 1500–1640* (Oxford 1974), pp. 25–7; F. R. Raines (ed.), *The Journal of Nicholas Assheton of Downham*, Chetham Society, old series, vol. 14 (1848). The analysis of Assheton's journal quoted is the work of Thelma Schwartz of the University of California (Berkeley). I am grateful to Ms Schwartz for undertaking this task during her year as a non-graduating student in St Andrews.

16 J. S. Morrill, *Cheshire, 1630–1660: County Government and Society During the 'English Revolution'* (Oxford 1974), p. 15; L. Stone, *The Family, Sex and*

Marriage in England 1500–1800 (London 1977), ch. 4; Clark, *English Provincial Society*, p. 278; R. O'Day, *The English Clergy: The Emergence and Consolidation of a Profession, 1558–1642* (Leicester 1979), p. 161; Grassby, 'Social mobility and business enterprise', p. 367; J. U. Nef, *The Rise of the British Coal Industry*, 2 vols. (London 1932), vol. 2, p. 39.

17 Macfarlane, *Family Life of Ralph Josselin*, chs. 7–10; H. J. Morehouse (ed.), 'The Diurnall of Adam Eyre', in *Yorkshire Diaries*, Surtees Society , vol. 65 (1875), *passim;* Wrightson and Levine, *Poverty and Piety*, pp. 99–103.

18 T. Parsons, 'The isolated conjugal family', in M. Anderson (ed.), *Sociology of the Family: Selected Readings*, 2nd edn (Harmondsworth 1980), p. 186 ff. The evidence of kin co-operation recently examined in Chaytor, 'Household and kinship', also falls within this narrow range.

19 Campbell, *The English Yeoman*, p. 382.

20 Macfarlane, *Origins of English Individualism,* pp.62–6; Orwin and Orwin, *The Open Fields*, ch. 10; Hoskins, *The Midland Peasant*, pp. 159–60.

21 B. A. Holderness, 'Credit in English rural society before the nineteenth century, with special reference to the period 1650–1720', *Agricultural History Review*, vol. 24 (1976); M. Spufford, *Contrasting Communities*, pp. 80, 105, 142, 212–13; cf. Hey, *English Rural Community*, pp. 55–7; Wrightson and Levine, *Poverty and Piety*, pp. 77, 100–1; A. Macfarlane (ed.), *The Diary of Ralph Josselin, 1616–1683*, British Academy, Records of Social and Economic History, new series, vol. 3 (1976), pp. 263–9; *idem*, *Family Life of Ralph Josselin*, pp. 55–6.

22 J. W. Willis Bund (ed.), *Worcestershire County Records, Division 1: Calendar of Quarter Sessions Papers*, 2 vols. (Worcester 1900), vol. 1 (1591–1643), p. 366.

23 Fletcher, *County Community in Peace and War*, p. 159; J. Raine (ed.), *Depositions and other Ecclesiastical Proceedings from the Courts of Durham*, Surtees Society, vol. 21 (1846), p. 244. For a valuable recent discussion of the importance of personal reputation and the role of gossip in the evaluation of people's standing in the community, see J. A. Sharpe, *Defamation and Sexual Slander in Early Modern England: The Church Courts at York*, Borthwick Papers, no. 58 (York 1980), esp. pp. 19–20.

24 Morehouse (ed.), 'The Diurnall of Adam Eyre', *passim*.

25 Macfarlane, *Family Life of Ralph Josselin*, pp. 149–50; Hodgson (ed.), *Wills and Inventories*, vol. 3, *passim*; Wrightson and Levine, *Poverty and Piety*, p. 100.

26 Macfarlane (ed.), *Diary of Ralph Josselin*, p. 361.

27 D. M. Palliser, 'The trade gilds of Tudor York', in Clark and Slack (eds.), *Crisis and Order*; A. D. Dyer, *The City of Worcester in the Sixteenth Century* (Leicester 1973), p. 177; M. J. Power, 'The urban development of East London, 1550 to 1700', (unpubl. PhD. thesis, University of London, 1971), p. 78; J. D. Marshall, 'Kendal in the late seventeenth and eighteenth centuries', *Transactions of the Cumberland and Westmorland Antiquarian and Archaeological Society*, new series, vol. 75 (1975), p. 190; Patten, *English Towns*, pp. 36–7.

28 Fletcher, *County Community in Peace and War*, pp. 46–53.
29 In approaching this problem I have benefited greatly from reading Howard Newby's analysis of deferential relationships in *The Deferential Worker: A Study of Farm Workers in East Anglia* (London 1977).
30 B. G. Blackwood, 'Lancashire cavaliers and their tenants', *Transactions of the Historic Society of Lancashire and Cheshire*, vol. 118 (1966), p. 19; *idem*, *The Lancashire Gentry*, p. 15; Mingay, *The Gentry*, pp. 121–2; Fletcher, *County Community in Peace and War*, p. 155.
31 J. Bankes and Eric Kerridge (eds.), *The Early Records of the Bankes Family at Winstanley*, Chetham Society, 3rd series, vol. 21 (1973), pp. 23–4, 26–8, 31, 35–6.
32 Cliffe, *The Yorkshire Gentry*, p. 46; Blackwood, *The Lancashire Gentry*, p. 15; A. B. Appleby, *Famine in Tudor and Stuart England* (Liverpool 1978), ch. 5; Watts, *Border to Middle Shire*, ch. 8.
33 R. Marchant, *The Church under the Law* (Cambridge 1969), p. 245; Laslett, *The World we have Lost*, pp. 185–7.
34 T. E. Gibson (ed.), *Crosby Records: A Cavalier's Note Book* (London 1880), p. 241; R. Parkinson (ed.), *The Autobiography of Henry Newcome*, 2 vols. Chetham Society, old series, vols. 26 and 27 (1852), vol. 1, pp. 84–5.
35 James, *Family, Lineage and Civil Society*, p. 27 ff.
36 R. B. Manning, *Religion and Society in Elizabethan Sussex: A Study of the Enforcement of the Religious Settlement, 1558–1603* (Leicester 1969), p. 113 ff.
37 K. Thomas, 'Work and leisure in pre-industrial society', *Past and Present*, no. 29 (1964); D. Brailsford, *Sport and Society: Elizabeth to Anne* (London 1969); C. Phythian-Adams, *Local History and Folklore: A New Framework*, Standing Conference for Local History (London 1975); R. W. Malcolmson, *Popular Recreations in English Society 1700–1850* (Cambridge 1973), ch. 1.
38 Everitt, 'Farm labourers', p. 348; Gibson (ed.), *Crosby Records*, p. 160; Sachse (ed.), *The Diary of Roger Lowe*, *passim*; Kussmaul, 'Servants in husbandry', p. 92; Parkinson (ed.), *Henry Newcome*, vol. 1, pp. 20, 43, 82.

Chapter 3: Family formation

1 M. M. Knappen (ed.), 'The diary of Richard Rogers', in *Two Elizabethan Puritan Diaries* (Chicago and London 1933), pp. 73–4.
2 T. F. Merrill (ed.), *William Perkins, 1558–1602 English Puritanist: His Pioneer Works on Casuistry* (The Hague 1966), p. 418. The best general study of the 'domestic conduct books' of the period remains C. L. Powell, *English Domestic Relations 1487–1653: A Study of Matrimony and Family Life in Theory and Practice as Revealed by the Literature, Law and History of the Period* (New York 1917 and 1972).
3 Merrill (ed.), *William Perkins*, pp. 419–20.
4 G. E. Howard, *A History of Matrimonial Institutions*, 3 vols. (London 1904), vol. 1, chs. 8 and 9; Merrill (ed), *William Perkins*, p. 420.
5 A. D. J. Macfarlane, 'The regulation of marital and sexual relationships in seventeenth-century England with special reference to the County of Essex'

(unpubl. MPhil. thesis, University of London, 1968), p. 70. It should be stressed that such estimates are very approximate.

6 P. Laslett, 'Introduction: comparing illegitimacy over time and between cultures', in P. Laslett, K. Oosterveen and R. M. Smith (eds.), *Bastardy and its Comparative History* (London 1980), p. 21; R. B. Outhwaite, 'Age at marriage in England from the late seventeenth to the nineteenth century', *Transactions of the Royal Historical Society*, 5th series, vol. 23 (1973); Elliott, 'Mobility and marriage', pt 3. For an admirable study of this problem, see D. Levine, *Family Formation in an Age of Nascent Capitalism* (New York, San Francisco, London 1977).

7 J. Hajnal, 'European marriage patterns in perspective', in D. V. Glass and D. E. C. Eversley (eds.), *Population in History: Essays in Historical Demography* (London 1965), pp. 101–43. Recent work suggests that this pattern did not apply to Mediterranean Europe in the pre-industrial period.

8 E. A. Wrigley, 'Fertility strategy for the individual and the group', in C. Tilly (ed.), *Studies in Fertility* (Princeton 1978).

9 Quoted in Macfarlane, *Origins of English Individualism*, p. 75. For examples of temporary and of retirement or inheritance-linked co-residence, see Chaytor, 'Household and kinship', p, 45; Spufford, *Contrasting Communities*, p. 113; Spufford, 'Peasant inheritance customs and land distribution in Cambridgeshire from the sixteenth to the eighteenth centuries', in J. Goody, J. Thirsk and E. P. Thompson (eds.), *Family and Inheritance: Rural Society in Western Europe 1200–1800* (Cambridge 1976), pp 174–5.

10 Wrightson and Levine, *Poverty and Piety*, p. 96; Hey, *English Rural Community*, pp. 204–5; C. Howell, 'Peasant inheritance customs in the Midlands, 1200–1700', in Goody, Thirsk and Thompson (eds.), *Family and Inheritance*, p. 145; Stone, *Crisis of the Aristocracy*, pp. 632–48; Mingay, *The Gentry*, pp. 109–10; Kussmaul, 'Servants in husbandry', pp. 175–92; Bankes and Kerridge (eds.), *Early Records of the Bankes Family*, p. 18; E. R. Brinkworth (ed.), *The Archdeacon's Court; Liber Actorum, 1584,* 2 vols., Oxford Record Series, vol. 23 (1942), vol. 29 (1946), vol. 1, p. 75, vol. 2, p. 160.

11 Stone, *The Family, Sex and Marriage*, pp. 4, 7–10, 117, 178–9, 187, 271–2 and *passim*. Since much of what follows is critical of Professor Stone's interpretation, it should be clearly stated that he himself recognized from the outset that his pioneering work was 'inevitably grossly over-simplified and over-schematized' (p. 4) and weakest when dealing with the experience of the common people. In the preface to the abridged version of the book (Harmondsworth 1979), he points out that 'Most sections treating the lower classes have been particularly ruthlessly trimmed, since, as reviewers were quick to point out, the evidence here was very weak.' Stone's book remains a treasury of information on the family lives of the English elite in the seventeenth and eighteenth centuries.

12 Powell, *English Domestic Relations*, pp. 128–9; Merrill (ed.), *William Perkins*, p. 431; J. Raine (ed.), *Injunctions and Other Ecclesiastical Proceedings of Richard*

Barnes, Bishop of Durham, 1575—1587, Surtees Society, vol. 22 (1850), p. 22; J.-L. Flandrin, *Familles, parenté, maison, sexualité dans l'ancienne société* (Paris 1976), p. 163.

13 Stone, *Crisis of the Aristocracy*, ch. 11; *idem, The Family, Sex and Marriage*, pp. 178–90.

14 Raines (ed.), *Journal of Nicholas Assheton*, p. 22; W. Notestein, *Four Worthies* (London 1956), p. 124; D. M. Meads (ed.), *The Diary of Lady Margaret Hoby 1599–1605* (London 1930), pp. 8–10, 21–32.

15 Stone, *Crisis of the Aristocracy*, pp. 594–600.

16 Fletcher, *County Community in Peace and War*, p. 30; Mingay, *The Gentry*, pp. 109, 111–12.

17 Powell, *English Domestic Relations*, pp. 174–6; A. Macfarlane, 'Modes of reproduction', *Journal of Development Studies*, vol. 14 (1978), p. 114.

18 S. Heller Mendelson, 'Debate: the weightiest business: marriage in an upper-gentry family in seventeenth-century England', *Past and Present*, no. 85 (1979), p. 130.

19 H. Maxwell Wood (ed.), *Wills and Inventories from the Registry at Durham*, vol. 4, Surtees Society, vol. 142 (1929), pp. 243–4.

20 R. Parkinson (ed.), *The Life of Adam Martindale, Written by Himself*, Chetham Society, old series, vol. 4 (1845), pp. 16, 21, 35, 211; Macfarlane (ed.), *Diary of Ralph Josselin*, pp. 7–8, 211; Parkinson (ed.), *Henry Newcome*, vol. 1, p. 10, vol. 2, pp. 215, 220.

21 Sachse (ed), *Diary of Roger Lowe*, pp. 16, 20, 21, 25, 26, 34, 45, 68, 79, 90, 97, 99, 119 and *passim*.

22 Parkinson (ed.), *Henry Newcome*, vol. 1, p. 49; *idem* (ed), *Adam Martindale*, p. 208; Raine (ed.), *Depositions and other Ecclesiastical Proceedings*, p. 227; Elliott, 'Mobility and marriage', pp. 303–4.

23 Macfarlane, *Family Life of Ralph Josselin*, p. 95 ff.; G. R. Quaife, *Wanton Wenches and Wayward Wives: Peasants and Illicit Sex in Early Seventeenth Century England* (London 1979), p. 46.

24 Brinkworth (ed.), *The Archdeacon's Court*, vol. 1, p. 53; Elliott, 'Mobility and marriage', pp. 305, 313.

25 Willis Bund (ed.), *Worcestershire County Records*, p. 267; Essex RO D/AEA 41 (November 1636); Thirsk and Cooper (eds.), *Seventeenth-Century Economic Documents*, p. 759.

26 Merrill (ed.), *William Perkins*, p. 421; A. C. Carter, 'Marriage counselling in the early seventeenth century: England and the Netherlands compared', in J. Van Dorsten (ed.), *Ten Studies in Anglo-Dutch Relations* (Leiden and London 1974), p. 105.

27 Stone, *Crisis of the Aristocracy*, pp. 613–18.

28 Fletcher, *County Community in Peace and War*, p. 30; Cliffe, *The Yorkshire Gentry*, p. 14; M. Slater, 'The weightiest business: marriage in an upper-gentry family in seventeenth-century England', *Past and Present*, no. 72 (1976), pp. 26, 31; Mingay, *The Gentry*, p. 109.

29 Mendelson, 'Debate: The weightiest business', pp. 127–9.

30 Meads (ed.), *Diary of Lady Margaret Hoby*, pp. 25, 28–9, 37; Bankes and Kerridge (eds.), *Early Records of the Bankes Family*, p. 19.
31 Quaife, *Wanton Wenches and Wayward Wives*, pp. 47, 93–4; Elliott, 'Mobility and marriage', p. 275; Raine (ed.), *Depositions and other Ecclesiastical Proceedings*, p. 234.
32 ibid., p. 109; Sachse (ed.), *Diary of Roger Lowe*, p. 105; Parkinson (ed.), *Adam Martindale*, pp. 21, 35.
33 Hey, *English Rural Community*, p. 214; Sachse (ed.), *Diary of Roger Lowe*, pp. 20–28, 37, 43–5, 61, 68.
34 Quoted in Elliott, 'Mobility and marriage', p. 335.
35 Parkinson (ed.), *Henry Newcome*, p. 10; *idem* (ed.), *Adam Martindale*, p. 16.
36 Macfarlane (ed.), *Diary of Ralph Josselin*, pp. 551, 555, 632.
37 Thirsk and Cooper (eds.), *Seventeenth-Century Economic Documents*, p. 183.
38 ibid., p. 759.
39 Laslett, Oosterveen and Smith (eds.), *Bastardy and its Comparative History*, chs. 1–3, 5–6; cf. Quaife, *Wanton Wenches and Wayward Wives*, ch. 3.
40 Wrightson and Levine, *Poverty and Piety*, p. 128; Essex RO Q/S Ba 2/17; Willis Bund (ed.), *Worcestershire County Records*, p. 251.
41 P. E. H. Hair, 'Bridal pregnancy in earlier rural England further examined', *Population Studies*, no. 24 (1970).
42 K. Wrightson, 'The nadir of English illegitimacy in the seventeenth century', in Laslett, Oosterveen and Smith (eds.), *Bastardy and its Comparative History*, pp. 177–9; Quaife, *Wanton Wenches and Wayward Wives*, ch. 4; K. Wrightson, 'Infanticide in earlier seventeenth century England', *Local Population Studies*, no. 15 (1975).
43 Quoted in Quaife, *Wanton Wenches and Wayward Wives*, p. 71.
44 Elliott, 'Mobility and marriage', pt 1, ch. 4, pt 3, ch. 3.
45 Blackwood, *The Lancashire Gentry*, p. 35; Fletcher, *County Community in Peace and War*, p. 48; Watts, *Border to Middle Shire*, p. 67; A. Macfarlane, *et al.*, *Reconstructing Historical Communities* (Cambridge 1977), p. 179; Hey, *English Rural Community*, pp. 201–3; Wrightson and Levine, *Poverty and Piety*, p. 77.

Chapter 4: Husbands and wives, parents and children

1 Macfarlane (ed.), *Diary of Ralph Josselin*, pp. 29, 410, 413; Campbell, *The English Yeoman*, p. 304; Essex RO D/ACA 18, fo. 71v.
2 Raine (ed.), *Depositions and Other Ecclesiastical Proceedings*, pp. 240–2.
3 Merrill (ed.), *William Perkins*, pp. 427–8; K. Davies, '"The sacred condition of equality"—how original were Puritan doctrines of marriage?', *Social History*, no. 5 (1977), pp. 566–7.
4 Powell, *English Domestic Relations*, pp. 147–159; W. Notestein, 'The English woman, 1580 to 1650', in J. H. Plumb (ed.), *Studies in Social History: A Tribute to G. M. Trevelyan* (London 1955 , pp. 73–8; Davies, 'Sacred condition of equality', p. 572; cf. B. Capp, *Astrology and the Popular Press: English Almanacs 1500–1800* (London and Boston 1979), p. 122 ff.

5 R. Thompson, *Women in Stuart England and America: A Comparative Study* (London and Boston 1974), ch. 8; Davies, 'Sacred condition of equality', pp. 566, 570; Merrill (ed.), *William Perkins*, pp. 423–27; Powell, *English Domestic Relations*, pp. 128–9, 133.

6 J. T. Johnson, 'English puritan thought on the ends of marriage', *Church History*, vol. 38 (1969); Powell, *English Domestic Relations*, ch. 4; Davies, 'Sacred condition of equality', pp. 564, 578.

7 Powell, *English Domestic Relations*, p. 169.

8 Parkinson (ed.), *Henry Newcome*, vol. 2, pp. 295–6.

9 Clark, *Working Life of Women*, p. 12 and ch. 3–5; J. D. Marshall (ed.), *The Autobiography of William Stout of Lancaster*, Chetham Society, 3rd series, vol. 14 (1967), p. 68; K. H. Burley, 'The economic development of Essex in the later seventeenth and early eighteenth centuries' (unpubl. PhD. thesis, University of London, 1957), pp. 110–13.

10 R. Weigall, 'An Elizabethan gentlewoman: the journal of Lady Mildmay, *c.* 1570–1617', *Quarterly Review*, vol. 215 (1911), p. 125; Notestein, *Four Worthies*, p. 147; Mingay, *The Gentry*, pp. 89–90; Clark, *Working Life of Women*, ch. 2; Wrightson and Levine, *Poverty and Piety*, p. 97; Spufford, *Contrasting Communities*, pp. 88–90, 112–13, 162–3; D. M. Stenton, *The English Woman in History* (London 1957), pp. 90, 100 ff.

11 Meads (ed.), *Diary of Lady Margaret Hoby*, pp. 62, 64, 65, 66, 110, 114, 135; Parkinson (ed.), *Henry Newcome*, vol. 1, p. 10; Macfarlane, *Family Life of Ralph Josselin*, pp. 108–9; Morehouse (ed.), 'The Diurnall of Adam Eyre', pp. 51, 99, 111.

12 Fletcher, *County Community in Peace and War*, p. 32; Notestein, 'The English woman', pp. 79–81; Elliott, 'Mobility and marriage', pp. 298–300, 302, 305, 311; Weigall, 'An Elizabethan gentlewoman', pp. 136–7; Notestein, *Four Worthies*, p. 139.

13 Parkinson (ed.), *Henry Newcome*, vol. 1, p. 296; cf. Macfarlane, *Family Life of Ralph Josselin*, p. 107.

14 Morehouse (ed.), 'The Diurnall of Adam Eyre', *passim*.

15 Knappen (ed.), 'Diary of Richard Rogers', pp. 81–3; Morehouse (ed.), 'The Diurnall of Adam Eyre', p. 99.

16 Stenton, *The English Woman*, p. 106; Davies, 'Sacred condition of equality', pp. 571–2; Powell, *English Domestic Relations*, pp. 133, 171.

17 Ely Diocesan Register, E14 (27 July 1652).

18 Willis Bund (ed.), *Worcestershire County Records*, p. 223. Dominant women were on occasion subjected to the public humiliation of 'rough music' or a 'riding' by malicious neighbours, a subject now being investigated by Dr M. J. Ingram.

19 K. Thomas, 'The double standard', *Journal of the History of Ideas*, vol. 20 (1959); Ingram, 'Ecclesiastical justice in Wiltshire', pp. 218–23, 239–40 and ch. 9; Sharpe, *Defamation and Sexual Slander*, pp. 15–20, 27–28.

20 Howard, *History of Matrimonial Institutions*, vol 2, ch. 11; Ingram, 'Ecclesiastical justice in Wiltshire', ch. 4.

21 ibid., p. 147 ff.; Sharpe, 'Crime and delinquency', p. 99; Fletcher, *County*

Community in Peace and War, p. 160; Willis Bund (ed.), *Worcestershire County Records*, p. 367.

22 Hey, *English Rural Community*, p. 214; Parkinson (ed.), *Henry Newcome*, vol. 1, pp. 21–2, 96; P. Laslett, *Family Life and Illicit Love in Earlier Generations: Essays in Historical Sociology*, pp. 161–2.

23 Slater, 'The weightiest business', pp. 34, 36; Meads (ed.), *Diary of Lady Margaret Hoby*, pp. 37, 39, 41–2 and *passim*; Carter, 'Marriage counselling', p. 116; Hey, *English Rural Community*, pp. 213–14; Macfarlane, *Family Life of Ralph Josselin*, p. 106 ff.

24 Mingay, *The Gentry*, p. 110, 113; Stenton, *The English Woman*, p. 34; M. Brigg, 'The Forest of Pendle in the seventeenth century', pt 2, *Transactions of the Historic Society of Lancashire and Cheshire*, vol. 115 (1963), p. 86; Spufford, *Contrasing Communities*, p. 113 and pp. 88–90, 111–19, 161–4 *passim*; Fletcher, *County Community in Peace and War*, p. 33; Wrightson and Levine, *Poverty and Piety*, p. 94; Hodgson (ed.), *Wills and Inventories*, vol. 3, pp. 22, 116.

25 Laslett, *Family Life and Illicit Love*, pp. 57–8.

26 Parkinson (ed.), *Henry Newcome*, vol. 1, p. 5; Marshall (ed.), *William Stout*, p. 74; Parkinson (ed.), *Adam Martindale*, p. 220.

27 Stone, *The Family, Sex and Marriage*, ch. 8.

28 Hair, 'Bridal pregnancy in earlier rural England', p. 60.

29 Macfarlane, 'Modes of reproduction', p. 111; *idem* (ed.), *The Diary of Ralph Josselin*, pp. 11, 12.

30 Macfarlane, *Family Life of Ralph Josselin*, pp. 84–6 and Appendix A; H. Blenkinsop (ed.), *Observations in Midwifery, by Percival Willughby* (London 1972); Parkinson (ed.), *Henry Newcome*, vol. 1, pp. 41, 53, 69, 74, vol. 2, p. 187.

31 E. A. Wrigley, 'Family limitation in pre-industrial England', *Economic History Review*, 2nd series, vol. 19 (1966); Wrightson and Levine, *Poverty and Piety*, pp. 49–56; Quaife, *Wanton Wenches and Wayward Wives*, pp. 133–4.

32 R. Schofield and E. A. Wrigley, 'Infant and child mortality in England in the late Tudor and early Stuart period', in C. Webster (ed.), *Health, Medicine and Mortality in the Sixteenth Century* (Cambridge 1979), pp. 61, 65.

33 Laslett, *The World we have Lost*, pp. 108–10.

34 Macfarlane, *Family Life of Ralph Josselin*, pp. 87–9; Powell, *English Domestic Relations*, p. 129; Stone, *The Family, Sex and Marriage*, pp. 159–61; J. E. Illick, 'Child-rearing in seventeenth-century England and America', in L. de Mause (ed.), *The History of Childhood* (New York 1974 and London 1976), pp. 307–11; V. Fildes, 'Weaning the Elizabethan child', 2 pts, *Nursing Times* (31 July 1980 and 7 August 1980).

35 M. J. Tucker, 'The child as beginning and end: fifteenth and sixteenth century English childhood', in L. de Mause (ed.), *History of Childhood*, pp. 229–30; I. Pinchbeck and M. Hewitt, *Children in English Society, Vol. 1: From Tudor Times to the Eighteenth Century* (London and Toronto 1969), pp. 7–22; Stone, *The Family, Sex and Marriage*, pp. 161–79, 194–5; Flandrin, *Familles*, p. 134.

36 B. A. Hanawalt, 'Childrearing among the lower classes of late mediaeval England', *Journal of Interdisciplinary History*, vol. 8 (1977). In approaching the problem of parent–child relations I have benefited from the opportunity to discuss these matters with Linda Pollock of the Department of Psychology, St Andrews University, whose research involves the intensive study of early diaries.

37 Merrill (ed.), *William Perkins*, p. 430.

38 L. de Mause, 'The evolution of childhood', in *idem* (ed.), *History of Childhood*, p. 35; Tucker, 'The child as beginning and end', pp. 242–3; Illick, 'Child rearing', pp. 308–11; R. A. P. Finlay, 'The population of London, 1580–1650', (unpubl. PhD. thesis, University of Cambridge, 1976), pp. 115–23; Wrightson, 'Infanticide', pp. 16–17; Pinchbeck and Hewitt, *Children in English Society*, pp. 175–6, 217–9. I must thank Valerie Fildes of the Department of Medical History, University College London, for her advice on the subject of nursing.

39 Macfarlane, *Family Life of Ralph Josselin*, p. 50; *idem* (ed.), *The Diary of Ralph Josselin*, p. 135; Wrightson and Levine, *Poverty and Piety*, pp. 40–1; Essex RO, Q/SR 227/28; Parkinson (ed.), *Henry Newcome*, vol. 1, pp. 82–5.

40 Macfarlane (ed.), *The Diary of Ralph Josselin*, pp. 113–14, 191, 201, 203, 447 and *passim*; Parkinson (ed.), *Adam Martindale*, p. 109; *idem* (ed.), *Henry Newcome*, vol. 1, pp. 43, 104–5, 147. The sole surviving section of Newcome's actual diary, covering the years 1661–3 provides yet more evidence of his preoccupation with the development of his children and his frequent anxiety on their behalf, together with evidence of similar attitudes on the part of other parents: T. Heywood (ed.), *The Diary of the Rev. Henry Newcome*, Chetham Society, old series, vol. 18 (1849), *passim*.

41 Parkinson (ed.), *Henry Newcome*, vol. 1, pp. 170–7, 181–4, vol. 2, pp. 200, 204, 215, 225, 228, 248, 252–4, 300, 302 and *passim*. Newcome's care and anxiety for Daniel is further illustrated in Heywood (ed.), *Diary of Henry Newcome*, pp. 18, 47, 53, 59, 60 and *passim*.

42 Macfarlane (ed.), *The Diary of Ralph Josselin*, p. 558.

43 Maxwell Wood (ed.), *Wills and Inventories*, vol. 4, pp. 70, 203.

44 Wrightson and Levine, *Poverty and Piety*, pp. 98–9; J. Thirsk, 'Younger sons in the seventeenth century', *History*, vol. 54 (1969), p. 361; Mingay, *The Gentry*, pp. 68, 109–10, 115–17; Chalklin, *Seventeenth-Century Kent*, pp. 55–7; Howell, 'Peasant inheritance customs', p. 140 ff.; Spufford, 'Peasant inheritance customs', pp. 157–169.

45 Wrightson and Levine, *Poverty and Piety*, pp. 39, 96–7; Spufford, 'Peasant inheritance customs', pp. 169–176; Macfarlane, *Family Life of Ralph Josselin*, pp. 48, 64; cf. Chaytor, 'Household and kinship', p. 32.

46 Macfarlane, *Family Life of Ralph Josselin*, pp. 48, 92.

47 M. Spufford, 'First steps in literacy: the reading and writing experiences of the humblest seventeenth-century spiritual autobiographers', *Social History*, vol. 4 (1979), pp. 413, 415.

48 ibid., pp. 422, 425; Thirsk and Cooper (eds.), *Seventeenth-Century Economic*

Documents, p. 754; Marshall (ed.), *William Stout*, p. 70; cf. Hey, *English Rural Community,* p. 215.

49 Kussmaul, 'Servants in husbandry', pp. 159, 165–72.

50 Spufford, 'Peasant inheritance customs', pp. 173–5; K. Thomas, 'Age and authority in early modern England', *Proceedings of the British Academy*, vol. 62 (1976), pp. 237–241.

51 Parkinson (ed.), *Adam Martindale*, p. 154; Macfarlane, 'Modes of reproduction', p. 117; *idem* (ed.), *The Diary of Ralph Josselin*, p. 183.

52 Parkinson (ed.), *Henry Newcome*, vol. 2, p. 235.

53 ibid., vol. 1, p. 105; Stone, *The Family, Sex and Marriage*, p. 171; Powell, *English Domestic Relations*, p. 129.

54 Merrill (ed.), *William Perkins*, p. 430; Spufford, 'First steps in literacy', pp. 415–16; Marshall (ed.), *William Stout*, pp. 70–1; Parkinson (ed.), *Adam Martindale*, pp. 6–8, 17–18, 24–5.

55 Pinchbeck and Hewitt, *Children in English Society*, pp. 17–18, 20; Merrill (ed.), *William Perkins*, p. 431; Parkinson (ed.), *Henry Newcome*, vol. 2, pp. 300–2; cf. Heywood (ed.), *Diary of Henry Newcome*, pp. 6, 14, 60.

56 On punishment in schools, see Stone, *The Family, Sex and Marriage*, pp. 163–6. For examples of punishment in gentry homes, see Illick, 'Child rearing', p. 337 n. 38. Josselin's diary and the autobiographies of Martindale and Stout make no reference to physical punishment in the home. Furnivall (ed.), *Harrison's Description of England*, pt 2, pp. 46–7, pt 3, pp. 155–6.

57 Parkinson (ed.), *Henry Newcome*, vol. 2, p. 248.

58 ibid., vol. 2, pp. 252–3; Parkinson (ed.), *Adam Martindale*, p. 213; Macfarlane (ed.), *The Diary of Ralph Josselin*, pp. 580, 582, 638; cf. Hey, *English Rural Community*, pp. 214–15.

Chapter 5: Population and resources

1 Furnivall (ed.), *Harrison's Description of England*, pt 1, pp. 239–42.

2 Thirsk and Cooper (eds.), *Seventeenth-Century Economic Documents*, pp. 79, 177–9, 752; R. H. Tawney and E. Power (eds.), *Tudor Economic Documents*, 3 vols. (London, New York, Toronto 1924), vol. 2, section 7, vol. 3, section 4.

3 R. M. Smith, 'Population and its geography in England 1500–1730', in R. A. Dodghson and R. A. Butlin (eds.), *An Historical Geography of England and Wales* (London 1978), pp. 205–7.

4 D. Palliser, 'Dearth and disease in Staffordshire, 1540–1670', in C. W. Chalklin and M. A. Havinden (eds.), *Rural Change and Urban Growth 1500–1800: Essays in English Regional History in Honour of W. G. Hoskins* (London 1974), p. 55; Skipp, *Crisis and Development*, p. 13; Spufford, *Contrasting Communities*, pp. 16–18, 25; Hoskins, *The Midland Peasant*, pp. 185, 211; Appleby, *Famine in Tudor and Stuart England*, p. 36.

5 For a very useful discussion of the possible interrelationships of these

variables, see R. S. Schofield, 'The relationship between demographic stucture and environment in pre-industrial western Europe', in W. Conze (ed.), *Sozialgeschichte Der Familie in Der Neuzeit Europas* (Stuttgart 1977), pp. 147–60.

6 J. D. Chambers, *Population, Economy and Society in Pre-Industrial England* (Oxford 1972); J. Hatcher, *Plague, Population and the English Economy 1348–1530* (London 1977).

7 L. Bradley, 'The most famous of all English plagues: a detailed analysis of the plague at Eyam, 1665–6', in *The Plague Reconsidered*, supplement to *Local Population Studies* (1977), pp. 74–7; R. Schofield, 'An anatomy of an epidemic: Colyton, November 1645 to November 1646', in *The Plague Reconsidered*, pp. 96, 107, 111–15, 119–120.

8 The best brief discussion of this demographic regime is D. S. Smith, 'A homeostatic demographic regime: patterns in West European family reconstitution studies', in R. D. Lee (ed.), *Population Patterns in the Past* (New York and London 1977), pp. 19–51.

9 F. J. Furnivall (ed.), *The Anatomie of Abuses in Ailgna by Philip Stubbes*, 2 pts (London 1877–82), pt 1, p. 97; T. Wright, *Queen Elizabeth and Her Times*, 2 vols. (London 1838), vol. 2, p. 407. I must thank Peter Clark for bringing the latter reference to my attention.

10 Smith, 'Population and its geography', p. 208. The population history of the later sixteenth and seventeenth centuries will shortly be illuminated by the publication of the results of the national survey of the Cambridge Group for the History of Population and Social Structure: E. A. Wrigley and R. S. Schofield, *The Population History of England, 1541–1971* (London forthcoming 1981).

11 R. B. Outhwaite, *Inflation in Tudor and Early Stuart England* (London 1969); E. H. Phelps-Brown and S. V. Hopkins, 'Seven centuries of the prices of consumables compared with builders' wages', *Economica*, vol. 92 (1954).

12 Spufford, *Contrasting Communities*, pp. 22–7 and ch. 4.

13 ibid., pp. 16–22 and ch. 5; Thirsk (ed.), *Agrarian History*, pp. 10, 13, 204, 403; B. Sharp, *In Contempt of All Authority: Rural Artisans and Riot in the West of England, 1586–1660* (Berkeley, Los Angeles, London 1980), pp. 159, 168–9.

14 Thirsk, 'Industries in the countryside'; J. H. C. Patten, 'Population distribution in Norfolk and Suffolk during the sixteenth and seventeenth centuries', *Institute of British Geographers Transactions*, no. 65 (1975), pp. 58, 62; Wrightson and Levine, *Poverty and Piety*, p. 44; Sharp, *In Contempt of All Authority*, pp. 161–2, 176–89; Nef, *Rise of the British Coal Industry*, vol. 2, pp. 135–51.

15 Clark and Slack, *English Towns in Transition*, pp. 83–4; Dyer, *City of Worcester*, p. 26; Smith, 'Population and its geography', p. 224; Power, 'Urban development of East London', p. 39.

16 Dyer, *City of Worcester*, ch. 3; A. L. Beier, 'Social problems in Elizabethan London', *Journal of Interdisciplinary History*, vol. 9 (1978), p. 205; E. A.

Wrigley, 'A simple model of London's importance in changing English society and economy 1650–1750', in P. Abrams and E. A. Wrigley (eds.), *Towns in Societies* (Cambridge 1978), pp. 220–1; P. Slack, 'The local incidence of epidemic disease: the case of Bristol, 1540–1650', in *The Plague Reconsidered*, pp. 49–51; *idem*, 'Social problems and social policies', in *The Traditional Community under Stress*, Open University, Course A322, English Urban History 1500–1780, block 3 (1977), pp. 79–80; P. Clark, 'The migrant in Kentish towns', pp. 142, 149; Smith, 'Population and its geography', p. 226; P. Corfield, 'Economic growth and change in seventeenth-century English towns', in *The Traditional Community Under Stress*, pp. 38–41.

17 F. J. Fisher, 'The development of the London food market, 1540–1640', in E. M. Carus-Wilson (ed.), *Essays in Economic History*, vol. 1 (London 1954); Chalklin, *Seventeenth-Century Kent*, pp. 165, 175; M. A. Havinden, 'Agricultural progress in open-field Oxfordshire', in W. E. Minchinton (ed.), *Essays in Agrarian History*, vol. 1 (Newton Abbot 1968), pp. 149–50.

18 Thirsk and Cooper (eds.), *Seventeenth-Century Economic Documents*, p. 343; James, *Family, Lineage and Civil Society*, pp. 73–4.

19 J. A. Chartres, *Internal Trade in England, 1500–1700* (London 1977), pp. 13–38; Dyer, *City of Worcester*, ch. 6; A. Hassell Smith, *County and Court: Government and Politics in Norfolk, 1558–1603* (Oxford 1974), p. 11.

20 A. Everitt, 'The marketing of agricultural produce', in Thirsk (ed.), *Agrarian History*, p. 506 ff.; J. Walter and K. Wrightson, 'Dearth and the social order in Early modern England', *Past and Present*, no. 71 (1976), p. 30 ff.

21 G. Batho, 'Landlords in England B: Noblemen, Gentlemen and Yeomen', in Thirsk (ed.), *Agrarian History*; Bowden 'Agricultural prices', pp. 674–94; Mingay, *The Gentry*, p. 40 ff.; E. Kerridge, *Agrarian Problems in the Sixteenth Century and After* (London 1969), pp. 38–9.

22 Batho, 'Landlords in England', p. 304; M. W. Beresford, 'Leeds in 1628: A 'ridinge observation' from the City of London', *Northern History*, vol. 10 (1975), pp. 135–6, 139; J. R. Sewell, 'A "short view" of some Northumberland manors, 1629', *Northern History*, vol. 14 (1978), pp. 160–2.

23 Batho, 'Landlords in England', pp. 293, 304; Bowden, 'Agricultural prices', pp. 684–7; Kerridge, *Agrarian Problems*, pp. 46–8.

24 Bankes and Kerridge (eds.), *Early Records of the Bankes Family*, *passim*; Bowden, 'Agricultural prices', pp. 690, 693; N. W. Alcock, *Stoneleigh Villagers, 1597–1650* (Coventry 1975), p. 7; Watts, *Border to Middle Shire*, pp. 71–2, 159 ff.

25 Bowden, 'Agricultural prices', pp. 675–9; Hassell Smith, *County and Court*, p. 16; Fletcher, *County Community in Peace and War*, pp. 13–14; J. Thirsk, 'Seventeenth-century agriculture and social change', in *idem* (ed.), *Land, Church and People: Essays presented to Professor H. P. R. Finberg, Agricultural History Review*, supplement (1970), p. 154; Thirsk and Cooper (eds.), *Seventeenth-Century Economic Documents*, p. 178. For the course of change in

agricultural technique, see J. Thirsk, 'Farming techniques', in *idem* (ed.), *Agrarian History* and E. Kerridge, *The Agricultural Revolution* (London 1967).

26 J. Thirsk, 'Enclosing and engrossing', in *idem* (ed.), *Agrarian History*; J. A. Yelling, 'Agriculture 1500–1730', in Dodghson and Butlin (eds.), *Historical Geography of England and Wales*, pp. 152–6; Thirsk and Cooper (eds.), *Seventeenth-Century Economic Documents*, p. 109.

27 Campbell, *The English Yeoman*, ch. 5; Bowden, 'Agricultural prices', pp. 659–71.

28 Fussell (ed.), *Robert Loder's Farm Accounts*, p. 47 ff.; Furnivall (ed.), *Harrison's Description of England*, pt 1, p. 298; Campbell, *The English Yeoman*, pp. 103–4.

29 Furnivall (ed.), *Harrison's Description of England*, pt 3, p. 131; Havinden, 'Agricultural progress in open-field Oxfordshire', *passim*; Thirsk, 'Enclosure and engrossing', pp. 237–8, 248.

30 Thirsk, 'Seventeenth-century agriculture', pp. 156–7; H. J. Habakkuk, 'La disparition du paysan anglais', *Annales ESC*, 20ᵉ Année, no. 4 (1965), pp. 657–8.

31 W. G. Hoskins, 'The rebuilding of rural England, 1570–1640', in *Provincial England* (London 1965), ch. 7; *idem*, *The Midland Peasant*, pp. 288–99; D. Portman, 'Vernacular building in the Oxford region in the sixteenth and seventeenth centuries', in Chalklin and Havinden (eds.), *Rural Change and Urban Growth*, pp. 135–68; Wrightson and Levine, *Poverty and Piety*, pp. 36–9; R. Machin, 'The great rebuilding: a reassessment, *Past and Present*, no. 77 (1977); J. Thirsk, *Economic Policy and Projects: The Development of a Consumer Society in Early Modern England* (Oxford 1978); Campbell, *The English Yeoman*, chs. 5–7.

32 Quoted in Skipp, *Crisis and Development*, p. 106; Thirsk and Cooper (eds.), *Seventeenth-Century Economic Documents*, p. 177.

33 ibid., p. 183; Furnivall (ed.), *Harrison's Description of England*, pt 1, p. 296.

34 Wrightson and Levine, *Poverty and Piety*, pp. 27–8.

35 Thirsk, 'Seventeenth-century agriculture', pp. 158–62, 171–3; Thirsk and Cooper (eds.), *Seventeenth-Century Economic Documents*, p. 184.

36 Thirsk, 'Seventeenth-century agriculture', pp. 156–7, 167–73; Spufford, *Contrasing Communities*, chs. 2–5; Hoskins, *The Midland Peasant*, pp. 196–9; N. S. B. Gras and E. C. Gras, *The Economic and Social History of an English Village (Crawley, Hampshire) A.D. 909–1928* (Cambridge, Mass. 1930). pp. 95–9; G. H. Tupling, *The Economic History of Rossendale*, Chetham Society, new series, vol. 86 (1927), pp. 75–6, 81, 95; Brigg, 'Forest of Pendle', pt 1, p. 72.

37 Everitt, 'Farm labourers', pp. 399, 401–2, 404, 406–10, 435, 462.

38 Ramsay, *The Wiltshire Woollen Industry*, ch. 5; B. E. Supple, *Commercial Crisis and Change in England, 1600–1642* (Cambridge 1959); Thirsk and Cooper (eds.), *Seventeenth-Century Economic Documents*, pp. 224–6; C. Hill, 'Pottage for freeborn Englishmen: attitudes to wage labour in the sixteenth and seventeenth centuries', in C. H. Feinstein (ed.), *Socialism, Capitalism and*

Economic Growth: Essays Presented to Maurice Dobb (Cambridge 1967), p. 339. The effects of periodic industrial crisis are well illustrated in Thirsk and Cooper (eds.), *Seventeenth-Century Economic Documents*, section 3.

39 C. Phythian-Adams and P. Slack, 'Urban crisis or urban change', P. Corfield, 'Economic growth and change in seventeenth-century English towns', and P. Slack, 'Social problems and social policies', all in *The Traditional Community Under Stress*; Marshall, 'Kendal', p. 203; Dyer, *City of Worcester*, pp. 160–1; Patten, *English Towns*, ch. 4; Beier, 'Social problems', pp. 210–11; Hill, 'Pottage for freeborn Englishmen', p. 341.

40 L. Stone, 'Social mobility in England, 1500–1700', *Past and Present*, no. 33 (1966); A. Everitt, 'Social mobility in early modern England', *Past and Present*, no. 33 (1966); Skipp, *Crisis and Development*, pp. 78–80.

41 C. Phythian-Adams, 'Urban decay in late-mediaeval England', in Abrams and Wrigley (eds.), *Towns in Societies*, p. 181; Hoskins, *The Midland Peasant*, pp. 189, 202, 212; Hey, *English Rural Community*, pp. 168–78; Skipp, *Crisis and Development*, pp. 80–2; Macfarlane, *Origins of English Individualism*, pp. 69–70, 77; Wrightson and Levine, *Poverty and Piety*, pp. 31–6; Spufford, *Contrasting Communities*, pp. 36–45; P. Slack, 'Poverty and politics in Salisbury 1597–1666', in Clark and Slack (eds.), *Crisis and Order*, pp. 166–178; Clark and Slack, *English Towns in Transition*, pp. 121–2.

42 Slack, 'Social problems and social policies', p. 86; Hull, 'Agriculture and rural society in Essex', pp. 475–8.

43 Thirsk and Cooper (eds.), *Seventeenth-Century Economic Documents*, p. 751; K. E. Wrightson, 'The puritan reformation of manners with special reference to the counties of Lancashire and Essex, 1640–1660', (unpubl. PhD. thesis, University of Cambridge, 1974), pp. 152, 154; P. Slack, 'Vagrants and vagrancy in England, 1598–1664', *Economic History Review*, 2nd series, vol. 27 (1974); A. L. Beier, 'Vagrants and the social order in Elizabethan England', *Past and Present*, no. 44 (1974); Beier, 'Social problems', pp. 204–9. The parish register entry quoted is from the parish register of Terling, Essex.

44 W. G. Hoskins, 'Harvest fluctuations and English economic history 1480–1619' and 'Harvest fluctuations and English economic history 1620–1759', *Agricultural History Review*, vol. 12 (1964), vol. 16 (1968); P. Bowden, 'Statistical appendix', in Thirsk (ed.), *Agrarian History*; C. J. Harrison, 'Grain price analysis and harvest qualities, 1465–1634', *Agricultural History Review*, vol. 19 (1971).

45 Batho, 'Landlords in England', pp. 292, 304; Bowden, 'Agricultural prices', p. 690.

46 Spufford, *Contrasting Communities*, chs. 3–4.

47 Supple, *Commercial Crisis and Change, passim.*

48 Slack, 'Social problems and social policies', *passim*.

49 Appleby, *Famine in Tudor and Stuart England*, chs. 1–8.

50 ibid., ch. 9; P. Slack, 'Mortality crises and epidemic disease in England 1485–1610', in Webster (ed.), *Health, Medicine and Mortality*, p. 34; *idem*,

'Social problems and social policies', p. 89; *idem*, 'Local incidence of epidemic disease', p. 57; Dyer, *City of Worcester*, p. 45; Watts, *Border to Middle Shire*, pp. 49, 169.

51 Skipp, *Crisis and Development*, ch. 4.

52 P. Laslett, 'Long-term trends in bastardy in England', in *Family Life and Illicit Love*, pp. 113, 115, 116–7, 125; Quaife, *Wanton Wenches and Wayward Wives*, pp. 56–7; D. Levine and K. Wrightson, 'The social context of illegitimacy in early modern England', in Laslett, Oosterveen and Smith (eds.), *Bastardy and its Comparative History*, pp. 170–2.

53. Bowden, 'Agricultural prices', p. 621.

54 Smith, 'Population and its geography', pp. 209–12, 216–18; Wrigley, 'Famility limitation', *passim*; Wrightson and Levine, *Poverty and Piety*, p. 63 ff.; Levine, *Family Formation*, ch. 7. Further evidence of a widespread desire to inhibit family size is provided by Dr Capp's discovery that almanacs of the mid to late seventeenth century provided advice on fertility-reducing herbal potions: Capp, *Astrology and the Popular Press*, p. 122.

55 Clark, 'Migration in England during the late seventeenth and early eighteenth centuries', pp. 73, 81.

56 Kerridge, *Agricultural Revolution*, pp. 289, 331–2; A. H. John, 'The course of agricultural change 1660–1760', and E. L. Jones, 'Agriculture and economic growth in England, 1660–1750: agricultural change', both in Minchinton (ed.), *Essays in Agrarian History*, vol. 1; A. B. Appleby, 'Grain prices and subsistence crises in England and France, 1590–1740', *Journal of Economic History*, vol. 39 (1979)

57 Appleby, *Famine in Tudor and Stuart England*, chs. 10–11; Skipp, *Crisis and Development*, chs. 7–8.

58 Figures quoted in Chalklin, *Seventeenth-Century Kent*, p. 255; J. Thirsk, 'The Farming regions of England', in *idem* (ed.), *Agrarian History*, p. 96; Burley, 'Economic development of Essex', pp. 335, 338, 358.

Chapter 6: Order

1 J. S. Cockburn, *A History of English Assizes, 1558–1714* (Cambridge 1972), p. 101; J. Samaha, *Law and Order in Historical Perspective: The Case of Elizabethan Essex* (New York and London 1974), p. 19; J. S. Cockburn, 'The nature and incidence of crime in England 1559–1625', in *idem* (ed.), *Crime in England*, pp. 52–3.

2 Lancashire RO, DP 353, 'The mss sermons of Christopher Hudson', fo. 48v; C. Hill, 'The many-headed monster', in *Change and Continuity in Seventeenth-Century England* (London 1974), p. 186.

3 Sharp, *In Contempt of All Authority*, p. 38; J. Walter, 'Grain riots and popular attitudes to the law: Maldon and the crisis of 1629', in J. Brewer and J. Styles (eds.), *An Ungovernable People: The English and Their Law in the Seventeenth and Eighteenth Centuries* (London 1980), p. 70.

4 Sharp, *In Contempt of All Authority*, pp. 120–1.

5 M. W. Beresford, 'The common informer, the penal statutes and economic regulation', *Economic History Review*, 2nd series, vol. 10 (1957–8), p. 222; A. W. Pollard and G. R. Redgrave (eds.), *A Short-Title Catalogue of Books Printed in England, Scotland and Ireland and of English Books Printed Abroad 1475–1640* (London 1969).

6 Hassell Smith, *County and Court*, pp. 60, 75, 113 ff.; M. G. Davies, *The Enforcement of English Apprenticeship: A Study in Applied Mercantilism* (Cambridge, Mass. 1956), *passim*; Fletcher, *County Community in Peace and War*, pp. 23, 137; G. C. F. Forster, 'The North Riding justices and their sessions, 1603–1625', *Northern History*, vol. 10 (1975), pp. 102–3; Clark, *English Provincial Society*, p. 146; Cockburn, *History of English Assizes*, pp. 158, 186.

7 Beresford, 'The common informer', p. 226; S. T. Bindoff, 'The making of the statute of artificers', in S. T. Bindoff, J. Hurstfield and C. H. Williams (eds.), *Elizabethan Government and Society: Essays Presented to Sir John Neale* (London 1961), pp. 85, 87; Cockburn, *History of English Assizes*, p. 58; Davies, *Enforcement of English Apprenticeship*, p. 231 ff.; E. M. Leonard, *The Early History of English Poor Relief* (Cambridge 1900), pp. 119, 145, 151.

8 Davies, *Enforcement of English Apprenticeship*, pp. 182–3; Forster, 'The North Riding justices', pp. 104, 110, 124; *idem*, 'Faction and county government in early Stuart Yorkshire', *Northern History*, vol. 11 (1976), *passim*; Watts, *Border to Middle Shire*, pp. 130, 202; Hassell Smith, *County and Court*, p. 112; Fletcher, *County Community in Peace and War*, pp. 56–7, 218, 221–2, 224.

9 Stone, *Crisis of the Aristocracy*, ch. 5; B. W. Beckinsale, 'The characteristics of the Tudor north', *Northern History*, vol. 4 (1969), p. 71; James, *Family, Lineage and Civil Society*, pp. 35, 45–51; Fletcher, *County Community in Peace and War*, pp. 22–4; Hassell Smith, *County and Court*, pp. 47–8, 93, 99, 108–9, 111, 314–15, 330–6; D. Hirst, *The Representative of the People? Voters and Voting in England under the Early Stuarts* (Cambridge 1976).

10 Cockburn, *History of English Assizes*, p. 186; Barnes, *Somerset 1625–40*, ch. 7; Higgins, 'Government of early stuart Cheshire', *passim*; Leonard, *Early History of English Poor Relief*, pp. 132, 150, 241 ff.; Hodgett, *Tudor Lincolnshire*, pp. 97–9; Forster, 'The North Riding justices', p. 116; Fletcher, *County Community in Peace and War*, p. 137 and ch. 8.

11 ibid., pp. 113–14, 132–3, 138, 154–5 and ch. 16; G. C. F. Forster, 'County government in Yorkshire during the Interregnum', *Northern History*, vol. 12 (1976); Blackwood, *The Lancashire Gentry*, ch. 3; A. L. Beier, 'Poor relief in Warwickshire 1630–1660', *Past and Present*, no. 35 (1966); V. Pearl, 'Puritans and poor relief: the London workhouse, 1649–1660', in Pennington and Thomas (eds.), *Puritans and Revolutionaries*, p. 210; A. M. Everitt, *The Community of Kent and the Great Rebellion* (Leicester 1966), chs. 5, 8; J. S. Morrill, *Cheshire, 1630–1660: County Government and Society During the 'English Revolution'* (Oxford 1974), chs. 3, 5, 6 and pp. 331–2; Wrightson, 'Puritan reformation of manners', chs. 7–10.

12 Tawney and Power (eds.), *Tudor Economic Documents*, vol. 1, p. 340.
13 J. C. M. Walker, 'Crime and capital punishment in Elizabethan Essex' (unpubl. BA dissertation, University of Birmingham, 1971), pp. 20–31, 41–3; J. H. Baker, 'Criminal courts and procedure at common law 1550–1800', in Cockburn (ed.), *Crime in England*, p. 17; Cockburn, *History of English Assizes*, p. 131; D. Hay, 'Property, authority and the criminal law', in D. Hay *et al.*, *Albion's Fatal Tree: Crime and Society in Eighteenth-Century England* (London 1975), p. 22; J. A. Sharpe, 'Crime in the county of Essex, 1620–1680: a study of offences and offenders at the assizes and quarter sessions' (unpubl. D.Phil. thesis, University of Oxford, 1979), p. 281 ff.: Dr Sharpe's thesis is shortly to be published as *Crime in Seventeenth-Century England: A County Study* (Cambridge); Tawney and Power, *Tudor Economic Documents*, vol. 1, p. 341.
14 M. J. Ingram, 'Communities and courts: law and disorder in early-seventeenth-century Wiltshire', in Cockburn (ed.), *Crime in England*, pp. 125–8; K. Wrightson, 'Two concepts of order: justices, constables and jurymen in seventeenth-century England', in Brewer and Styles (eds.), *An Ungovernable People*, pp. 30–1.
15 ibid., pp. 23–5, 29–30.
16 Parkinson (ed.), *Adam Martindale*, pp. 123–6.
17 Furnivall (ed.), *Harrison's Description of England*, pt 1, p. 229; Cockburn, 'Nature and incidence of crime', p. 55, 57; Sharpe, 'Crime in the county of Essex', pp. 186, 205–7.
18 C. Haigh, *Reformation and Resistance in Tudor Lancashire* (Cambridge 1975), p. 53; Raines (ed.), *Journal of Nicholas Assheton*, pp. 9–13.
19 Cockburn, 'Nature and incidence of crime', p. 56 ff.; Sharpe, 'Crime in the county of Essex', pp. 190–203.
20 ibid., ch. 10; Cockburn, 'Nature and incidence of crime', pp. 59–60; Wrightson and Levine, *Poverty and Piety*, pp. 122–5.
21 Furnivall (ed.), *Harrison's Description of England*, pt 1, pp. 229–30; Cockburn, *History of English Assizes*, p. 97; *idem*, 'Nature and incidence of crime', pp. 55, 60; Samaha, *Law and Order*, pp. 20–1.
22 Cockburn, 'Nature and incidence of crime', pp. 64–6; Beier, 'Social problems', p. 220.
23 Walker, 'Crime and capital punishment', pp. 84–5.
24 Cockburn, 'Nature and incidence of crime', pp. 61–4, 67–70; Macfarlane *et al.*, *Reconstructing Historical Communities*, pp. 185–6; Ingram, 'Communities and courts', p. 129 ff.; Sharpe, 'Crime and delinquency', p. 100 ff.; *idem*, 'Crime in the county of Essex', pp. 268, 296–306, 342; Ramsay, *Wiltshire Woollen Industry*, p. 77; Forster, 'The North Riding justices', p. 123; Wrightson and Levine, *Poverty and Piety*, pp. 39, 120–2.
25 Walker, 'Crime and capital punishment', p. 55.
26 Fussell (ed.), *Robert Loder's Farm Accounts*, p. 56; J. A. Sharpe, 'Enforcing the law in the seventeenth-century English village', in V. A. C. Gattrell, B. Lenman and G. Parker (eds.), *Crime and the Law: The Social History of*

Crime in Western Europe since 1500 (London 1980), pp. 105–6; cf. Walter and Wrightson, 'Death and the social order', p. 26 n. 10; Ingram, 'Communities and courts', p. 134.

27 A. J. Willis and M. J. Hoad (eds.), *Portsmouth Record Series 1: Borough Sessions Papers, 1653–1688* (London and Chichester 1971), pp. 15, 20, 23, 156, 161, 162.

28 Wrightson, 'Two concepts of order', pp. 36–9.

29 ibid., pp. 34–7, 39–41; Wrightson and Levine, *Poverty and Piety*, pp. 125–7, 132–4; Ingram, 'Ecclesiastical justice in Wiltshire', p. 374; Fletcher, *County Community in Peace and War*, p. 168; Alcock, *Stoneleigh Villagers*, p. 5; Skipp, *Crisis and Development*, p. 40; F. G. Emmison (ed.), *Early Essex Town Meetings: Braintree, 1619–1636: Finchingfield, 1626–1634* (London and Chichester 1970), p. 101 and *passim*.

30 Quoted in Everitt, 'Farm labourers', p. 441.

31 The following discussion of alehouses and their regulation is based upon K. Wrightson, 'Alehouses, order and reformation in rural England, 1590–1660', paper to the conference of the Society for the Study of Labour History, 1975, forthcoming in E. Yeo and S. Yeo (eds.), *Popular Culture and Class Conflict 1590–1914: Explorations in the History of Labour and Leisure* (Brighton 1981). For a complementary study which employs much urban evidence, see P. Clark, 'The alehouse and the alternative society', in Pennington and Thomas (eds.), *Puritans and Revolutionaries*.

32 A. Dent, *The Plaine Mans Path-way to Heaven* (London 1601), pp. 165–6; Lancashire RO, DP 353, 'Mss sermons of Christopher Hudson', fo. 46; R. Young, *The Blemish of Government, the Shame of Religion, the Disgrace of Mankind or a Charge drawn up against Drunkards* (London 1658), p. 6; S. Hammond, *Gods Judgements upon Drunkards* (London 1659), p. 26.

33 Essex RO Q/SR 259/10; Lancashire RO QSB/1/277/48; Essex RO Q/SR 264/103. For detailed examples of the local conflicts underlying such petitions, see Wrightson and Levine, *Poverty and Piety*, pp. 134–9, 177–9; Wrightson, 'Two concepts of order', pp. 39–44.

34 Thirsk, 'Seventeenth-century agriculture', p. 151 ff.; Hey, *English Rural Community*, pp. 6–8; S. Webb and B. Webb, *English Local Government from the Revolution to the Municipal Corporations Act: Vol. 1, The Parish and the County* (London 1906), pp. 43–9, 52, 176–227; Nef, *Rise of the British Coal Industry*, pp. 135, 150–1; Thirsk, 'Farming regions', pp. 111–12; H. Fishwick (ed.), *Lancashire and Cheshire Church Surveys*, Lancashire and Cheshire Record Society, vol. 1 (1878), p. 126; Sewell, '"Short view" of some Northumberland manors', p. 159.

35 What follows owes much to discussions with John Walter of the University of Essex. On the particular question of enclosure riots, Mr Walter generously made available to me his unpublished paper, '"The poor man's friend and the gentleman's plague"? Agrarian disorder in early modern England'.

36 Walter and Wrightson, 'Dearth and the social order', p. 26 (the number of Essex riots given here is nine; this figure has subsequently been corrected by John Walter to ten); Sharp, *In Contempt of All Authority*, pp. 10–13;

P. Clark, 'Popular protest and disturbance in Kent, 1558–1640', *Economic History Review*, 2nd series, vol. 29 (1976).

37 Walter, 'Poor man's friend', pp. 8, 10–14; J. S. Morrill, *The Revolt of the Provinces: Conservatives and Radicals in the English Civil War 1630–1650* (London 1976), p. 34; Sharp, *In Contempt of All Authority*, pp. 86–96, 104.

38 ibid., pp. 36, 39; C. S. L. Davies, 'Peasant revolt in France and England: a comparison', *Agricultural History Review*, vol. 21 (1973), p. 133.

39 ibid., p. 132; Sharp, *In Contempt of All Authority*, pp. 7–8.

40 Walter and Wrightson, 'Dearth and the social order', pp. 29–31; Walter, 'Grain riots and popular attitudes', p. 51; Chalklin, *Seventeenth-Century Kent*, p. 20; Sharp, *In Contempt of All Authority*, pp. 145–9, 176–9, 190–1.

41 ibid., pp. 13, 19, 22; Walter and Wrightson, 'Dearth and the social order', p. 27.

42 Walter, 'Poor man's friend', pp. 4–9. A number of riots also took place in towns in response to the enclosure of town commons.

43 ibid., pp. 14–15; Spufford, *Contrasting Communities*, p. 122 ff.

44 Walter and Wrightson, 'Dearth and the social order', pp. 32, 41; Sharp, *In Contempt of All Authority*, pp. 42, 71.

45 Davies, 'Peasant revolt', p. 131; Walter, 'Poor man's friend', pp. 15–19; Sharp, *In Contempt of All Authority*, pp. 32, 95–6, 105; Clark, 'Popular protest', p. 378.

46 Walter and Wrightson, 'Dearth and the social order', pp. 31, 33–4; Walter, 'Grain riots and popular attitudes', pp. 51–4, 62–3; *idem*, 'Poor man's friend', p. 24; Clark, 'Popular protest', pp. 376, 380.

47 Davies, 'Peasant revolt', pp. 127, 130; Walter, 'Poor man's friend', pp. 20, 21–2; Sharp, *In Contempt of All Authority*, pp. 97–104 and ch. 5; Walter, 'Grain riots and popular attitudes', pp. 54, 55–8, 72, 76–7.

48 Sharp, *In Contempt of All Authority*, chs. 3, 9 and pp. 107–17; Clark, 'Popular protest', p. 381; Walter and Wrightson, 'Dearth and the social order', pp. 35–42; Walter, 'Grain riots and popular attitudes', *passim*, esp. pp. 81–4.

49 E. P. Thompson, 'The moral economy of the English crowd in the eighteenth century', *Past and Present*, no. 50 (1971); Sharp, *In Contempt of All Authority*, ch. 9; Walter, 'Poor man's friend', p. 25.

50 Pearl, 'Puritans and poor relief', pp. 209–10; Maxwell Wood (ed.), *Wills and Inventories*, vol. 4, pp. 18–19; Wrightson and Levine, *Poverty and Piety*, p. 179.

51 R. W. Malcolmson, '"A set of ungovernable people": the Kingswood colliers in the eighteenth century', in Brewer and Styles (eds.) *An Ungovernable People*, pp. 85–9, 91.

Chapter 7: Learning and godliness

1 J. M. Lloyd Thomas (ed.), *The Autobiography of Richard Baxter*, Everyman edn (London and New York 1931), pp. 3–4, 6.

2 ibid., pp. 4–5, 7.
3 L. Stone, 'The educational revolution in England, 1560–1640', *Past and Present*, no. 28 (1964), pp. 70–3; D. Cressy, 'Educational opportunity in Tudor and Stuart England', *History of Education Quarterly*, vol. 16 (1976), pp. 501–6.
4 Stone, 'Size and composition of the Oxford student body', pp. 6–8; Prest, *The Inns of Court*, pp. 5–7; Stone, 'Educational revolution', pp. 42, 47, 51–2, 73; Spufford, *Contrasting Communities*, p. 193; Skipp, *Crisis and Development*, p. 83; Hodgett, *Tudor Lincolnshire*, p. 139.
5 Stone, 'Size and composition of the Oxford student body', p. 17; Clark, *English Provincial Society*, p. 200; Fletcher, *County Community in Peace and War*, p. 35; R. O'Day, 'The reformation of the ministry, 1558–1642', in R. O'Day and F. Heal (eds.), *Continuity and Change: Personnel and Administration of the Church in England, 1500–1642* (Leicester 1976), p. 72; Spufford, *Contrasting Communities*, pp. 184–7.
6 Cressy, 'Educational opportunity', p. 307; Marshall (ed.), *William Stout*, p. 72; Stone, 'Educational revolution', p. 67; *idem*, 'Size and composition of the Oxford student body', p. 20; Prest, *The Inns of Court*, p. 27.
7 Spufford, 'First steps in literacy', pp. 415–16. For further evidence on the acquisition of literacy, see Cressy, *Literacy and the Social Order*, ch. 2.
8 Marshall (ed.), *William Stout*, pp. 68–70.
9 Spufford, 'First steps in literacy', p. 425.
10 M. H. Curtis, *Oxford and Cambridge in Transition, 1558–1642* (Oxford 1959), ch. 3; Stone, 'Size and composition of the Oxford student body', pp. 17–24; Dyer, *City of Worcester*, pp. 347–8; Campbell, *The English Yeoman*, pp. 263, 265, 275; Spufford, 'First steps in literacy', pp. 417–18, 429; Marshall (ed.), *William Stout*, p. 71; Parkinson (ed.), *Adam Martindale*, p. 24.
11 Cressy, 'Educational opportunity', pp. 310, 312; Stone, 'Size and composition of the Oxford student body', pp. 19, 37; Prest, *The Inns of Court*, pp. 30, 44–5.
12 R. S. Schofield, 'The measurement of literacy in pre-industrial England', in J. Goody (ed.), *Literacy in Traditional Societies* (Cambridge 1968), pp. 317–24; Cressy, 'Educational opportunity', pp. 314–15; James, *Family, Lineage and Civil Society*, p. 103; Spufford, *Contrasting Communities*, pp. 199–200. I owe the Leicestershire figures to the generosity of Dr R. S. Schofield in allowing me to quote unpublished material from the literacy files of the Cambridge Group for the History of Population and Social Structure. For a thorough treatment of the whole problem of literacy levels, see Cressy, *Literacy and the Social Order, passim.*
13 James, *Family, Lineage and Civil Society*, pp. 98, 100; Curtis, *Oxford and Cambridge in Transition*, chs. 4–5; Stone, 'Size and composition of the Oxford student body', pp. 24–6; Prest, *The Inns of Court*, pp. 151–69.
14 Curtis, *Oxford and Cambridge in Transition*, ch. 10; Stone, 'Educational revolution', p. 63; J. H. Gleason, *The Justices of the Peace in England,*

1558–1640 (Oxford 1969), pp. 86–8; Cliffe, *The Yorkshire Gentry*, p. 77; Stone, 'Size and composition of the Oxford student body', pp. 48–55. Such developments were not incompatible with the simultaneous enhancement of a sense of regional identity as a result of the connections of particular counties with individual colleges, as is suggested by V. Morgan, 'Cambridge university and "the country" 1560–1640', in Stone (ed.), *The University in Society*, vol. 1, pp. 183–243.

15 Stone, *Crisis of the Aristocracy*, pp. 672, 702–24; Mingay, *The Gentry*, pp. 156, 163; Morgan, 'Cambridge university and "the country"', p. 183; Cliffe, *The Yorkshire Gentry*, p. 82; P. Laslett, 'The gentry of Kent in 1640', *Cambridge Historical Journal*, vol. 9 (1947), p. 149; James, *Family, Lineage and Civil Society*, pp. 98, 104.

16 D. Cressy, 'Literacy in seventeenth-century England: more evidence', *Journal of Interdisciplinary History*, vol. 8 (1977), p. 150. In what follows my argument is greatly influenced by that of T. Laqueur, 'The cultural origins of popular literacy in England, 1500–1850', *Oxford Review of Education*, vol. 2 (1976).

17 Figures from Dr R. S. Schofield of the Cambridge Group for the History of Population and Social Structure. cf. Cressy, 'Literacy in seventeenth-century England: more evidence', pp. 143–4. Illiteracy levels in the period 1641–4 for 414 parishes have now been published in Cressy, *Literacy and the Social Order*, pp. 191–201.

18 Laqueur, 'Cultural origins of popular literacy', pp. 255, 260–1; Breton quoted in Campbell, *The English Yeoman*, p. 265; Sachse (ed.), *Diary of Roger Lowe, passim*; Maxwell Wood (ed.), *Wills and Inventories*, vol. 4, p. 188; Wrightson, 'Two concepts of order', p. 27.

19 Spufford, 'First steps in literacy', pp. 418–20; Laqueur, 'Cultural origins of popular literacy', p. 267; N. Bownde, *The Doctrine of the Sabbath plainely layde forth* (London 1595), pp. 241–2.

20 Spufford, 'First steps in literacy', p. 416; Laqueur, 'Cultural origins of popular literacy', p. 255.

21 Parkinson (ed.), *Adam Martindale*, p. 5; Spufford, 'First steps in literacy', pp. 416, 421; Marshall (ed.), *William Stout*, pp. 80–1 (my italics).

22 Capp, *Astrology and the Popular Press*, pp. 23–4, 33–4, 41, 61.

23 Laqueur, 'Cultural origins of popular literacy', pp. 261–3; Brigg, 'The Forest of Pendle' pt 2, pp. 82–3; Skipp, *Crisis and Development*, p. 82; P. Clark, 'The ownership of books in England, 1560–1640: the example of some Kentish townsfolk', in L. Stone (ed.), *Schooling and Society* (Baltimore 1976); W. H. Rylands, 'Booksellers and stationers in Warrington, 1639 to 1657', *Transactions of the Historic Society of Lancashire and Cheshire*, new series, vol. 1 (1885).

24 Macfarlane, *Reconstructing Historical Communities*, p. 191; G. H. Kenyon, 'Petworth town and trades, 1610–1760', pt 1, *Sussex Archaeological Collections*, vol. 96 (1958), p. 70; Lloyd-Thomas (ed.), *Richard Baxter*, p. 4; Spufford, 'First steps in literacy', p. 425; Parkinson (ed.), *Henry Newcome*,

vol. 1, p. 10; Sachse (ed.), *Diary of Roger Lowe*, p. 99; Morehouse (ed.), 'The Diurnall of Adam Eyre', pp. 4, 10, 23–4.

25 Spufford, 'First steps in literacy', pp. 418 n. 43, 419; Morehouse (ed.), 'The Diurnall of Adam Eyre', *passim*.

26 K. Thomas, *Religion and the Decline of Magic: Studies in Popular Beliefs in Sixteenth and Seventeenth Century England* (London 1971), pp. 73, 75–6; J. Bossy, 'The Counter-Reformation and the people of Catholic Europe', *Past and Present*, no. 47 (1970), p. 62.

27 F. R. Raines (ed.), *The State, Civil and Ecclesiastical of the County of Lancaster about the year 1590*, Chetham Society, *Chetham Miscellany*, vol. 5 (1875), pp. 4, 5–7; James, *Family, Lineage and Civil Society*, p. 52, 125; E. M. Guest, 'Pre-Christian survivals in connection with crosses in the North of England', *Folklore*, vol. 52 (1941), p. 224 and *passim*; Thomas, *Religion and the Decline of Magic*, pp. 70–73.

28 The following discussion of magic, religion and the problem of misfortune is based upon Thomas, *Religion and the Decline of Magic*, pp. 5, 75–6, 185 and chs. 4, 7–9 *passim*.

29 Morehouse (ed.), 'The Diurnall of Adam Eyre', p. 84; Macfarlane (ed.), *The Diary of Ralph Josselin*, pp. 23–4; Parkinson (ed.), *Adam Martindale*, p. 154.

30 The following discussion of witchcraft is based upon Thomas, *Religion and the Decline of Magic*, chs. 14–17 and A. Macfarlane, *Witchcraft in Tudor and Stuart England, a Regional and Comparative Study* (London 1970).

31 C. L'Estrange Ewen, *Witchcraft and Demonianism* (London 1933), pp. 229–31.

32 A. D. J. Macfarlane, 'Witchcraft in Tudor and Stuart Essex', in Cockburn (ed.), *Crime in England*, p. 87.

33 Thomas, *Religion and the Decline of Magic*, p. 164; Bownde, *Doctrine of the Sabbath*, p. 200.

34 Merrill (ed.), *William Perkins*, pp. 70–1; Dent, *Plaine Mans Pathway*, pp. 25, 275, 309, 370 and *passim*; R. Bolton, *Two Sermons Preached at Northampton* (London 1639), p. 81.

35. Merrill (ed.), *William Perkins*, p. 43. Such characterizations of popular attitudes were part of the stock in trade of the reforming preachers. For the particular examples quoted here and similar allegations, see ibid., p. 70; Dent, *Plaine Mans Pathway*, pp. 58, 95, 124–5, 146, 165; J. Northbrooke, *Spiritus est Vicarius Christi in Terra* (London 1579), 'To the Christian and faithfull Reader'.

36 W. Haller, *Foxe's Book of Martyrs and the Elect Nation* (London 1963); C. Fetherston, *A Dialogue agaynst Light Lewde and Lascivious Dauncing* (London 1582), unpaginated; W. Gouge, *Gods Three Arrows: Plague, Famine, Sword* (London 1631).

37 Hodgett, *Tudor Lincolnshire*, p. 175; Haigh, *Reformation and Resistance*, p. 231; W. G. Hoskins, 'The Leicestershire country parson in the sixteenth century', in *Essays in Leicestershire History* (Liverpool 1950), p. 19; Manning,

Religion and Society in Elizabethan Sussex, p. 178; D. Lambert, 'The lower clergy of Lancashire, 1558–1642' (unpubl. MA thesis, University of Liverpool, 1964), pp. 127–8, 142; Watts, *Border to Middle Shire*, pp. 86–8.

38 O'Day, *The English Clergy*, pp. 27, 127; Manning, *Religion and Society in Elizabethan Sussex*, pp. 178, 183–5. For the whole question of ecclesiastical finances and resultant problems, see C. Hill, *Economic Problems of the Church, from Archbishop Whitgift to the Long Parliament* (Oxford 1956).

39 Morrill, *Cheshire, 1630–1660*, p. 6; Lambert, 'Lower clergy of Lancashire', p.xxiv; P. Collinson, 'Cranbrook and the Fletchers: popular and unpopular religion in the Kentish Weald', in P. Newman Brooks (ed.), *Reformation Principle and Practice: Essays in Honour of Arthur Geoffrey Dickens* (London 1980), p. 174.

40 O'Day, *The English Clergy*, pp. 9–13 and chs. 4–10; Hodgett, *Tudor Lincolnshire*, p. 178; Ingram, 'Ecclesiastical justice in Wiltshire', pp. 72–7; Fletcher, *County Community in Peace and War*, p. 71; A. G. Dickens, *The English Reformation* (London 1967), p. 419; Hill, *Economic Problems*, ch. 11; *idem, Society and Puritanism in Pre-Revolutionary England (London 1964)*, chs. 2–3.

41 O'Day, *The English Clergy*, pp. 4–7, 126, 159–66, 185–6, 189–90.

42 R. Houlbrooke, *Church Courts and the People during the English Reformation* (Oxford 1979), chs. 1, 7, 8; J. C. Coldeway, 'Early Essex drama; a history of its rise and fall, and a theory concerning the Digby Plays' (unpubl. PhD. thesis, University of Colorado, 1972), p. 156; Brinkworth (ed.), *The Archdeacon's Court*, vol. 1, pp. 43–4, 51, 54–5, 124–5; Essex RO D/ACA 25, fo. 167v; E. R. C. Brinkworth, *Shakespeare and the Bawdy Court of Stratford* (London and Chichester 1972), p. 150; R. Halley, *Lancashire: its Puritanism and Nonconformity* (Manchester and London 1869), pp. 271–2.

43 Thomas, *Religion and the Decline of Magic*, pp. 257–63, 455–60; R. Marchant, *The Church under the Law* (Cambridge 1969), pp. 204–35; Ingram, 'Ecclesiastical justice in Wiltshire', pp. 87, 336 ff.

44 J. R. Kent, 'Attitudes of members of the House of Commons to the regulation of "personal conduct" in late Elizabethan and early Stuart England', *Bulletin of the Institute of Historical Research*, vol. 46 (1973); K. Thomas, 'The puritans and adultery: the act of 1650 reconsidered', in Pennington and Thomas (eds.), *Puritans and Revolutionaries*, p. 273; Clark and Slack, *English Towns in Transition*, pp. 150–1; R. C. Richardson, *Puritanism in North-West England: A Regional Study of the Diocese of Chester to 1642* (Manchester 1972), p. 158; Ingram, 'Ecclesiastical justice in Wiltshire', pp. 102–3; Hassell Smith, *County and Court*, p. 223; A. H. A. Hamilton, *Quarter Sessions from Elizabeth to Anne* (London 1878), pp. 73, 115; T. G. Barnes, 'County politics and a puritan cause celebre; Somerset churchales 1633', *Transactions of the Royal Historical Society*, 5th series, vol. 9 (1959), p. 109.

45 Spufford, *Contrasting Communities*, pp. 334–43; Wrightson and Levine,

Poverty and Piety, pp. 155, 158; C. Z. Weiner, 'The beleaguered isle: a study of Elizabethan and early Jacobean anti-Catholicism', *Past and Present*, no. 51 (1971); J. Bossy, *The English Catholic Community, 1570–1850*, pp. 100, 175 and *passim*.

46 Wrightson and Levine, *Poverty and Piety*, pp. 142–3, 155–62, 180–1; Ingram, 'Ecclesiastical justice in Wiltshire', pp. 102–3; T. Young, *Englands Bane, or the Description of Drunkenness* (London 1634), p. 65; Fishwick (ed.), *Lancashire and Cheshire Church Surveys*, p. 126.

47 G. Widley, *The Doctrine of the Sabbath* (London 1604), p. 127; J. Angier, *An Helpe to Better Hearts for Better Times* (London 1647), pp. 69–70 and *passim* [preached 1638]; Bownde, *Doctrine of the Sabbath*, p. 175.

48 ibid., p. 173; Ingram, 'Ecclesiastical justice in Wiltshire', pp. 90–1; Thomas, *Religion and the Decline of Magic*, pp. 160–2; Bolton, *Two Sermons Preached at Northampton*, p. 81; D'Ewes quoted in Thomas, p. 163.

49 N. Tyacke, 'Puritanism, Arminianism and Counter-Revolution', in C. Russell (ed.), *The Origins of the English Civil War* (London 1973); Barnes, 'County politics and a puritan cause celebre', pp. 119–20.

50 T. Case, *Gods Waiting to be Gracious unto His People* (London 1642), pp. 11, 94; N. Proffett, *Englands Impenitencie under Smiting* (London 1645), Epistle and p. 46.

51 Morrill, *Cheshire, 1630–1660*, ch. 6; Hamilton, *Quarter Sessions from Elizabeth to Anne*, p. 138 ff.; Forster, 'County government in Yorkshire during the Interregnum', pp. 97–9; Fletcher, *County Community in Peace and War*, ch. 6; Wrightson, 'Puritan reformation of manners', chs 7–11; C. Hill, 'Propagating the Gospel', in *Change and Continuity in Seventeenth-Century England*.

52 Parkinson (ed.), *Henry Newcome*, vol. 1, pp. 74, 86; R. Younge, *A Hopefull Way to Cure that Horrid Sinne of Swearing* (London 1645), p. 412; W. Harrison, *The Difference of Hearers* (London 1614), 'To the Bishop of Chester'; Dent, *Plaine Mans Pathway*, p. 124.

53 R. Baxter, *The Reformed Pastor* (London 1656), pp. 357, 431–432.

54 Parkinson (ed.), *Adam Martindale*, pp. 122–3; *idem* (ed.), *Henry Newcome*, vol. 1, p. 53.

55 Lloyd Thomas (ed.), *Richard Baxter*, p. 84.

56 For the ferment of religious ideas in this period, see C. Hill, *The World Turned Upside Down: Radical Ideas During the English Revolution*. (London 1972). For detailed local examples, see Spufford, *Contrasting Communities*, ch. 11; Wrightson and Levine, *Poverty and Piety*, pp. 162–4.

57 Macfarlane (ed.), *The Diary of Ralph Josselin*, pp. 236, 252, 376, 424.

58 H. Fishwick (ed.), *The Note Book of the Rev. Thomas Jolly*, Chetham Society, New Series, vol. 33 (1895), pp. 120–3, 128, 132; *idem* (ed.), *Lancashire and Cheshire Church Surveys*, p. 165.

59 Ingram, 'Ecclesiastical justice in Wiltshire', p. 106; P. Tyler, 'The church courts at York and witchcraft prosecutions. 1567–1640', *Northern History*, vol. 4 (1969), pp. 102 n. 72, 103 n. 73. For attitudes to the clergy, see O'Day, *The English Clergy*, ch. 14.

60 Parkinson (ed.), *Adam Martindale*, pp. 156–7; *idem* (ed.), *Henry Newcome*, p. 121.
61 Chalklin, *Seventeenth-Century Kent*, p. 227; Spufford, *Contrasting Communities*, pp. 223–30, 300–6; Wrightson and Levine, *Poverty and Piety*, pp. 165–171.
62 Laslett and Harrison, 'Clayworth and Cogenhoe', p. 162; Chalklin, *Seventeenth-Century Kent*, p. 224; Macfarlane (ed.), *The Diary of Ralph Josselin*, pp. 495, 500, 502, 503, 505.
63 Thomas, *Religion and the Decline of Magic*, chs. 18, 22.
64 ibid., pp. 162, 666.

Index